Chile's Salmon Industry

Akio Hosono • Michiko Iizuka • Jorge Katz
Editors

Chile's Salmon Industry

Policy Challenges in Managing Public Goods

Springer

Editors
Akio Hosono
JICA Research Institute
Shinjuku-ku
Tokyo
Japan

Michiko Iizuka
MERIT
United Nations University
Maastricht
Limburg
The Netherlands

Jorge Katz
University of Chile
Santiago
Chile

ISBN 978-4-431-55765-4 ISBN 978-4-431-55766-1 (eBook)
DOI 10.1007/978-4-431-55766-1

Library of Congress Control Number: 2016934849

Springer Tokyo Heidelberg New York Dordrecht London

Printed on acid-free paper

Springer Japan KK is part of Springer Science+Business Media (www.springer.com)

Foreword

Aquaculture is growing and becoming more important globally. It now makes up almost 50 % of the global fish harvest in what is called the "Blue Revolution," to draw a comparison with agriculture's "Green Revolution." One of the most impressive examples of the Blue Revolution is Chile's salmon farming and processing industry, which achieved its phenomenal development from scratch. In its initial phase, the Chilean semi-public agency Fundación Chile as well as pioneering private firms were the major actors in establishing the industry, while the cooperation programs of Chile and Japan fulfilled the catalytic role.

This book takes a historical and holistic approach in understanding the evolutionary development of Chile's salmon industry, focusing on learning and capacity development, environment sustainability and institutions, as well as social welfare and inclusiveness. The study aims to respond to questions such as how to create new economic activities whilst overcoming the initial difficulties of acquiring knowledge and technological capabilities, and how to use natural resources in a sustainable manner while promoting new economic activities.

This book is the outcome of a research program conducted by the Japan International Cooperation Agency Research Institute (JICA-RI) with participation of researchers and professionals from the University of Chile, United Nations University Maastricht Economic and Social Research Institute (UNU-MERIT) and JICA-RI. I am convinced that this publication will offer insightful lessons that can be applied to other natural resource-based sectors and industries facing similar challenges during the course of development.

Tokyo, Japan

Akihiko Tanaka
Former President
Japan International Cooperation Agency

Acknowledgements

The editors are most grateful to the staff of the Japan International Cooperation Agency (JICA) Research Institute and the JICA office in Chile. We would especially like to thank Akihiko Tanaka, president of JICA, Hiroshi Kato, vice-president of JICA, and Ichiro Tambo, director of the JICA Research Institute for encouraging us to prepare this volume.

We would like to thank institutions to which editors and other authors belong, among others, the University of Chile and United Nations University Maastricht Economic and Social Research Institute (UNU-MERIT).

This volume has also benefitted from the input of the many key people who kindly accepted our invitations to be interviewed and gave us valuable information on Chile's salmon industry development.

We are also grateful to Keiichi Tsunekawa and Naohiro Kitano for their continuous support for our study. We are thankful to Yasuhiko Sato, chief editor of the JICA Research Institute, together with Koji Yamada, Haruko Kamei, Maiko Takeuchi, and Aiko Oki for providing professional assistance during the preparation of this volume.

Akio Hosono
Michiko Iizuka
Jorge Katz

Contents

List of Tables

List of Figures

Editors and Contributors

Editors

Akio Hosono is senior research adviser of Japan International Cooperation Agency Research Institute (JICA-RI). He holds a doctorate in economics from the University of Tokyo. After graduation he served in a variety of posts such as vice-president at Tsukuba University in Tsukuba Science City, Japanese ambassador to El Salvador, and professor at the National Graduate Institute for Policy Studies (GRIPS) in Tokyo, professor at the Research Institute of Economics and Business Administration at Kobe University to name a few. He became a senior advisor at JICA in 2007. He served as director of JICA-RI from 2011 to 2013. Major publications: Chandy, Hosono, Kharas, and Linn (eds.), *Getting to Scale: How to Bring Development Solutions to Millions of Poor People* [Brookings Press 2013]; Saavedra, Hosono and Stallings (eds.), *Regional Integration and Economic Development* [Palgrave 2003]; Hosono and Saavedra (eds.), *Development Strategies in East Asia and Latin America* [Macmillan Press 1998].

Michiko Iizuka is a research fellow at United Nations University, Maastricht Economic and Social Research and Training Center for Innovation and Technology (UNU-MERIT), located in Maastricht, the Netherlands. She is a policy specialist in the field of development, innovation and sustainability. Before 2008, she worked as a researcher at International Development Center of Japan and as an environmental officer at the United Nations Economic Commission for Latin America and the Caribbean (UN-ECLAC). She has also provided consultancy works for UNIDO, ECLAC, EU, JICA, DFID and WWF-UK. Her main areas of interest are: innovation systems in the context of developing countries; the role of innovation policy in the development process; the impact of global institutions such as standards and global agreements on local capacity building; and agriculture, natural resources and environmental policy. She has a D.Phil in science, technology and innovation policy from the Science Policy Research Unit (SPRU) and M.Phil from the Institute of Development Studies (IDS), both at the University of Sussex. She also holds a postgraduate diploma in environmental management from Imperial College, University of London.

Jorge Katz received his first degree in economics at the University of Buenos Aires in 1964 and completed his tertiary education in England, obtaining a D.Phil degree in economics at Nuffield College, Oxford, in 1967. His doctoral dissertation *Production Functions, Foreign Investment and Growth*—carried out under the supervision of Professor Sir John Hicks—was published by North-Holland in 1969. After returning to Argentina he was appointed as lecturer at the University of Bs. As, where he taught on industrial organization and economic development. He acted as visiting professor at the University of Sussex (UK) and also at the University of Yale (US) in 1970s. As from 1994 and until 2003 he was director of the Division of Production, Productivity and Management, at ECLAC, the UN Economic Commission for Latin America and the Caribbean, in Santiago de Chile. In 2003 he was appointed as professor at the University of Chile where he currently lectures on innovation and economic development. He presently works on macro-to-micro interactions and structural change in the process of economic growth, looking at the cases of Argentina, Brazil, Chile and Colombia on a comparative basis. Also on topics of natural resource based economic development, examining cases such as salmon farming in Chile, soybean production in Argentina, flowers in Colombia and else.

Contributors

Pedro Roje Associate Researcher, Research Department, Central Bank of Chile.

Valentina Vera Departamento de Ingeniería Industrial, Universidad de Chile; División de Proyectos Externos.

Juan Pablo Zanlungo Departamento de Ingeniería Industrial, Universidad de Chile; División de Proyectos Externos.

Chapter 1
Introduction

Michiko Iizuka, Akio Hosono, and Jorge Katz

1 Overview

The Chilean salmon industry accounts for around one third of salmon production in the world, and is, along with Norway, one of the two largest producers of salmon (SalmonChile 2008). For a country which is still very much dependent upon copper exports, exports of salmon currently provide a significant proportion of Chilean export revenue (5 %). The fish is an exotic species to Chile, and the miraculous speed in which the country became a top exporter was thus achieved through intensive learning efforts in collaboration with various stakeholders, beginning as early as the 1960s.

This book originated with the idea to keep a good historical account of the development of the Chilean salmon farming industry from its inception to its present situation. The history itself is compelling, and as the story unfolded, we came across various insightful lessons that could be applied to other natural resources-based sectors, which face similar questions of industrial development via capacity building, environmental sustainability, institutional development, and social inclusion. We consider that these issues are important for developing countries, especially those rich in natural resources such as Chile.

This book describes the development of salmon farming industry in chronological order. Following the development of a non-traditional industry, we came across questions that are perhaps common to many developing countries. First, how to

M. Iizuka (✉)
Maastricht Economic and Social Research and Training Center for Innovation and Technology (UNU-MERIT), United Nations University, Maastricht, The Netherlands
e-mail: iizuka@merit.unu.edu

A. Hosono
Japan International Cooperation Agency Research Institute (JICA-RI), Tokyo, Japan

J. Katz
University of Chile, Santiago, Chile

A. Hosono et al. (eds.), *Chile's Salmon Industry*,
DOI 10.1007/978-4-431-55766-1_1

create new economic activities in a natural resource rich country overcoming the initial difficulties of acquiring knowledge and technological capabilities? Second, how to use natural resources in a sustainable manner while promoting new economic activities? Third, how to create institutions that enable the industry to develop while meeting with other societal challenges? Fourth, how to make development of new economic activity more equitable and socially inclusive?

The chapters in this book are arranged in four distinctive thematic headings that represent policy challenges in managing public goods—knowledge development, environmental sustainability, institutions, and social welfare (inclusiveness)—using the case of salmon farming in Chile to illustrate the complex mechanisms involved in each challenge. Below we explain why we chose to focus on these four areas and how these themes are linked to our argument.

1.1 Knowledge

Knowledge, its pure form, has non-exclusive and non-rival properties (Stiglitz 1999). This means that while knowledge requires a substantial amount of investment, once it is created its owners have limited power to appropriate it because everyone can access and use it simultaneously without diminishing others' utility. Hence, under the market mechanism, investment in knowledge always stays at a suboptimal level (David 1993). Public institutions such as Intellectual Property Rights[1] (IPR), by creating means of appropriation, encourage investment in knowledge creation by firms while at the same time ensuring access to that knowledge via a licensing mechanism (David 1993; Verspagen 2003)[2]; however, it is also reported that IPR can discourage the diffusion of knowledge and subsequent network effects.[3] Knowledge transfer and diffusion are critical issues for developing countries trying to diversify their economic activities in order to catch up. Knowledge diffusion also encourages a critical mass of entrepreneurs, an important precondition for creating an industry.

[1] Different types of Intellectual Property Rights, such as copyright, trademarks, patents, industrial designs and trade secrets exist and their distinctive characteristics determine the diffusion process. With regards to patent protection, various discussion were being made on its effects that varies depending on the length of protection (Nordhaus 1969), breath (how wide a patent should cover) (Mazzoleni and Nelson 1998) and hight (extent of novelty) (Odagiri et al. 2010).

[2] However, this point is not relevant for developing countries because the desired benefits of IPR are often insignificant due to their weak economic and technological structures (van Wijk and Junne 1993). Van Wijk and Junne (1993, 22) argue that in "developing countries the privileges created by the industrial property systems failed both to stimulate inventions among their own nationals and did not encourage the rapid transfer, appropriate adaptation or widespread diffusion of imported technology."

[3] This is especially true for developing countries after the TRIPs agreement that came into effect in 1995; this restricts design of IPR regimes to their own purposes, unlike the case of many developed nations (OECD 2013).

Natural resource sectors, in particular, have much more difficulty investing in knowledge than other productive sectors such as manufacturing and services due to the high degree of site specificity caused by the biological nature of this type of production. In addition to the above, there is the general difficulty appropriating the benefits from knowledge generation.[4] These conditions create higher barriers to investment in knowledge under the market mechanism in general, and especially for activities based on natural resources such as agriculture (Pardey et al. 2010).[5] The policy challenge, at the early stage of industrial activities, is to promote the knowledge creation and diffusion.

Knowledge creation and diffusion within the Chilean salmon farming industry took place in the form of technical transfer supported by government and international cooperation. Chile's success in salmon farming is often associated with its open market policy in the mid-1980s; however, Chaps. 2 and 3 of this book demonstrate that a long iterative process of technological transfer and diffusion, with state initiative, preceded the takeoff of Chile's salmon industry.

1.2 Sustainability (Environment and Natural Resources)

Environmental resources—such as clean water, air, biodiversity, to name just a few—make significant contributions to economic activities, but the value of these services is not explicitly included in production functions (Costanza et al. 1992; Hawken et al. 1999; UNEP 2011). The importance of these services is often recognized after negative externalities have occurred through exploitative use by the productive sector beyond the environmental carrying capacity. Although the urgency of transforming the current productive structure into a sustainable and inclusive one is well recognized under the concept of a 'green economy'[6] (UNEP 2011), we still observe overexploitation of environmental resources due to weak or absent institutions. The policy challenge for sustainable development is to create institutions that are capable of monitoring and managing resources by identifying sustainable levels of their use (carrying capacity) while supporting dynamic growth of the productive sector.

As Chap. 5 explains, in Chile, the sanitary crisis of the salmon industry in 2007 was the result of overexploitation of environmental resources in coastal areas by salmon firms and the weakness of regulatory institutions to control firms'

[4] Knowledge in agriculture is often a combination of tacit and codified knowledge. It is easily diffused unless it is protected in the form of genetics.

[5] It is for this reason that agricultural research and extension services are financed publicly in many countries.

[6] UNEP defines a green economy as one that results in 'improved human well-being and social equity, while significantly reducing environmental risks and ecological scarcities' (UNEP 2010, quoted in UNEP 2011, 9). The document states that a green economy is low-carbon, resource-efficient, and socially inclusive.

exploitative behavior. Currently, policy efforts are being made to create institutions based on scientific evidence at the local level.

1.3 Institutions

"Institutions" in broad terms shape the behavior of individuals in the society (Greif 2006; Aoki 2007). Scott (1995) makes a useful distinction among regulatory, normative, and cognitive levels of institutions. The regulatory institutions include government regulations that serve as "rules of the law" following the seminal works by Williamson (1975, 1985, 1998). The normative institutions, or "the way things are done" are embedded in business practices, policies or ethical standards rather than rules or governing structures that constrain behavior. The cognitive institutions reflect the way people interpret and make sense of the world around them, including cultures, value systems, religions and norms (North 1990, 1991). Meeting societal challenges often requires changing institutions in all three levels. Sometimes this does not happen so easily or in an aligned manner and policy interventions are made often at either the regulatory—by means of regulation—or normative levels but not so much on cognitive level. Ostrom (1990) describes the emergence of institutions at the cognitive level in the cases of small communities managing natural resources through game-theoretical interactions among the stakeholders. The question is how institutions like the one described by Ostrom (1990) can emerge.

In Chile, the sanitary crisis in 2007 created the situation in which policy needed to intervene and create changes in existing institutions surrounding the salmon farming industry to ensure sustainability. The regulatory institutions appeared as the Aquaculture law in 2010. The implementation of such institutions at the regulatory level required accompanying normative and cognitive changes in institutions. Such institutional change is a complex and evolving process as can be seen by the case described in Chap. 5, with regard to sanitary regulations, and in Chap. 6, with regard the process of change in institutions before and after the crisis in 2007.

1.4 Inclusiveness (Social Welfare)

Inclusiveness of the economic and political institutions is important for economic development (Acemoglu et al. 2005; Acemoglu and Robinson 2012). Economic growth based on natural resources often leads to increasing inequality due to the absence of good institutions that can allocate "ownership," "access," and "profits" associated with use of resources in an equitable manner (Auty 1990, 2001). Here the policy challenge is how to incorporate inclusive mechanisms and institutions to ensure the welfare of vulnerable populations in tandem with development of new industry based on natural resources.

The Chilean salmon farming industry has made huge contributions to the regional economy. In addition some attempts have been made to support marginalized populations and artisanal fisheries. But in terms of inclusive growth, much remains to be done if this industry is to contribute significantly to the equity and welfare enhancement of Southern Chile (Chap. 7). This chapter also reflects on collaboration between the public and the private sector, corporate social responsibility and tries to trace out a future developmental pathway for this industry.

2 Organization of the Book

In this book, each chapter covers one period of development in the Chilean salmon industry, and also refers to the one of the questions mentioned in the above section of this chapter.

2.1 Chapter 2: Genesis of Chilean Salmon Industry

With growing global competition, developing countries are now struggling to survive by swiftly meeting the changing demands of the market or identifying emerging market niche, with both their static and "dynamic" comparative advantages determined by existing and changing factors and endowments such as labor, technology/knowledge/skill, natural resources, geographical location, and capital. These countries are increasing the flow of information and knowledge through frequent exchanges via the global market; improved ICT and increased movement of workers are considered to facilitate this "discovery" process (Rodrik 2007) of finding the right match between the market demand and what can be produced effectively by the country to compete in the global market. Yet in reality, some countries fall behind while others forge ahead. What can explain such differences in outcome? How can certain countries succeed in transforming their economic structures to be more productive while others cannot?

This chapter aims to present an illustrative case on how the salmon industry acquires and diffuses knowledge during its inception phase. The salmon farming industry in Chile had achieved phenomenal development from scratch that could be described as a miracle by any industrial standards (Katz 2006; Iizuka 2007; Hosono 2010). Although numerous references have been made to the successful inception of the Chilean salmon industry (Chang 2011; Rodrik 2007, for example) these focus on the growth period of this industry from the mid-1980s onwards, when Chile adopted an open trade policy. This chapter pays attention to the years prior to this. What happened in terms of domestic capability building before rapid growth came about? This chapter illustrates how the industry accumulated the knowledge necessary for its foundation. To transfer necessary knowledge, the Chilean government utilized bi-lateral technical cooperation schemes wisely in the late 1960s and 1970s, in particular the "Japan-Chile Salmon Project," together with timely pro-active intervention from public or semi-public agencies such as Fundación Chile, CORFO, IFOP and SAG. This gestation period creating a knowledge base was critical in understanding successful industry development in the subsequent period.

2.2 Chapter 3: The Chilean Salmon Industry Takes Off: From the Commercialization to the Early Development Phase

Technological transfer does not automatically create domestic capabilities. Once the knowledge base is established, entrepreneurs are needed to actually implement existing knowledge into practice, overcoming various local specific barriers. Hence, the next challenge for establishing new industries is how to attract entrepreneurs to invest in this new economic activity. As entrepreneurs are risk averse, it is necessary to decrease the entry risk and provide incentives.

The knowledge base needed for salmon farming has been gradually built since the 1970s through "The Japan-Chile Salmon Project" in Coihaique and Ensenada Baja, as well as among private pioneering firms (Domsea Pesquera, Pscicultura Lago Llanquihue Ltd., and Nichiro). The identification of viable salmon farming technology for Chile in 1979 and the success of Fundación Chile in producing 1000 t in 1988 transmitted clear message that this industry was indeed commercially viable to potential entrepreneurs. The intermediary mechanisms for technological transfer such as Fundación Chile and "Japan-Chile Salmon Project" played crucial roles in the diffusion of knowledge to attract a critical mass of entrepreneurs. Their success in doing so resulted from their approach to the diffusion of knowledge and technology as "public goods" instead of more exclusive "club goods" available to only a small number of people. Furthermore, export success cannot be discussed without market access. For instance, in exporting to Japan, Chilean producers were able to acquire market access without causing major trade frictions with existing domestic salmon producers in Japan because buyers and intermediaries not only supported Chilean firms in complying with necessary requirements such as sanitary standards but also carefully adjusted the type and timing of products to be introduced to the market. Here the case of access to the Japanese market is explained in detail.

2.3 Chapter 4: The Development of Salmon Aquaculture in Chile into an Internationally Competitive Industry: 1985–2007

The growth of industry accompanied by an increase in exports and foreign direct investment (FDI) further induce the structural transformation of industry. The

Chilean salmon farming industry was not an exception. During the growth and globalization phase, scale and complexity increased both at the industry and firm levels. At the industry level, diverse stakeholders—suppliers of inputs and services, universities and research organizations, regulatory organizations, and industrial associations, among others—were now contributing to the enhancement of competitiveness on the global market. Beyond any doubt we can say that this has been a fairly successful process of "dynamic interdependence" between multiple forces in society. These actors were involved in creating further changes such as an oligopoly and the introduction of stronger regulatory control measures and new political dynamics from suppliers of inputs and services, as each interact with the global market. At the firm level, on the other hand, a production structure was created to achieve economic efficiency to compete in a competitive market; however, from the hindsight this may not have been accompanied with the capability to cope with long term problems. Hence, from this period, the industry started to show unbalanced growth, with the rapid growth of capacity for efficient production (i.e. effectively extracting the resources) and the slow or stagnant development of the capability to solve long-term problems (i.e. developing technological/scientific capabilities, and figuring out carrying capacity at local level) creating the conditions for the sanitary collapse which occurred next.

2.4 Chapter 5: Environmental Collapse and Institutional Restructuring: The Sanitary Crisis in the Chilean Salmon Industry

Industries based on natural resources need to balance their extractive activities with the environment's pace of re-generation. A good balance is hard to find because the optimal point is not static but instead dynamically evolves over a long period with a complex web of cause and effect. This chapter, using the case of the salmon industry in Chile, seeks to explain first, how an environmental catastrophe (such as sanitary crisis by ISA[7] in 2007) happened in Chile where regulations to protect the environment and natural resources are secondary to economic growth; and second, how efforts to create appropriate management institutions (standards, regulations, and systems) aim to prevent the future occurrence of such a sanitary crisis. The Chilean case will demonstrate how natural resource-based activities need to be supported not only by advanced production technology, but also by scientific knowledge of the local environment so that appropriate local regulatory institutions to manage the use of common resources are established.

[7] Infectious salmon anaemia (ISA) is a disease that causes the sanitary problem for farmed Atlantic salmon.

2.5 Chapter 6: Transformation of Institutions: Crisis and Change in Institutions for Chilean Salmon Industry

In the event of a major catastrophe, institutions[8] will experience some changes to adjust to the new environment. The institutional change takes place in either a top-down fashion—whereby the change is initiated with the formal institution (i.e. change in the laws or regulations) and translates into industrial structural change accompanied with a change in firm behavior—or a bottom up fashion—whereby the changes in firm behavior and industrial dynamics require formal institutions to change. This chapter pays attention to the process of institutional change through the case of the sanitary crisis of the Chilean salmon industry.

The formal institutional change in response to the sanitary crisis in 2007 is observed in the passing of the Aquaculture Law (Ley Aquacultura, Ley No. 20.434) in 2010. This modification of the law granted more authority to the government, namely to the Undersecretariat of Fisheries (SubPesca) and the National Fisheries Service (SERNAPESCA), to ensure the sustainable management of aquaculture. The passing of the law seems to confirm that this is the top-down transformation of institution. However, real institutional changes do not take place unless each actor is motivated to change. Hence the chapter examines each stakeholder within the industry, including industrial associations, firms, regulatory institutions, suppliers, regional actors, labor unions, NGOs, and the media, to reveal the complex picture behind the top-down transformation. This examination suggests in fact that the change was the result of both bottom-up and top-down processes, confirming that effective change in institutions requires facilities to ensure dialogue among stakeholders, including those from the public and private sectors as well as civil society.

2.6 Chapter 7: Public Goods, Regulation and the Expansion of the Natural Resource Exploitation Frontier: The Future of Salmon Farming in Chile

This chapter takes up the findings from previous chapters to extend the discussion in an attempt to draw a future image of natural resource-based activities, particularly referring to Chilean salmon industry. Recently we have observed strong growth in natural resource-based activities in developing countries owing to the commodity boom. In the context of such growth, the chapter pays attention to the two issues, environmental sustainability and inclusiveness, having learned that the "successfully" developed Chilean salmon industry neither become an inclusive nor

[8] In this chapter it is defined as "a system of social factors that conjointly generate a regularity of behaviour" (Grief 2006, 30), or "self sustaining salient pattern of social interactions, as represented by meaningful rules that every agent knows and are incorporated as agents' shared beliefs about how the game is played and to be played" (Aoki 2007, 6).

environmentally sustainable industry. In dealing with issue of inclusiveness, there was some isolated success in Chile, such as Creo Antofagasta and Chinquihue Foundation, but these are not enough to address the issue of inclusiveness from the societal perspective. To improve environmental sustainability, understanding the mechanism of environmental degradation from the local perspective and creating appropriate institutions are essential to shape sustainable productive activities for the long term. The Chilean salmon industry has undergone this process through a trial and error manner, introducing institutions such as a "risk score" and "neighborhoods" that are based on a scientific understanding of ecological balance in the region where the activity is situated. It is yet to be determined whether these institutions will successfully change the behavior of stakeholders involved in this sector. The chapter reveals that the role of public sector in assuming the responsibilities for making productive activity sustainable and inclusive from a social point of view is increasingly important. At the same time, the chapter claims that this can only be possible through building strong partnerships with both the private sector and civil society.

2.7 Chapter 8: Conclusion and Policy Implications

This chapter summarizes the lessons learned from each chapter and tries to extend the discussion beyond the case of the Chilean salmon industry by linking back to the theory and practical policy issues. The four themes that are important in creating industry yet are difficult to manage without policy interventions are highlighted again. These themes are: knowledge development, environmental sustainability, institutions, and social welfare/ inclusiveness. Reflection on the lessons learned from each chapter demonstrates the need for policy intervention throughout the whole development of industry, though such policies must take into account the developmental stages of industry.

3 Background of the Case

3.1 About the Salmon Farming

This book deals with the case of salmon farming in Chile. Technologies for fish farming on a commercial scale were established relatively recently in the 1960s and increased rapidly in the 1980s. Since the 1980s, farmed fish and shellfish have higher growth rates than any other aquatic organism harvested in the world (FAO 2012: fish stat database). While the total fish harvest in the world increased by around 80 % from 1990 to 2012 (102.8 million tons to 182.9 million tons), the harvest of farmed fish increased more than five times from 16.8 million tons to 90.43 million tons. Farmed fish corresponds to almost half of the total harvest of fish today (Nihon Keizai Shinbun 2014a). The growth of fish farming has important implications for food security. Given that the majority of countries entering into aquaculture are developing countries, this case is increasingly relevant for these "late comers" to this activity. This section will illustrate the process of salmon farming to increase understanding of this sector.

There is major distinction made in salmon farming between rearing methods. The first method established in the late nineteenth century is called "ocean ranching."[9] This method takes advantage of salmon being an anadromous fish—born in freshwater, spending most of its life in the sea and then returning to fresh water to spawn—by enhancing brood stock artificially through hatcheries to increase the catch (returned salmon) in the future. This method was widely used in the USA (Alaska), Canada, Japan and USSR. Another method consists of rearing salmon entirely in the floating cage after the fresh water rearing (fresh water farming) to smolt. This method was applied for the first time in Norway in the late 1960s, in Japan in the beginning of 1970s and applied also in Chile in the late 1970s. This latter method is explained in more detail below.

The farmed salmon is carefully reared in the controlled fresh water tank and sea cage for its entire life: it is fed and inspected for possible diseases with managed control over its entire life cycle. During this process the climatic, geographical, and environmental conditions greatly affect the growth of the fish, which is unlike what occurs in the manufacturing sector. In salmon farming in particular, differences in water quality, temperature, luminosity, and combinations thereof, defined by the given geographical location, provide the basic competitive edge for the performance of the industry as well as individual firm.

In aquaculture, there is complexity that comes with the rearing of a living animal (fish) in artificial form, from reproduction to final growth. In the case of salmon, this is particularly true since the salmon's life cycle is long and it is sensitive to change in the surrounding environment. At the same time the industry, which provides perishable food for human consumption, requires carefully planned logistics and inspections to maintain quality in health and sanitation. This involves combinations of different bodies of knowledge and the capability to apply them flexibly according to changing situations at local and global level. These factors clearly suggest that attaining success in this industry cannot be attributed solely to the given natural conditions and market opportunity but also to the constant efforts made in organizing the production system to build capability.

[9] This method was established for the first time in the Murakami district of Niigata Prefecture in the eighteenth century (mid Edo era of Japan). It took 30 years to establish the systematic method of ranching through efforts led by Buheiji Aoto of Murakami-han, where salmon rearing and processing industries florished (Nihon Keizai Shinbun 2014b).

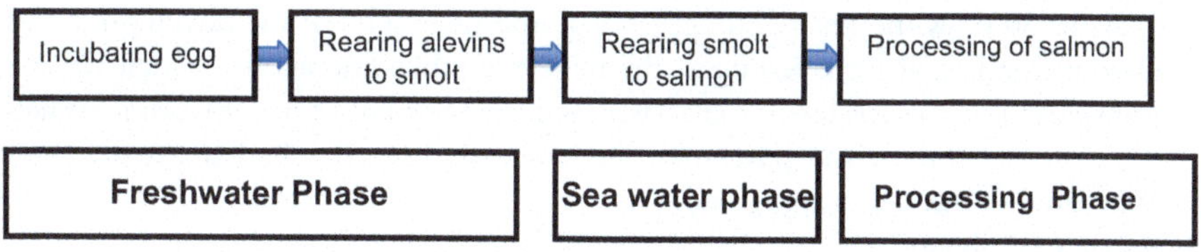

Fig. 1.1 The main line of production

The production of salmon consists of three central stages. These are: the freshwater phase (pisciculture and hatchery), the seawater phase (farming at the cultivation center), and the processing phase. Each phase involves different industrial activities but each needs to be constantly connected to all others to produce the final product, since without coordinated efforts there will be a huge loss in both quantity and quality of the products. The freshwater phase produces important inputs such as eggs, alevins and smolt for the cultivation center. This in turn rears the smolt to adult fish and provides salmon and trout as input to the processing plant. In the processing phase, the salmon are slaughtered, cut, processed, and packaged. In each phase, there exists a complex web of suppliers of products as well as services.

The main line of production can be seen as Fig. 1.1.

1. **Freshwater phase**

   In nature, salmon changes its physiology annually in relation to the environmental photoperiod. Such change allows salmon to grow in seawater and reproduce in freshwater. After the spending some time[10] in the ocean, the fish finally reach maturity and are ready to reproduce. During this period, the matured fish start to return to their original freshwater river to reproduce. Once the fish finds water without a current, the female fish starts to lay eggs and the male adds its sperm to complete fecundation.

   The aquaculture process tries to imitate this process artificially with some modifications, by selecting better quality salmon to take the eggs and reproduce for future genetic improvement. Once the selected salmon start to show signs of maturation, they are transferred in trucks with oxygen-equipped tanks from the seawater site to the freshwater site and kept for 6 months until ovulation begins. The male sperm is artificially extracted a day before the ovulation of the female and stored for artificial fertilization. The female salmon produce 1000 eggs per each kg of its weight. Hence, the female coho salmon of 5–6 kg would produce 5000 eggs and the Atlantic salmon of 7–8 kg would produce 8000 eggs, while a trout salmon would produce 8000–9000 eggs.

[10] The duration of time spent in the ocean varies from 1 to 4 years dependent on the species of salmon.

After 30 days the fertilized eggs reveal the first signs of the development of alevin: first it will form red eggs, then close and become alevin, which will be transported to the freshwater site such as a river or lake for cultivation. When these alevin attain 55–80 g in tanks, they are called smolt, which are ready to be cultivated in the sea farming site.

2. **Sea water phase**
Once the smolt (whitefry) have passed the freshwater phase, with a weight of around 55–80 g, it is transported in special trucks with water tanks to the coast where the cultivation center is located. There, the fish are kept in a cage or net for the rearing phase in the ocean. This starts between the 10th and 13th months, depending upon the type of salmon.

Maintaining the center involves many different specialists, who are usually subcontracted under supervision from the cultivation center. The strength of firms in this phase lies in the regional web of relationships established with suppliers to coordinate and collaborate amongst different stakeholders.

Due to technological progress that allows for the reproduction of salmon at any time of the year, this phase is in operation all year round with salmon at different stages of growth, through the introduction of knowledge and techniques above as well as some technological advancements leading to enhanced productivity. For instance, the introduction of auto feeders, which are programmed to adjust the amount of feed based on calculations of the speed of the current, temperature, topography, and luminosity, are increasingly being used in large farms to increase efficiency in production and to decrease the feed wastage to prevent future contamination of the water and seabed, coincides with increases in the scale of production. The provision of complementary inputs, such as large nets and infrastructure to install the large nets also supported larger-scale production which reduced the labor cost per unit of production.

3. **Processing phase (cutting and packaging)**
After harvesting, the salmon are transported to the processing plant in containers full of ice and water or through well boats. Once the fish enter the plant, they are manually weighed and processed, which consists of removing their heads and internal organs. Later, they go through a tunnel of washing and reweighing. After that, they are hanged, frozen and glazed, all by hand, and finally enter the packaging and labelling machine.

The degree of product elaboration varies depending upon the destination market. This phase can be highly profitable. Some firms utilize technology through processing machinery while others use the labor force to meet special processing needs, which is still difficult to do by machinery, such as removing fish bones from the fillet. In such respects, the availability of relatively cheap labor compared to other salmon producing countries is an advantage for Chilean producers.

Some processing plants started as subcontractor for extractive fishery; however, as the salmon farming export increased, many of them were converted into salmon processing plants. This transition required meeting higher standards for the purpose of exports. The productivity of the plants has improved tremendously, from 200–500 kg/hour to 3000–4000 kg/hour due to the incorporation of new and high-tech machinery.

4 Conclusion

There are increasing discussions on the role of policy in economic development. Most scholars accept that some policy intervention is needed, but views tend to differ significantly as to how far and in what way intervention should be implemented. This book aims to focus on policy interventions to manage public goods where market forces fail to allocate resources in an optimal way. We use the case of Chilean salmon farming, an industry that by many indicators stands as a significant success in recent decades, to discuss issues of public policy. The case concerns four themes—knowledge, environment/natural resources, institutions, and inclusiveness (social welfare)—where policy intervention has been seen as particularly important for successful and sustainable economic development.

This book illustrates the Chilean salmon farming industry. Its development has been naturally influenced by various factors including sectoral specificity, historical path dependence of the country, "windows of opportunity," and the particular moment in the history. Each story of industrial development is a unique combination of various factors, though many scholars were nonetheless able to draw some lessons for countries to follow. It must be stated that we do not aim to give a standard set of prescriptions for successful economic development based on natural resources. Rather, the book tries to give a full account of how different forms of actions were taken while interacting with external factors. The case therefore aims to describe the complex nature of the policy mix in design and implementation.

We take this strategy because we feel that due to increasing specialization in the field of social science, policy discussion on economic activities has become highly segmented and often falls short of giving the full picture for a discussion of policy issues. This is problematic for policy studies as the aim is to deal with a problem that is embedded in the complex web of interactions among numerous agents. The book aims to fill this gap by looking at policy intervention both holistically and historically through the development of the Chilean salmon industry.

We are fully aware that what we are doing in this book—a retrospective study on industrial development on one industrial sector in particular country—is limited in its ability to fully answer the real-life challenges policy makers face every day, that is, having to make difficult decisions in a set of constantly changing situations with imperfect information and uncertain prospects. Yet we hope this book can contribute to articulating their challenges for further discussions involving a wider audience who can move the agenda forward.

Box: Fish Production: The Role of Aquaculture and Salmon Farming in the Global Context

The practices of fish production and patterns of consumption have undergone substantial changes over the past four decades. On the production side, aquaculture has demonstrated fast growth while capture fishery has remained stagnant. Aquaculture provided close to half (47 %) of all fish supplies destined for direct human food consumption in 2012 (Marine Harvest 2014). Parallel to changes in fish production methods, there were significant increases in per capita consumption of fish at the global level, with quantities almost doubling from 9.9 kg in the 1960s to 18.9 kg in 2011 (FAO 2008, 2014). This means that aquaculture has played a significant role in meeting changes in fish consumption in order to keep up with global changes in diet—due to increases in protein intake—and population growth. It is expected that aquaculture will continue to play an important role in meeting the growing demand for fish around the world. According to World Bank (2013a), 62 % of fish destined for human consumption will come from aquaculture by 2030.

Figure 1.B1 shows the fish (all fish) produced by different types of production methods (captured or aquaculture) and by countries grouped by economic levels from 1985 to 2012. This figure demonstrates two important trends. First, it demonstrates the stagnant growth of capture fishery in contrast to the rapid growth of aquaculture, as mentioned above. Second, it shows the shifts of fish production activities from developed countries to developing countries. For capture fisheries, developed countries demonstrated an overall decline while developing countries showed some increase. This contrast is clearer in terms of aquaculture, where 'other developing countries' showed strong growth, while the other two groups, 'developed' and 'least developing' countries, remained stagnant.

In fact, if detailed statistics at the country level for aquaculture are examined, the top ten producing countries in 2012 (excluding aquatic plants and non-food products) were mainly developing countries such as China (41.1 million tons), India (4.2 million tons), Viet Nam (3.1 million tons), Indonesia (3.1 million tons), Bangladesh, Norway, Thailand, Chile, Egypt and Myanmar. These countries, in total, constituted 88 % of global aquaculture production in volume (FAO 2014). In terms of global exports of these fishery resources, developing countries currently export 77 % (in value terms) of fish products (FAO 2014). Among these developing countries, China was by far the top producing country in 2012 (FAO 2014).

Salmonids constituted 4.2 % of global seafood supply in 2012 (Marine Harvest 2014). 'Salmon' is the common name for several species of fish under the family Salmonids that are either captured or farmed. Each species of salmon is produced differently. For instance, Atlantic salmon and rainbow trout are commonly farmed; pink, chum, and sockeye salmon are commonly

(continued)

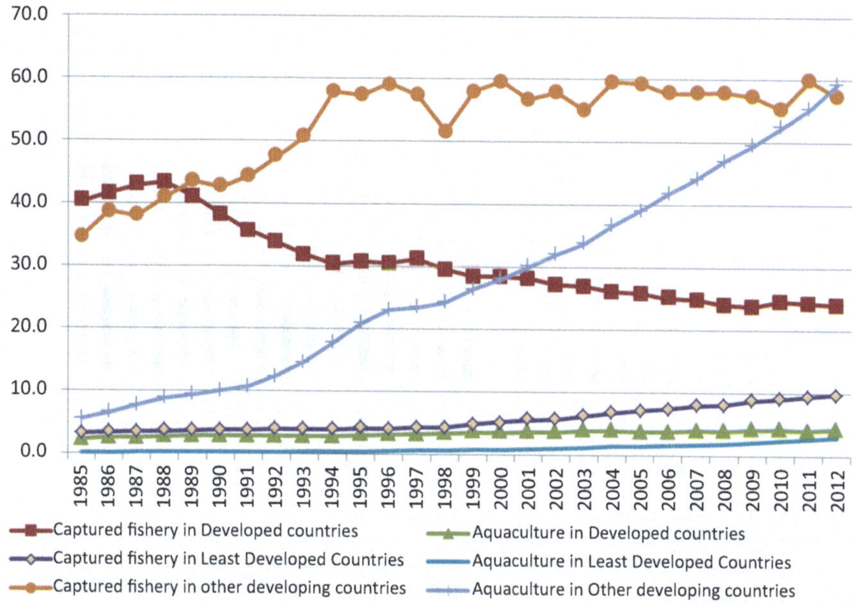

Fig. 1.B1 Fish production by production methods and economic levels of countries from 1985 to 2012 (in million tons) (Source: Authors, based on FAO (2014) Fishery and Aquaculture Statistics 2012. Note: The definition of 'developed' 'other developing' and 'least developing countries' follows UN Country classification prepared by Development Policy and Analysis Division (DPAD) of Department of Economic and Social Affairs of the United Nations Secretariat (UN/DESA))

captured; while coho (silver) and chinook (king) are mainly farmed, with a only small quantity of them still being captured (Marine Harvest 2012). Hence, when compared, the major species of 'farmed salmon' are Atlantic salmon, rainbow trout and coho salmon, the main species produced in Chile and Norway.[11]

Farming techniques for salmon were developed in the 1960s. Production grew gradually over the years with establishment of the industry in Norway in the 1980s followed by Chile in the 1990s. As mentioned in Chap. 4 of this book, Chile has been the number two exporter of farmed salmon after Norway since the 1990s (Fig. 1.B2).

The pattern of increases in production corresponds well with the overall growth trends in aquaculture production (Fig. 1.B2). Historically, the rapid development of salmon farming in Chile is not just interesting in itself but also has wider implications related to global issues such as food security, sustainability and equality between Northern and Southern countries.

[11] In Norway and Chile as well as in other countries, rainbow trout is farmed in the sea and is widely known as 'trout salmon' or 'steelhead'.

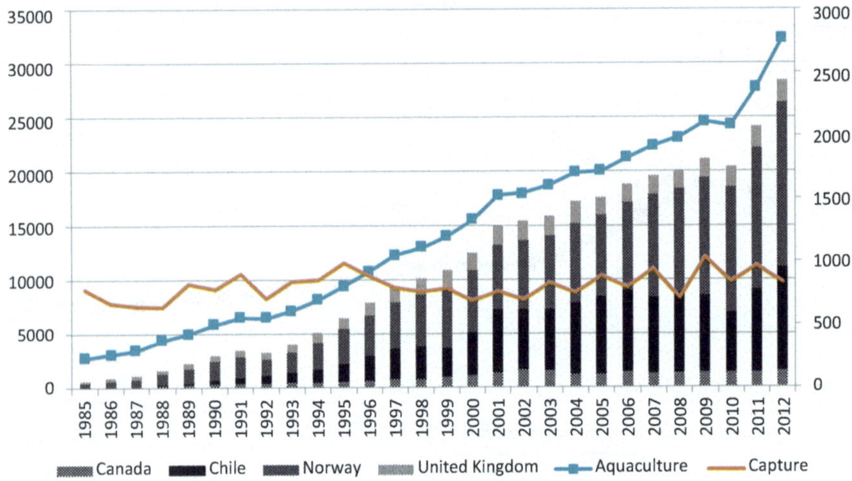

Fig. 1.B2 Increases in the production of farmed salmon by country (right axis) and global production of fish by different methods (capture and aquaculture) (in thousand tons) (*Source*: Authors, based on FAO (2014). Note: *Right axis* indicates production at country level; *left axis* indicates production at global level based on different production methods)

Bibliography

Acemoglu, D., and J. Robinson. 2012. *Why nations fail*. London: Profile Books.

Acemoglu, D., S. Johnson, and J. Robinson. 2005. Institutions as a fundamental cause of long-run growth. In *Handbook of economic growth*, vol. 1A, ed. P. Aghion and S. Durlauf, 385–472. Amsterdam: Elsevier.

ADB. 2012. In chapter 8

Aghion, P., and P. Howitt. 1992. A model of growth through creative destruction. *Ecoometrica* 60(2): 323–351.

Agosin, M.R. 1999. Trade and growth in Chile. *Cepal Review* 68: 72–100.

Amsden, A. 1989. *Asia's next giant: South Korea and late industrialization*. Oxford: Oxford University Press.

Aoki, M. 2007. Endogenizing institutions and institutional changes. *Journal of Institutional Economics* 3: 1–31.

Argote, M. 2003. *Chile Performance: La mas complete guia para hacer negocios en Chile*. Santiago: Editorial Puyehue.

Auty, R. 1990. *Resource-based industrialization: Sowing the oil in eight developing countries*. New York: Oxford University Press.

Auty, R. 2001. *Resource abundance and economic development*. Oxford: Oxford University Press.

Barton, J., and W. Murrray. 2009. Grounding geographies of economic globalization: Globalized spaces in Chile's non-traditional export sector, 1980–2005. *Tijdschrift voor Economische en Sociale Geografie* 100(1): 81–100.

Bell, M., and K. Pavitt. 1995. The development of technological capabilities. In *Trade, technology and international competitiveness*, ed. I.U. Haque, 69–102. Washington, DC: World Bank.

Chang, H.J. 2003. Kicking away the ladder – Infant industry promotion in historical perspective. *Oxford Development Studies* 31(1): 21–32.

Chang, H-J. 2011. Industrial policy: can we go beyond an unproductive confrontation? In *Annual World Bank conference on development economics 2010: Global lessons from East Asia and the global financial crisis*, eds. Justin Yifu Lin, Boris Pleskovic. Washington, DC: World Bank.

Cimoli, M., and J. Katz. 2003. Structural reforms, technological gaps and economic development: A Latin American perspective. *Industrial and Corporate Change* 12(2): 387–411.

Cimoli, M., G. Dosi, R.R. Nelson, and J. Stiglitz. 2006. *Institutions and policies shaping industrial development: An introductory note*. LEM Papers Series 2006/02, Laboratory of Economics and Management (LEM). Pisa: Sant'Anna School of Advanced Studies. http://ideas.repec.org/p/ssa/lemwps/2006-02.html. Accessed 23 Oct 2008.

Cimoli, M., G. Dosi, and J. Stiglitz. 2009. *Industrial policy and development: Political economy of capabilities, accumulation*. Oxford: Oxford University Press.

Costanza, R., R. d'Arge, R. de Groot, S. Farberk, M. Grasso, B. Hannon, K. Limburg, S. Naeem, R. O'Neill, J. Paruelo, R. Raskin, P. Suttonkk, and M. van den Belt. 1992. The value of the world's ecosystem services and natural capital. *Nature* 387: 253–260.

Cozzens, S. and J. Sutz. 2012. Innovation in informal settings: A research agenda. *Mimeo*, 28 July. http://www.crdi.ca/EN/Lists/Publications/Attachments/1130/IID%20Framework%20July%2029.pdf. Accessed Sept 2013.

Daly, H., and J.B. Cobb. 1994. *For the common good: Redirecting the economy toward community, the environment, and a sustainable future*. Boston: Beacon.

David, P. 1993. Intellectual property institutions and the panda's thumb: Patents, copy rights and trade secrets in economic theory and history. In *Global dimensions of intellectual property rights in science and technology*, ed. M.B. Wallerstein, Me. Mogee, and R.A. Schoen, 19–64. Washington, DC: National Academy Press.

De Ferrati, D.M. 2002. *From natural resource to the knowledge economy: Trade and job quality*. Washington, DC: World Bank.

ECLAC. 2000. *Panorama de la Insercion International de America Latin y el Caribe*. Santiago: Economic Commission for Latin America and Caribbean, United Nations.

ECLAC. 2002. *Globalization and development, Santiago, Chile Economic Commission for Latin America and Caribbean*. United Nations.

FAO. 2008. *The state of world fisheries and aquaculture*. Rome: FAO.

FAO. 2014. *Fishery and aquaculture statistics 2012*. Rome: FAO.

Fu, X., C. Pietrobelli, and L. Soete. 2011. The role of foreign technology and indigenous innovation in the emerging economies: Technological change and catch up. *World Development* 39(7): 1204–1212.

Greif, A. 2006. *Institutions and the path to the modern economy: Lessons from medieval trade*. New York: Cambridge University Press.

Hardin, G. 1968. The tragedy of the commons. *Science* 162: 1243–1248.

Hausmann, R., and D. Rodrik. 2005. Self-discovery in a development strategy for El Salvador. *Economia* 6(1): 43–101.

Hawken, P., A. Lovins, and H. Lovins. 1999. *Natural capitalism: Creating the next industrial revolution*. Boston: Little Brown Publications.

Hosono, A. 2010. *Nambei Chili wo sake yushutsu taikoku ni kaeta Nihonjintachi* (The Japanese who transformed Chile into a major salmon exporter). Tokyo: Daiyamondo-sha.

Howells, J. 2006. Intermediation and the role of intermediaries in innovation. *Research Policy* 35: 715–728.

Iizuka, M. 2007. *Global standards and local producers knowledge governance and the rise of the Chilean salmon industry*. PhD dissertation, University of Sussex.

Katz, J. 2001. Structural reforms and technological behavior: The sources and nature of technological change in Latin America in the 1990s. *Research Policy* 30: 1–19.

Katz, J. 2006. Economic, institutional and technological forces inducing the successful inception of salmon farming in Chile. In *Technology, adaption and exports: How some countries got it right*, ed. V. Chandra, 193–224. Washington, DC: World Bank.

Koh, L.P., and D.S. Wilcove. 2007. Cashing in palm oil for conservation. *Nature* 448: 993–994. *The World Economy* 8(2): 93–108.

Lenzen, M., D. Moran, K. Kanemoto, B. Foran, L. Lobefaro, and A. Geschke. 2012. International trade drives biodiversity threats in developing nations. *Nature* 486: 109–112.

Lin, J. 2011. New structural economics: A framework for rethinking development. *The World Bank Research Observer* 26: 193–221.
Lin, J.Y., and H. Chang. 2009. DPR debate: Should industrial policy in developing countries conform to comparative advantage or defy it? *Development Policy Review* 27(5): 483–502.
Lundvall, B.Å. 2010. *National systems of innovation–towards a theory of innovation and interactive learning*. New York: Anthem Press.
Marine Harvest. 2012. *Salmon farming industry handbook 2012*. Oslo: Marine Harvest ASA.
Marine Harvest. 2014. *Salmon farming industry handbook 2014*. Oslo: Marine Harvest ASA.
Martinez-Alier, J. 1990. *Ecological economics: Energy, environment and society*. Oxford: Basil Blackwell.
Mazzoleni, R., and R.R. Nelson. 1998. The benefit s and cots of strong patent protection: A contribution to the current debate. *Research Policy* 27: 273–284.
Meller, P., and R.E. Saez. 1997. *Auge Exportador Chileno: lecciones y desafios futuros*. Santiago: Cieplan y Dolmen.
Montero, C. 2004. *Formación y Desarrollo de un Clúster Globalizado: El Caso de la Industria del Salmón en Chile*. Santiago: ECLAC, United Nations.
Naunde, W. 2010. *New challenges for industrial policy*. Working paper No 2010/107, UNWIDER, September, 2010.
Nelson, R. 2008. What enables rapid economic progress: What are the needed institutions? *Research Policy* 37: 1–11.
Nelson, R., and B. Sampat. 2001. Making sense of institutions as a factor shaping economic performance. *Journal of Economic Behavior and Organization* 44: 31–54.
Nihon Keizai Shinbun. 2014a. Consumption of fish filled by farming. *Nihon Keizai Shinbun*. 3rd November 2014
Nihon Keizai Shinbun. 2014b. Salmon cultue nurtured by Castle Town, Niigata Murakami. *Nihon Keizai Shinbun*. 18th November 2014
Nissanke, M., and E. Thorbecke. 2010. Globalization, poverty and inequality in Latin America: Finding from case studies. *World Development* 38(6): 797–802.
Noman, A., K. Botchwey, H. Stein, and J.E. Stigliz. 2012. *Good growth and the governance in Africa: Rethinking development strategies, the initiative for policy Dialogue*. Oxford: Oxford University Press.
Nordhaus, W.D. 1969. *Invention, growth and welfare, a theoretical treatment of technological change*. Cambridge: MIT Press.
North, D. 1990. *Institutions, institutional change and economic performance*. Cambridge/ New York: Cambridge University Press.
North, D. 1991. Institutions. *The Journal of Economic Perspectives* 5(1): 97–112.
Odagiri, H., A. Goto, A. Sunami, and R.R. Nelson. 2010. *Intellectual property rights, development, and catch up*. Oxford: Oxford University Press.
OECD. 2007. *Chile OECD reviews of innovation policy*. Paris: OECD.
OECD. 2012. *Innovation and inclusive development: Discussion report*. Paris: OECD.
OECD. 2013. *Perspectives on global development 2013: Industrial policies in a changing world shifting up a gear*. Paris: OECD Development Center.
Ostrom, E. 1990. *Governing the commons: Evolution of institutions for collective action*. New York: Cambridge University Press.
Ostrom, E., J. Burger, C.B. Field, R.B. Norgaard, and D. Policansky. 1999. Revisiting the commons: Local lessons, global challenges. *Science* 284: 278–282.
Pardey, P.G., J.M. Alston, and V.W. Ruttan. 2010. The economics of innovation and technical change in agriculture. In *Handbook of economics of technical change*, ed. B.H. Hall and N. Rosenberg, 939–984. Amsterdam: Elsevier.
Pietrobelli, C., and R. Rabellotti. 2011. Global value chains meet innovation systems: Are there learning opportunities for developing countries? *World Development* 39(7): 1261–1269.
Rodrik, D. 2001. *Development strategies for the 21st century*. Paper presented at the Annual World Bank Conference on Development Economics 2000, Washington, DC, April 8.

Rodrik, D. 2007. *One economics, many recipes: Globalization, institutions, and economic growth.* Princeton: Princeton University Press.

Rodrik, D., and R. Hausmann. 2003. Economic development as self-discovery. *Journal of Development Economics* 72: 603–633.

Romer, R.M. 1987. Growth based on increasing returns due to specialization. *American Economic Review* 77(2): 56–62.

Romer, R.M. 1990. Endogenous technological change. *Journal of Political Economy* 98(5,2): S71–S102.

Sato, J. 2011. *State inaction in resource governance: Natural resource control and bureaucratic oversight in Thailand.* JICA-RI Working Paper No 36. Tokyo: JICA Research Institute.

Scott, W.R. 1995. *Institutions and Organizations. Ideas, Interests and Identities.* Los Angeles, Sage.

Stiglitz, J.E. 1999. Knowledge as a global public good. In *Global public goods: International cooperation in the 21st century*, ed. I. Kaul, I. Grunberg, and M. Stern. New York: Office of Development Studies (ODS), Bureau for Development Policy (BDP), United Nations Development Programme (UNDP).

UN/DESA. 2012. *Statistical annex, country classification.* New York: UN/DESA. http://www.un.org/en/development/desa/policy/wesp/wesp_current/2012country_class.pdf#page=10&zoom=auto,-12,726. Accessed 3 June 2015

UNEP. 2011. *Towards a green economy: Pathways to sustainable development and poverty eradication—A synthesis for policy makers.* Accessed 28th Jun 2012. www.unep.org/greeneconomy.

Van Wijk, J., and G. Junne. 1993. *Intellectual property protection of advanced technology. Changes in the global technology system: Implications and options for developing countries.* Maastricht: UNU/INTECH.

Verspagen, B. 2003. Intellectual property rights in the world economy. In *Economics, law and intellectual property*, ed. O. Granstrand, 489–518. Boston: Kluwer Academic Publishers.

Wade, R. 1990. *Governing the market: Economic theory and the role of government in East Asia's industrialization.* Princeton: Princeton University Press.

Wade, R. 2010. After the crisis: Industrial policy and the developmental state in low-income countries. *Global Policy* 1(2): 150–161.

Wade, R. 2012. Return of industrial policy. *International Review of Applied Economics* 26(2): 223–239.

Warwick, K. 2013. *Beyond industrial policy: Emerging issues and new trends.* OECD Science, Technology and Industry Policy Papers, No. 2, Paris: OECD Publishing.

Williamson, John. 1999. *What should the bank think about Washington Consensus?* Paper prepared as a background to the World Bank's World Development Report, 2000, Jul 1999.

Williamson, O. 1975. *Markets and hierarchies: Analysis and antitrust implications.* New York: Free Press.

Williamson, O. 1985. *The economic institutions of capitalism.* New York: Free Press.

Williamson, O. 1998. The institutions of governance. *The American Economic Review* 88(2): 75–79.

World Bank. 1993. *The East Asian miracle: Economic growth and public policy.* Washington, DC: World Bank.

World Bank. 2013a. *Fish to 2030.* Washington, DC: World Bank.

World Bank. 2013b. *World development report 2013.* Washington, DC: World Bank.

Chapter 2
Genesis of Chilean Salmon Farming

Akio Hosono

1 Introduction: Creating New Industry and Transforming Economic Structures in Developing Countries?

Industrial development and economic transformation have recently been attracting renewed attention. Among the significant and growing research on industrial policy, however, only a small proportion has focused on the early phases of industrial development—an essential area, as this nascent phase is quite different from the later stages of industrial development. The existing literature places importance on the accumulation of knowledge and capabilities (Cimoli et al. 2009) and creation of a learning society (Stiglitz and Greenwald 2014). Knowledge creation, capability building and learning processes are crucial factors that cannot be optimally managed via market forces. Consistent under-investment in these areas by the private sector provides a basis for arguments justifying policy intervention. However, there is no clear consensus in the existing policy-related literature regarding the type of policy interventions necessary for industrial development, the degree and duration (Rodrik 2007) or the selection of areas for intervention (Lin and Chang 2009).

This Chapter tries to answer the question of what needs to be done to establish and foster a new industry and to identify the conditions that play a role in its successful development within a relatively short period of time. It does so by presenting an illustrative case study of the Chilean salmon industry at its inception phase—from its early period up to the establishment, or commercialization, of the salmon industry. As some research (Katz 2005; Iizuka 2008; Hosono 2010) has shown, this industry has achieved rapid development in a way that could be described as almost miraculous: a start-from-scratch process in a country where the production of salmon on a commercial scale had not existed before. Although

A. Hosono (✉)
Japan International Cooperation Agency Research Institute (JICA-RI), Tokyo, Japan
e-mail: hosono.akio@jica.go.jp

A. Hosono et al. (eds.), *Chile's Salmon Industry*,
DOI 10.1007/978-4-431-55766-1_2

numerous existing studies have paid attention to the growth period of this industry after the open economic policy was put in place, very few have paid attention to the gestation period before the actual emergence of the industry, particularly with regard to how knowledge creation, capacity building and learning took place in order to prepare for the takeoff of this industry.

Chile has pursued market-oriented economic policies since the mid-1970s. This means that policy interventions are supposed, in theory, to be restricted to ensuring that the market functions correctly (trade and foreign investment liberalization, privatization, deregulation and so forth) while scant attention is given to more proactive policy interventions to promote the development of so-called soft and hard infrastructure (Lin 2012a, b). These are areas that are often considered to be public goods, and require significant investment. In the case of Chile in the 1970s and 1980s, the government did not promote policies towards directly fostering the development of industries. However, it is clear that the Chilean salmon industry did not develop as a result of voluntary investments from the private sector at the outset. Noting that the major export items for Chile include copper, grapes, fish and timber, Rodrik (2007, 109) argued that the diversification of export products from the traditional production of copper had hitherto not been achieved in a laissez-faire market.

This and the following chapters will also serve the purpose of presenting previously undisseminated information showing the important roles played by both Fundación Chile and Japan-Chile scientific and technical cooperation.[1] Together with other agencies, industry experts and individuals, there was an effort made towards social, economic and institutional change. At the same time, these chapters explicitly address the topic of Japanese influence, as the Japanese market imported more than half of the Chilean total salmon exports during the early development phase of salmon industry. In presenting this case, the author hopes to contribute to existing discussions on viable public policy interventions for economic development.[2]

[1] As such, these chapters do not explore other sources of capability and knowledge enhancement, as they will be examined in the following chapters of the book.

[2] There has been a dispute over the role of government in the development of an industry since the argument for infant industry protection was put forward. For example, *The East Asian Miracle: Economic Growth and Public Policy* (World Bank 1993) reintroduced the neoclassical view that the market should play the central role in the economy, with a limited role for government. It also presents some arguments critical of this view. Then it analyzes cases in Asia and advocates "market-friendly" strategies. More recently, Dani Rodrik and his colleagues have put forward an "industrial policy for the twenty-first century" (Rodrik 2007). Joseph Stiglitz and his colleagues advocate "industrial policies in the new millennium" (Cimoli et al. 2009). Some of these studies make note of and introduce the development of the Chilean salmon industry, among other cases.

2 Essential Requirements for the Industrial Development of the Chilean Salmon Industry

In order to analyze the development of the Chilean salmon industry, we need to first look at both the supply and demand-side conditions. The supply-side conditions refer to the ability to competitively produce and supply products on the global market. The requirements for these conditions include not only favorable natural conditions and the availability of sufficient capital and labor to support the industry but also appropriate technology/innovation and trained industrial personnel. The demand-side conditions relate to the existence or the cultivation of the market. In the case of the Chilean salmon industry, the natural conditions, capital, and labor were generally favorable. What was lacking was the technology and trained industrial personnel. Introducing and developing technology may be no easy task for the private sector. Personnel with the necessary skills to sustain an industry will not be trained overnight, and costs for the private sector are likely to be significant, as they require long-term investment (Fig. 2.1).

The development of the Chilean salmon industry can be divided into four phases or periods: a "preparatory phase" in the 1960s and 1970s, an "establishment phase", from the end of the 1970s into the 1980s, an early development phase, in which the industry began to expand as innovations spread in the early 1990s, and a "fully-fledged development" phase from the second half of the 1990s and the beginning of this century. As noted earlier, much of the existing literature only really focuses on the latter periods in detail. Figure 2.2 summarizes the analytical framework of these four phases.

Existing studies stress that technology and industrial personnel training/capacity building are the most important of all factors (Iizuka 2006).[3] These studies identified trained personnel, technology and, later, the development of an innovation system as three major factors necessary for developing an industry. Yet the importance and role of supply-side requirements will necessarily differ between the early preparatory period and later periods after takeoff has occurred.

In the preparatory phase, emphasis must be placed on introducing and transferring technology from overseas. This requires establishing a basic skill and knowledge base to undertake the new activities required for the industry. It is not easy for private companies by themselves to venture into new activities due to high risk and uncertainty. The conditions may be even more difficult for firms in developing countries. Hence in this phase, the role of public policy is crucial, particularly in identifying, introducing and diffusing knowledge with the aim of creating a basic knowledge base. From this point, the learning process during this gestation period should be considered differently to those of after the take off in view of degrees of risks and uncertainty involved.

[3] In addition to the work by Iizuka (2006), research focused on the clusters of the salmon industry has been carried out by Montero (2004), Maggi Campos (2006), and others.

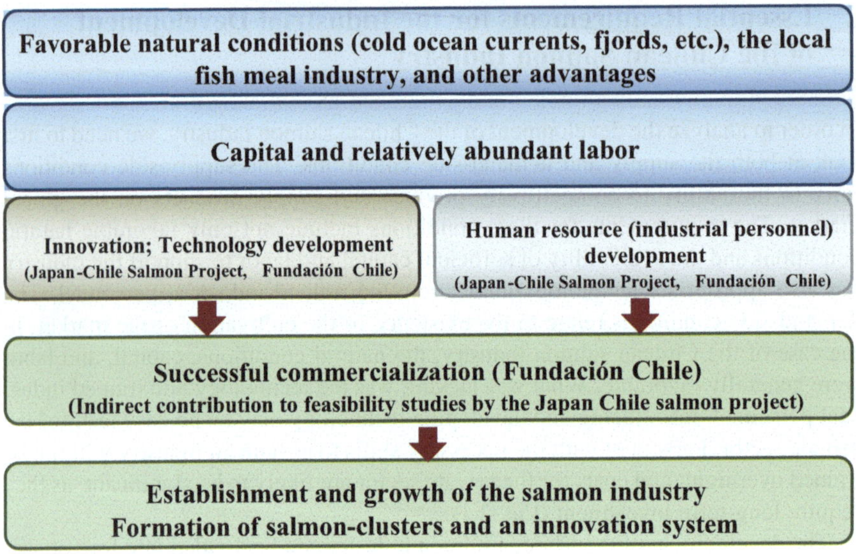

Fig. 2.1 Requirements for and processes involved in the establishment and growth of the Chilean salmon industry (*Source*: Created by the author)

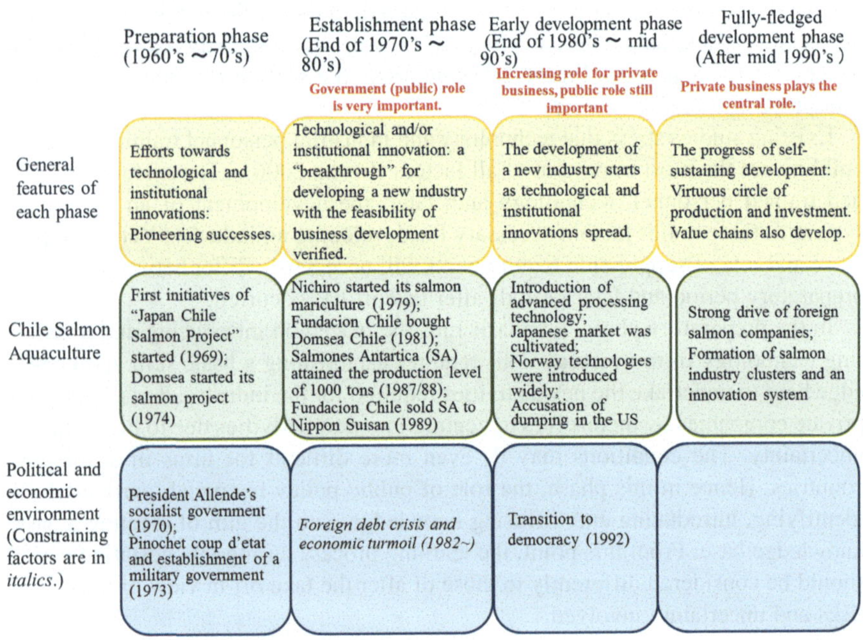

Fig. 2.2 Four phases of development of the salmon industry in Chile: an analytical framework (*Source*: Prepared by the author)

As Rodrik (2007) emphasizes in his work, investors are most likely to think twice about investing in a new industry if technologies that have been developed over much time and expense are not protected by patents or other methods of intellectual property control. This is because the uncontrolled copying of such technologies will undermine confidence that sufficient profit will be returned to investors in compensation for the high risks and development costs. Private companies will have to train industrial personnel in-house if no institutions for training such personnel are available. That increases costs substantially, and they will be unable to recover those costs if trained employees are lured away by other companies. This is why governments need to play a role in establishing education and training institutions or similar facilities during these early phases.

The above describes the situation for the Chilean salmon farming industry during the preparatory and establishment phases. The under-investment in knowledge creation necessary for the establishment of a new industry was met by governmental or semi-governmental initiatives, such as the "Japan-Chile Salmon Project" and Fundación Chile's Salmones Antártica project. The former initiative was implemented through an international technical cooperation scheme between Chile and Japan. The Chilean Ministry of Agriculture and Livestock, SERNAP (National Fisheries Service) and IFOP (Fisheries Development Institute), and JICA (Japan International Cooperation Agency) were jointly in charge of the program under an agreement between the Chilean and Japanese governments. The second initiative will be explained below.[4]

Because the Japan-Chile Salmon Project took place under the auspices of the two governments, technologies transferred/adapted/developed were treated as public goods that were made freely available and diffused in what was later to become the salmon industry in Chile. Similar steps were taken by Fundación Chile, a semi-governmental corporation but in this case strong emphasis was placed on developing the commercial feasibility of salmon farming for export markets.

[4] Andres Couve Rioseco, director of the Fishing and Hunting Division of SAG between 1967 and 1970, signed an agreement between the University of Washington in Seattle and SAG thanks to an encounter with Dr. Earnest Salo, professor of the School of Fisheries at that university. The agreement was to select the right rivers to introduce coho and chinook salmon between Valdivia and Puerto Montt. As for this and other initiatives undertaken before the Japan-Chile Salmon Project, see TechnoPress and SalmonChile (2003).

3 Phases of Birth and Growth of a New Industry: Preparation, Establishment, Early Development and Fully-Fledged Development

The development of an industry in a market economy requires ensuring a sustainable cycle of expanding production in which private entrepreneurs invest in that industry and reinvest the profits from such investments. It therefore calls for the critical stage of commercialization as a precondition for entrepreneurs to invest. In other words, it is essential to demonstrate the commercial feasibility of the industry for private companies. This role was effectively performed by Fundación Chile.

In this and the following chapters, the 10-year period from 1979 to 1988 is considered to be when the establishment phase of the Chilean salmon industry took place, a period when its commercial feasibility was established. During this period, salmon farming in the private sector was started off by the Japanese fishery Nichiro (now Maruha Nichiro Seafoods, Inc.) followed by Mytilus. Later, Salmones Antártica attained a production level of 1000 tons of sea-farmed salmon. Fundación Chile sold this company to Nippon Suisan Kaisha, another Japanese fishery company, at the end of this phase.

In terms of industrial development, the establishment phase (or the commercialization phase) is preceded by a preparatory phase. In the case of the Japan-Chile Salmon Project, the most important objectives in this phase included introducing technologies crucial for the establishment and development of the salmon industry, developing the institutional capacity to develop technologies on their own, and training technicians and industrial personnel through these processes in Chile. The initiatives taken by Fundación Chile, Japan-Chile Salmon Project as well as of other entities were the major drivers of technological transfer, institutional capacity building, and human resources development in the preparatory and commercialization phases.

The establishment/commercialization phase is followed by the development phases, in which production expansion is primarily driven by the private sector's self-sustained investment. The early stages of these phases or the "early development phase" generally entail many difficulties. Failure to overcome these difficulties in this phase may stall industrial development altogether. In other words, the key to sustained production expansion after demonstration of feasibility is whether the private sector will be able to successfully address such challenges on its own.

Among the challenges to be addressed in the Chilean salmon industry were cultivating the market, increasing the competitiveness of the products through quality assurance and other means, and establishing a Chilean brand. Chile first successfully commercialized coho salmon farming. This species played a pivotal role in the early stages of development of the Chilean salmon industry, during which time Japan accounted for more than 55 % of its market. It was therefore crucial to develop distribution channels in the Japanese market and assure the quality and regulatory standards suitable for this market. In a later challenge, as the Chilean salmon industry began increasing its exports to the United States, it was confronted with a dumping accusation.[5]

4 Starting from Scratch: Internalization of Basic Technologies of Salmon Farming in Chile

Basic technologies for salmon aquaculture were introduced and consolidated in Chile through at least the three following conduits: Japan-Chile Salmon Project; Domsea Farms and Fundación Chile projects as well as initiatives by private companies. The first two initiatives started with a *raise and release method of aquaculture* in which the firm artificially released salmon juveniles raised in freshwater into the river and waited until grown salmon returned to the river after remaining for 1–4 years in the sea.[6] Both initiatives faced difficulties because of the low return rates of salmon. In the case of the Domsea Farms project, in addition to achieving a higher and profitable return rate, the company needed to see the establishment of a law that would guarantee the ownership of the returned salmon to the companies that had released them, as its aim was to put salmon stocking on a commercial footing.

In the case of Domsea Farms, although the rate of return remained below 1 %, this return rate was still high enough to continue the propagation process, including extracting and incubating eggs, raising them into juveniles and releasing them (Mendez and Munita 1989, 192). In the case of the Japan-Chile salmon project, the rate of return was even lower and efforts were made to introduce mariculture (sea farming): that is, farming salmon in floating net pens in the sea in which salmon are reared to adulthood, stripped of eggs, the hatchlings from the eggs raised into juveniles, which in turn are released. In the following sections, a historical account is given, explaining in detail the process of internalizing salmon aquiculture in conjunction with the above-mentioned initiatives.

[5] The dumping accusation was brought to the U.S. Department of Commerce by main US salmon producers (TechnoPress and SalmonChile 2003, 274).

[6] Raise and release (or ranching) method is based on the release of small fish (smolt) and the capture of adult stock. Salmonid species such as Pacific and Atlantic salmons and steelhead trout are anadromous and have a good homing instinct. In this method, the profit/benefit depends on rate of return of adult salmon.

4.1 Japan-Chile Salmon Project: The First Structured Government Salmon Initiative

Southern Chile was poor until the 1980s. In particular, Chiloé Island, situated at around 42°–43° south in the Los Lagos region, Coihaique in the Aysén region,[7] and the vast coastal zone of fjords to the south with little access to arable land or fish of high value.[8] Chiloé was often derided as "an island that produces only potatoes," and the people were particularly badly off. Artisanal fishers there had to live off the land through a mixture of semi-agricultural and semi-fishing activities. Many other artisanal fishers lived on other, isolated islands in the region, which were even more impoverished. Without opportunities or hope for the future, many young people left the islands.

In the face of above tough socio-economic conditions, the salmon stocking project was developed as a way to alleviate the poverty in the Southern region during the 1960s by the government. The Chilean government conceived of the idea of raising artisanal fishers out of poverty by allowing them to catch fish of higher value, particularly by releasing juvenile salmon so that they would return as adults as they do in the Northern Hemisphere. At that time, the Japan Fisheries Association (JFA[9]) was looking for an alternative source of salmon in the North Pacific Ocean, with production expected to dwindle as a result of restrictions on operating areas and fishing seasons by both the United States and the Soviet Union. Chile was one of the candidates for an alternative fishery site chosen by the JFA. Hence, the interests of JFA and Chile coincided, leading to the launch of a technological cooperation program of fry and stock salmon in Chile.

A series of fishery cooperation projects was conducted between 1969 and 1989 by Chilean government and Japanese government through Japan International Cooperation Agency (JICA), and other entities including its predecessor, Overseas Technical Cooperation Agency (OTCA) as well as Chilean public organizations, with a focus on introducing salmon in Chile (Mendes and Munita 1989, 41). To begin with, Mr. Pablo Aguilera, an officer of SAG, Ministry of Agriculture received training in 1970 for 6 months at the Nemuro Branch of the Hokkaido Salmon Hatchery, Japanese Fisheries Agency as part of OTCA's training program in Japan. In 1972, this developed into more comprehensive technical cooperation activities,

[7] Coihaique is also known as Coyhaique and Aysén is also known as the Aisén Region.

[8] Cusk-eel and New Zealand hake are high-quality fish, but the catches are low.

[9] According to the Maruha Nichiro Salmon Museum, salmon and trout fishing in the North Pacific was resumed in 1952, however, due to several restrictions by USA and the Soviet Union in 1960s, the allowable catch was gradually decreased, and the future of the northern-sea fishery was causing considerable concern among stakeholders. Because of this, the Japan Fisheries Association sent the first salmon and trout mission to Chile in 1969 to explore the possibility of transplanting Japanese salmon. The mission was sent twice, and later, a technical cooperation program was implemented.

including technical transfer, with the dispatch of experts and the provision of salmon eggs.

In 1979, this set of activities was upgraded to the Chile Aquaculture Project under the framework of Project-Type Technical Cooperation, a major category of JICA's assistance schemes at that time. In 1984, the project was extended by 3 years toward stock buildup with emphasis on delayed release, feed development, and fish disease control. The follow-up period between 1988 and late 1989 focused on the development of technologies for domestic seed (salmon eggs) production. During almost two decades of "the Japan Chile Salmon Project",[10] a total of 52 experts from Japan were sent to Chile to transfer a diverse type of knowledge and skills with regards to salmon farming and stocking. Hence, intensive technological transfer/development activities took place. This is how the Japan-Chile Salmon Project[11] was implemented.

It was the first structured project of considerable scale in which the government of Chile was proactively involved, with the goal of introducing technology and knowledge for salmon farming—an operation that had to be started from scratch. Necessary equipment and parts all had to be airlifted to Coihaique, where this project was based, a remote city that was far from any major city in Chile. This involved not only the transfer of the technology of hatchery process and rearing of fry but also adaptation of the technology to the local area by identifying the suitable sites in Southern Chile through a trial and error process. This site selection process required careful judgment, because the success of the project depended heavily on its outcome. Of utmost importance was securing good quality water. The site was decided on after comparing and weighing several candidate sites.[12] The first two professionals sent from Japan were Mr. Ariaky Nagasawa and Dr. Yoshikazu Shiraishi.

The Japan-Chile Salmon Project had to secure salmon eggs to be hatched into juveniles. This required prior selection of suitable species of salmon. Some 150,000 cherry salmon eggs were transported by air in specially designed containers. The air transport of a large number of salmon eggs 20,000 km to the other side of the planet was no doubt the first time such an operation had been taken. It was a real challenge for the senders as well. The trial incubation of these cherry salmon eggs from

[10] In this and the following Chapters, the whole series of Japan-Chile official cooperation are referred to as "the Japan Chile Salmon Project".

[11] The project started in 1972 as a technical cooperation project, Chile Aquaculture Project, but Japan began to accept trainees from Chile in 1970, as described in the text.

[12] The hatchery was completed 4 years later and was named "Dr. Shiraishi Hatchery (Piscicultura Doctor Shiraishi)." Dr. Shiraishi suddenly passed away on November 10, 1972 after he decided on the site for the hatchery. A month before his death he wrote, "I thought that as a salmon and trout researcher, I would be most happy if I could play a role in carrying out the project and making it successful. Putting my knowledge to good use for people in the world is the most I could hope for as a fisheries researcher... As a scientist, I have come to harbor high hopes that I will be able to make the most of what I had learned, and, hopefully, create salmon and trout fisheries in the Southern Hemisphere as in the northern waters" Shiraishi (1973) (written October 5th 1972). Translation is by the author.

Fig. 2.3 View of Dr. Shiraishi Hatchery at Coihaique (Photo by Akio Hosono)

Hokkaido was successful. The success of the trial incubation paved the way for the shipment of one million eggs of chum salmon from Japan.

In March 1974, 645,000 out of the dispatched one million eggs of chum salmon hatched. In May, the first release was made. The year 1976 saw completion of building the Coihaique hatchery—the so-called Dr. Shiraishi Hatchery—by the Chilean government. With a Japanese grant, state-of-the-art laboratory equipment was installed in the facility. Following a study mission to Chile in late 1978, Japan decided to expand the project under the framework of Project-Type Technical Cooperation for a period of 5 years from 1979 (Fig. 2.3).[13]

Meanwhile, Chile created the Undersecretariat of Fisheries (SubPesca) and the National Fisheries Service (SERNAP, Servicio Nacional de Pesca) in 1978 as a result of institutional reforms by the Chilean government. These two offices were assigned as the Chilean counterpart organizations for the Japan Chile Salmon Project.[14] In this way, a new cooperation framework was established in 1979.

[13] Nagasawa worked for the Fisheries Agency after he returned to Japan, but he returned to the project in 1978 when Chilean Government strongly requested Nagasawa's dispatch for the project to a member of the House of Representatives, Shin Sakurai, during his visit to Chile.

[14] The Undersecretariat of Fisheries is Subscretaria de Pesca (SubPesca for short) in Spanish, and is responsible for fisheries. The Ministry of Economy is in Santiago, the capital, while the Undersecretariat of Fisheries is in Valparaíso, a port 100 km away from Santiago. SERNAPESCA/SERNAP is a shortened form of Servicio Nacional de Pesca, and the literal translation would be National Fisheries Service, but it is close to the Fisheries Agency of Japan.

It was deemed necessary to build a breeding facility designed to increase the size of the fish before releasing them, based on the analysis that hatchery-raised juveniles were too small in size and were often eaten by predators, making the return of adult fish after ocean migration difficult. Consequently, in 1981 another hatchery, designed primarily to raise juveniles, was constructed on the coastal area near Puerto Aisén called Ensenada Baja, 65 km from Coihaique. The construction was financed by the Japanese government. This made it possible to hatch eggs and raise juveniles (at the Dr. Shiraishi Hatchery) and then to further rear the juveniles (at Ensenada Baja Hatchery) until they grew large enough to be released. The implementation of this phase was carried out by a team of nine, consisting of Chilean and Japanese experts, a joint undertaking by JICA and SERNAP.[15]

The Japan Chile Salmon Project endeavored to raise salmon to adulthood in floating cages in a fjord to obtain offspring in Ensenada Baja in 1979. This attempt paid off handsomely. The salmon grew to 3–4 kg in weight, matured, and produced fertilized eggs. This was how the Japan-Chile Salmon Project obtained the second generation of transplanted chum salmon—the first recorded case of chum salmon in South America. The Project expanded on this technique and came to produce by itself a far greater amount of seeds than it had by hatching eggs brought from Hokkaido. The locally produced seeds better suited the seasons, environment, and climate in Chile. The domestic production of chum salmon in 1982 by the Japan-Chile Salmon Project was a remarkable feat. It was a major milestone for the project. The success of seed (eggs) production—a cycle of adult rearing, egg stripping, fertilization, incubation, and juvenile raising, and releasing—was not achieved overnight. As far as sea farming (mariculture) was concerned, project members had already accumulated experience in trial releases of chum salmon from the cages when they reached a certain length (such as 10, 15, or 20 cm). In other words, they practiced "delayed release," in which juveniles were raised to be of a larger size and then released with seasonal adjustments (for additional information regarding the "delayed release" process, see BOX of this Chapter).

Accumulation of know-how on sea farming came about as follows. In the trial and error process of improving the return rate of salmon, they were experimenting the impact of the size of juveniles at the moment of release. For this, chum salmon, from Hokkaido was used. Chum salmon is characterized by its short growing period in fresh water and this makes it possible to release juveniles when they are small, unlike coho salmon. While this makes production cycle shorter, small chum juveniles thus released were often eaten by other fish. To deal with this problem, project members transported juveniles from the freshwater hatchery in Coihaique to sea cages in Ensenada Baja for further rearing and conducted experiments in which the larger juveniles were released and their return levels were checked. In the

[15] As mentioned above, the Japan Chile Salmon Project in this book refers to a series of cooperation activities, including this Japan Chile joint project, which was terminated in late 1989, and other preceding activities. The Chilean counterpart organization was SERNAP (National Fisheries Service) until 1987, and IFOP (Fisheries Development Institute, Instituto de Fomento Pesquero in Spanish) between 1988 and 1989.

process of this experimentation, they raised the juveniles until they reached different sizes before releasing them and checked the necessary amount of feed and the return rate for each size. They then analyzed the correlation between juvenile size at release and return rate. These experiments were made to determine the optimal size at release with the necessary amount of feed taken into account.

At the end of this trial and error process of experimentation, sufficient experience of rearing salmon in cages in the sea had been accumulated, in preparation for commencing the sea farming of adults. This experience, together with an already established system for domestic egg production was a particularly significant achievement in the process of establishing a Chilean salmon industry. First and foremost, that meant being able to secure safe, disease-free eggs for seed production. It also meant that egg supply shortage problems arising from the seasonal differences between the Northern and Southern hemispheres had been overcome.[16]

4.2 Domsea Farms, the First Foreign Company to Start Salmon Stocking in Chile

In 1976, the year the Dr. Shiraishi Hatchery was completed in Coihaique, Mr. Jon Lindbergh, from the US state of Washington, made up his mind to conduct salmon stocking in Chile.[17] At that time, Lindbergh was a director at Domsea Farms, a subsidiary of Union Carbide. Founded in 1969, Domsea Farms reportedly had a department called "New Adventurers" created by Lindbergh and Mr. Dick Nobel. On learning that salmon farming had started in Norway, Lindbergh tried to do the same in the United States. Due to legal and other constraints, this proved difficult to put into practice, and he instead chose Chile.[18] By the middle of 1976 it became clear that Chile was suitable for salmon farming, and Lindbergh developed the idea of transplanting salmon from the Northern Hemisphere to the Southern Hemisphere.

Lindbergh instructed the Chilean branch of Union Carbide[19] to start making preparations. A staff member at the branch visited the Fisheries Protection Division of the Agricultural and Livestock Service[20] (SAG, Servicio Agrícola Ganadero), which advised him to locate the project on Chiloé Island. Located some 500 km

[16] In the Northern Hemisphere, salmon typically migrate out to sea in summer after hatching from eggs in spring. In the case of eggs brought from the Northern Hemisphere, releases were made in autumn in Chile, because the seasons are reversed. Research found, however, that some released juveniles spent the winter in rivers. It that case, it would take 3 years to reach adulthood.

[17] Jon Lindbergh was the second son (among the six children) of Charles Lindbergh, famous for having completed the first nonstop transatlantic flight.

[18] This and following paragraphs regarding Domsea Farms are based on an interview with Ricardo Rodríguez in February 2008 and Mendez and Munita (1989).

[19] To be precise, Union Carbide Comercial Chile Ltda.

[20] División de Protección Pesquera del Servicio Agrícola Ganadero (SAG).

north of Coihaique, Chiloé Island has a somewhat warmer climate, where the temperature does not reach minus 20 °C in winter as it does in Coihaique. The island had a much larger population and is linked by ferry with the mainland of Chile. In November 1976, Domsea Farms brought in 500,000 coho salmon eggs to Lake Popetan in Chiloé, but 90 % of them died due to unexpected rises in temperature. A replacement batch of 200,000 died out due to a subsequent storm.

The company found the most appropriate place for a hatchery at Curaco de Vélez. This hatchery later proved to be a trailblazer for Chile, along with the Dr. Shiraishi Hatchery. While the Dr. Shiraishi Hatchery focused on cherry salmon and chum salmon, this hatchery of Domsea Farms incubated coho salmon, with the eggs brought in from Washington State, USA. In 1978, the company released 200,000 coho juveniles and 170,000 chinook juveniles. In 1979, 30 coho salmon returned.[21] The return rate, however, did not suffice for Domsea Farms. Moreover, because its aim was to put salmon stocking on a commercial footing, the company needed to see the establishment of a law that would guarantee the ownership of the returned salmon for companies that had released them, which Domsea Farms was never able to obtain.

Meanwhile, the release operation continued. Returns, however, continued to be elusive; some of the released salmon returned in good years but almost none in bad years. The rate of return remained below 1 %. Yet the low return rate was high enough to continue the propagation process, including extracting and incubating eggs, and raising them into juveniles and releasing them. In 1979, the company was renamed Domsea Pesquera Chile Limitada.

After the ephemeral joy at the confirmation of the returns, Union Carbide, the parent company, decided to step out from the salmon project. As it was primarily focused on chemical production, Union Carbide had little interest in propagating salmon. The company approached several food producing companies with the idea of selling. As a result, the Chiloé hatchery was sold to Campbell Soup Co., a long-established American food company in 1979. Campbell bought Domsea Pesquera but showed no interest in the salmon project. The person in charge of the project, Griff Evans, returned home, and Ricardo Rodríguez who remained in Curaco de Vélez had no choice but to continue the operations with his locally hired assistant. Rodríguez then went to Norway to study farming facilities there, returning home with fish cages.

In this way, two salmon projects, though different in nature, were simultaneously underway between 1978 and 1979: one in Coihaique and Ensenada Baja, Aisén Region; and the other on Chiloé Island, Los Lagos Region. It was just at this time that a Japanese company Nichiro started salmon sea farming in Puerto Montt.

---

[21] This species is characterized by its behavior of not going far into the ocean before returning home.

4.3 *Nichiro: The Pioneer in the Commercialization and Mariculture of Salmon Farming in Chile*

In 1978, Nichiro Fisheries ("Nichiro", later Maruha Nichiro) set up Nichiro Chile, which in 1979 launched salmon sea farming, near the city of Puerto Montt (facing Chiloé Island), the first of its kind by a private company in the country.[22] This was a groundbreaking event that surprised fisheries experts at home and abroad who were familiar with the situation. The funds necessary for this investment in Chile were provided by a Japanese government entity for concessional financial cooperation, OECF (Overseas Economic Cooperation Fund, that later merged with Japan International Cooperation Agency, JICA). The funding was decided bearing in mind the possible synergy with Japan-Chile Salmon Project mentioned above.

Among the team at Nichiro were Mr. Yuji Nemoto and Mr. Akinori Niinuma, who later joined the Japan-Chile Salmon Project. Nemoto, who had been involved in the culture of cherry, sockeye, and coho salmon in Miyagi Prefecture and Sado Island in Niigata Prefecture, Japan, took charge of the local management of coho salmon farming (Nemoto 2002). Niinuma, who had been a veteran long-time member of the well-known salmon and trout fishing fleet that operated in the North Pacific fisheries, got involved in this coho salmon mariculture project (Furukawa 1987).

Nichiro had already accumulated aquaculture technology in Japan. In 1971, it started a freshwater culture of chum, pink, cherry, sockeye, and coho salmon with the establishment of its wholly owned subsidiary called "Nichiro Yougyo." By December 1973, the company had conducted freshwater farming with 200,000 eyed eggs of coho salmon imported from Washington State, USA. In autumn 1975, it obtained fertilized eggs through artificial spawning of freshwater-reared coho salmon, the first of its kind in Japan.

In the meantime, in 1974 the company started mariculture trials in which coho juveniles that had been raised in fresh water at a fish farm in Fujinomiya were cultured in cages in Kurihama Bay in the city of Yokosuka. In autumn 1975, it transported juveniles from Fujinomiya to Shizugawa-cho, Miyagi Prefecture and launched a mariculture feasibility study. This project harvested and shipped 2.4 tons of adults in 1976 and 5.3 tons in 1977, turning the project into a commercially feasible business. In that year, this coho salmon farming business started its full-fledged operations in partnership with the Shizugawa Fisheries Cooperative and other fisheries coops in Miyagi Prefecture and the neighboring prefecture of Iwate.[23]

---

[22] At first, salmon farming was started near Angelmo port in Puerto Monttt, but later it was moved to a suburb, Chinquihue.

[23] The description of Nichiro's aquaculture business in this Chapter is based on information provided by the article "*Sake no Yoshoku Jigyo*" [Salmon Aquaculture Business] in the Salmon Museum of Maruha Nichiro, an online virtual museum.

The aquaculture business grew steadily, with Nichiro's sales of farmed coho salmon reaching 1,000 tons in 1982. Tying up with fisheries cooperatives that practiced mariculture, the company provided seeds, feed, and technology, and sold the farmed salmon through its distribution channels across Japan. Such accumulated experience and technology of Nichiro was put to effective use for the mariculture business in Chile.

Nichiro Chile had started coastal surveys using fishing boats to select optimal farming grounds since early 1978, finally deciding on Puerto Montt. In December 1978, the company launched the aquaculture business with eyed eggs of coho salmon from the United States. After successful farming, in 1980 it harvested Chile's first sea-farmed coho salmon, totaling 130 tons.[24] Though small in size, Nichiro's aquaculture business in Chile was a milestone because it was the first to demonstrate the commercial feasibility of mariculture in Chile.

Mr. Mitsuo Sakai at the National Research Institute of Far Seas Fisheries, who participated in the Japan-Chile Salmon Project by JICA and the Fisheries Development Institute in Chile (IFOP), said: "In the early 1980s, two companies emerged to launch commercial production in Chile: Nichiro Chile and Mytilus, both coho farming pioneers. It is safe to say that this was the beginning of the history of salmon farming in Chile" (Sakai 1999).[25] As Mr. Akira Kudo of Mitsubishi Corporation stated, "The first and memorable commercial production in Chile was made by a Japanese company. Mitsubishi Corporation also took part in this project, importing and selling the first shipped coho salmon" (Kudo 2008, 42).[26]

The Chilean government thanked Nichiro for having contributed to the development of the Chilean economy and industry through coho salmon farming. It awarded the Bernardo O'Higgins Order to the president of Nichiro.[27] The project by Nichiro had an impact on both the Japan-Chile Salmon Project in Coihaique and the Domsea Farms' project on Chiloé Island. The relationship among pioneering companies and institutions is illustrated in Fig. 2.4.

[24] Abiding by the conditions of its business license, Nichiro Chile released 10 % of smolt raised. In 1980, 17,000, and in 1981, 10,000 juveniles were released in Correntoso River. As a result of these releases, homing was reported. TechnoPress/SalmonChile (2003), P. 26.

[25] Mytilus' activities will be discussed later in this chapter.

[26] The relationship between Mitsubishi and Nichiro has continued since Nichiro obtained the rights for the Northern-sea fishery. Nichiro caught the fish, and Mitsubishi sold canned fish and crab. According to Makihara (former President of Mitsubishi Corporation)'s article "*Watashi no Rirekisho* [My resume]," in *Nikkei Shimbun* dated September 17, 2009, canned salmon was processed on a depot boat, which accumulated 8,000–9,000 tons of salmon. Depot boat fishery in the North Pacific usually operated for sockeye salmon from late May to early June, chum salmon and humpback salmon until mid-July, and then coho salmon.

[27] Maruha Nichiro Salmon Museum.

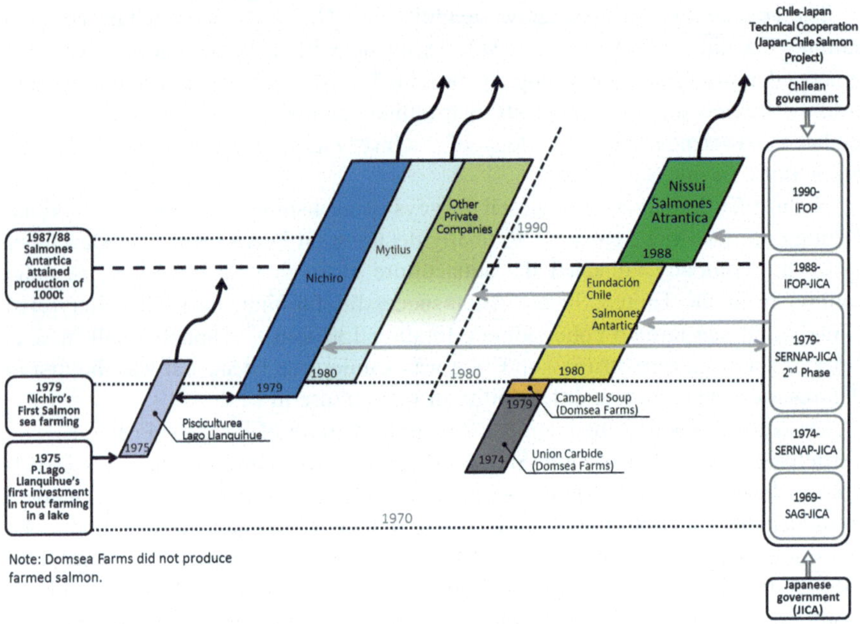

Fig. 2.4 Pioneer companies and institutions in the establishment and early development phases of Chilean salmon industry (Note: Domesea farms did not produce farmed salmon. *Source*: Compiled by the author based on the descriptions in the main text)

4.4 Piscicultura Lago Llanquihue, Chile's First Freshwater Trout Farming Company

For aquaculture in its floating cages in the sea, the Nichiro team needed freshwater facilities to rear in juveniles from eggs the company imported. Such facilities were provided by a local company called Piscicultura Lago Llanquihue ("Llanquihue Ltd."), the first privately-owned Chilean freshwater trout farming company, founded in 1975 by two men: Mr. Alfredo Valenzuela, and Mr. Alfonso Muena.

Valenzuela was familiar with sea cage farming, as he had once been in Japan for training as a staff member at the Agricultural and Livestock Service (SAG) of the Chilean Ministry of Agriculture and Livestock.[28] The two men wanted to become independent from government bodies and set up their own company. Strapped for funds, they convinced the governor of the Los Lagos Region, a former general who had assumed office right after the 1973 coup. They were granted a loan of 100,000 dollars from the Production Development Corporation (CORFO, Corporacion de Fomento de Produccion).

[28] For more information on this and the following paragraphs, see Mendez and Munita (1989).

This company, founded in 1975, faced a plethora of difficulties from the outset. The eggs the company first imported were all dead on arrival. In 1977, 60 % of the trout to be exported to France died. That same year, a storm so violent that it was described as one that would statistically only occur once every 35 years hit the region, forcing the company to abandon all the trout it was raising. This invited fierce criticism from locals. These events suggest how hard it was for the struggling private company to put aquaculture business on a commercial footing. The next year, in 1978, the company successfully exported freshwater trout to France for the first time. The company, however, remained deeply in debt. This difficult situation continued until 1979 when Nichiro approached them for collaboration.

5 Salmon Mariculture (Sea Farming) Found Feasible

Nichiro incubated and reared imported coho eggs at facilities of Llanquihue Ltd. The first batch of imported eggs was dead on arrival. The company, however, successfully incubated the second batch of 200,000 eggs and raised them until they became juveniles in fresh water.

In November 1979, these smolts—juvenile salmon that had grown enough for adaptation to the marine environment (approximately the size of a sardine or herring)—were transferred to Nichiro's floating cages off the fishing port of Angelmó near Puerto Montt for rearing (Basulto del Campo 2003) Obviously, the first to witness this success by Nichiro were Valenzuela and Muena. In particular Muena was mindful that salmon cage farming was commercially feasible, and worked hard so that Mytilus could expand its business to include salmon farming.

Also around this time, Rodríguez at Domsea Farms began to secretly build marine floating cages on Chiloé Island. As mentioned above, he had gone to Norway to study fish farming and had returned home with fish cages. He realized that he needed to feed the fish.[29] Rodríguez had first tried to import feed from the United States but realized that doing so would be costly. Then he went to see Valenzuela and Muena for advice on how to procure feed within Chile.

In the Aisén Region, on the other hand, the Japan-Chile Salmon Project started mariculture in Ensenada Baja, 65 km away from Coihaique. Securing feed was also an important issue for the team in Coihaique. The Japan-Chile Salmon Project created a feed section and set up a laboratory. The project also built a feed factory and began feed production there. By providing a variety data on feed, these efforts provided a foundation from which the Chilean aquaculture feed industry has developed into what it is today.

[29] From the interview with Ricardo Rodríguez and Mendez and Munita (1989, 94).

5.1 *Mytilus Joins Mariculture*

Having witnessed Nichiro's success in mariculture, Muena realized the commercial feasibility of salmon cage farming and tried to go ahead with this kind of aquaculture. He left Llanquihue Ltd. and joined a project in 1980 that had been launched by the Regional Secretary for Planning and Coordination (SERPLAC, Secretaria Regional de Planificación y Coordinación) in Los Lagos to oversee and evaluate the mariculture of mussels, oysters, and salmon. His main task was to find sites suitable for cultivation. One of the companies that showed interest in salmon farming was Mytilus, which had been cultivating mussels ("chorito" in Chile).

In late 1979, Mytilus imported 110,000 coho eggs, raised them into juveniles at a hatchery in Rio Sur, and cultivated them in the sea, at the port of Domeyko. In doing so Mytilus became the first Chilean company to domestically produce eggs, a total of 200,000.[30] Cultivation in four places, including Maullín and Angelmó, was hampered by high mortality due to seaweed plague in 1983 and by problems with fishmeal for feed. Later, however, the company began to successfully export farmed salmon to the United States.

5.2 *Pioneering Private Companies Expand Coho Salmon Exports to Japan*

These developments indicate that Nichiro and Mytilus (which was later renamed Mares Australes) were the private company pioneers that first put salmon mariculture on a commercial footing, although their production levels were low.[31] Nichiro had started exports to Japan in 1985 with just 30 tons. By 1988, exports to Japan from four Japanese buyers, including those who bought from other companies, topped 1000 tons for the first time.

The company that followed these pioneers, rapidly increasing production to become the largest salmon cultivator in Chile, was Salmones Antártica, an affiliate of Fundación Chile. By 1988, this company's production reached 1000 tons. The Chilean salmon industry thus had reached a point where a firm foundation had been established, and the industry was ready to take off. Details of this will be discussed in the next chapter.

---

[30] TechnoPress/SalmonChile (2003, 27–28). Mytilus changed its name to Sociedad Pesquera Mares Australes (Mares Australes for short) in 1983. Later, it was acquired by Mainstream. Pablo Aguilera, JICA's counterpart, and a leader of the Japan Chile Salmon Project from the beginning, joined Mares Australes when the project ended.

[31] Some may think Nichiro was the first private company and the successful pioneer of salmon mariculture in Chile, but Nichiro was a foreign company, thus Mytilus could be considered the national pioneer of salmon mariculture.

6 Concluding Remarks: Technological Contributions by Japan-Chile Salmon Project, Fundación Chile and Private Companies

The preceding sections have reviewed the development of the salmon industry in the 1970s and 1980s in Chile. Here, we summarize the technological contributions to the Chilean salmon industry made by the Japan-Chile Salmon Project, Fundación Chile (from the acquisition of Domsea to the disposal of Salmones Antártica), and Chilean and foreign private companies, in its preparatory, establishment (commercialization), and early growth phases. Figure 2.5 shows the major contributing technologies in the areas of freshwater fry farming (from eggs to smolts), seed production (typically domestic egg production), and sea farming (mariculture). Figure 2.6 focuses on processing technology, feed production technology, and fish disease control technology, which will be discussed in Chap. 3.

As mentioned in Sect. 2 of this chapter, the binding constraints for the Chilean salmon farming industry to emerge were technology and industrial personnel training. This chapter aimed to respond to the questions such as: How was the required technology introduced? How was the technological capability built and industrial personnel trained? How did the industry overcome the lack of frontier (cutting edge) knowledge, technical know-how and information? How was the

		Contributions by the Japan-Chile Salmon Project	Contributions byFundación Chile (Including Salmones Antártica and Domsea Farms)	Contributions by the private sector
Seed production and freshwater farming technology	General (Freshwater culture from eggs to juveniles)	Pioneered building of a hatchery and rearing juveniles from eggs (at Dr. Shiraishi Hatchery)	*Domsea*Farms *and Fundacbn Chile* reared juveniles from eggs for stocking purposes	PisciculturaLago Llanquihue farmed fry for mariculture for the first time as a private company in 1978-79
	Domestic egg production technology (Egg stripping, fertilization, domestic Production of safe eggs)	Pioneered building of a Hatchery and produced domestic eggs (at Dr. Shiraishi and Ensenada Baja Hatcheries)		
Mari-culture (sea farming) technology	General	Sea-farmed salmon for eggs in the early 1980s.	*SalmonesAntártica/ FundaciónChile* put large-scale sea cage farming of salmon on a commercial footing in the mid1980s	*Nichiro* successfully commercialized mariculture for the first time in Chile in 1979. *Mytilus* followed suit.
	Large cages and automatic feeders			*Norwegian firms* introduced salmon technology into Chile through the sale of equipment followed by investment, mainly in the 1990s.

Fig. 2.5 Contributions to the development of seed production/freshwater farming and mariculture (sea farming) technologies (*Source*: Compiled by the author based on descriptions in the main text)

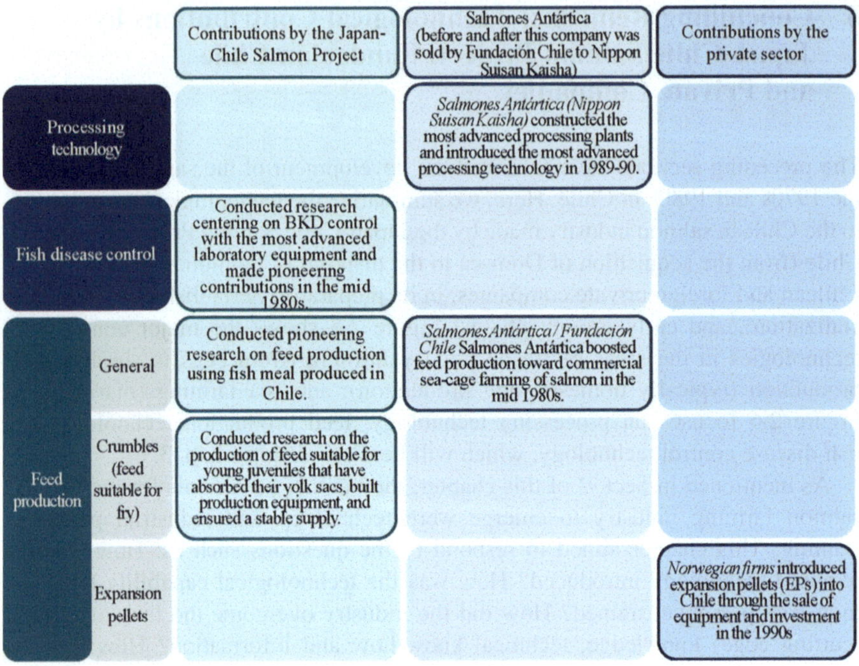

Fig. 2.6 Contributions to the development of technologies for processing, feed production, and fish disease control (*Source*: Compiled by the author based on descriptions in the main text)

technology diffused? Answers to the above questions are summarized in Figs. 2.5 and 2.6. As explained in the earlier section, the Chilean salmon industry had natural advantages in factors of production such as the natural conditions, capital, and available cheap labor. With technological adaptation and development, the value of these endowments changed, enabling Chile to attain a new comparative advantage. However, improving technological levels through increasing R&D, professionals and trained industrial personnel were still lagging behind. Investing in technology with high-level professionals is not an easy task for a firm, especially if it is still a relatively young firm. Industrial personnel will not be trained overnight, and the costs will be significant. In the preparatory phase of the Chilean salmon industry, these factors were all constraints on further development.

Fundación Chile and the Japan-Chile Salmon Project filled the missing gap of investment for knowledge in a rather spontaneous manner. The latter project was implemented for 20 years starting from 1969 as a collaboration between the National Fisheries Service (SERNAP), the Fisheries Development Institute (IFOP), and Japan International Cooperation Agency (JICA) under a bilateral cooperation agreement. Because the Japan-Chile Salmon Project was managed by the public sector, technologies developed and personnel trained by the project were treated as 'public goods' that were free to be diffused to anyone. This allowed salmon firms to save on the cost of investment in knowledge development and allowed many entrepreneurs to enter into the sector. The Fundación Chile also played a similar role, as will be discussed in the following chapter.

Box: Delayed Release

The "delayed release" ("liberación diferida" in Spanish) method was introduced and developed step by step by the Japan Chile Salmon Project. The first pilot experiment of sea farming was carried out in October 1979. Two hundred sixty-six thousand Chum salmon fry, incubated in the Dr. Shiraishi Hatchery in Coyhaique, were transported to Ensenada Baja, where the fry were reared first in a freshwater pond and then in a 5 × 5 m cage in the sea. In 1980, one million eyed eggs were brought to Ensenada Baja and incubated in ponds and then reared in five cages in the sea.

The project made an important progress in 1981, particularly due to the inauguration of the Ensenada Baja hatchery and related facilities. 1.55 million Chum salmon fry were brought from Coyhaique and reared in a pond and cages in sea. A delayed release of salmon with a size of 300 g was carried out. In this year, sea farming of Chum salmon in Puerto Aguirre was also started.

The new installations were fully utilized in 1982 and the project got the second generation of transplanted chum salmon. It was the first recorded case of producing eggs of chum salmon in South America. The project expanded on this technique and came to produce by itself a far greater amount of seeds than it had by hatching eggs from Hokkaido. As it was emphasized in the Sect. 4.1 of this Chapter, the locally produced seeds were better suited to the seasons, environment, and climate in Chile. The domestic production of chum salmon in 1982 by the Japan-Chile Salmon Project was a remarkable feat. It was a major milestone for the project.

There had been no antecedents in Japan of rearing Chum salmon for 6 months and implementing delayed release. As such, it could be considered a case of 'innovative solutions' in the local context through a step-by-step learning process by the team headed by Mr. Nagasawa of the project. The Evaluation Team for Japan Chile Salmon Project sent to Chile in 1984 noted that, "As it is a method which had no antecedents in Japan, there still remained challenges. Nevertheless we considered that the Project has sufficient capabilities to implement the method." The Team concluded the 'delayed release' should be given high priority among activities of the Japan Chile Salmon Project (JICA 1984).

Acknowledgements A number of articles and books written in Japanese are not included here (see Hosono 2010). The author wrote Chaps. 2 and 3 drawing on not only the references listed here and articles and books in Japanese, but also on approximately 80 h of interviews with Chileans and Japanese considered to be the key people in the development of the Chilean salmon industry. The author is most grateful to all those who kindly accepted his invitation to be interviewed and/or gave him valuable information. They are, among others, Pablo Aguirela, Shizuo Akaboshi, Carlos Alvarez, Fernando Aldea, Gustavo Araya, Rodrigo Benito, Roberto Bravo, Patricio Bustos, Emilio

Bruggemann, Mario Castillo, Raul Castro, Jorge Ruiz Cerda, Alejandro Cobarrubia, Luis Hernan Cortes, Sergio Contreras, Benjamin Eyzaguirre, Ramon Figueroa, Maria Soledad Guarda, Atsushi Harada, Evelin Henriquez, Jose Miguel Hernandez, Tatsuyoshi Hirata, Tazuko Ichinohe, Juan Enrique Illanes, Fumio Kawano, Shigeru Kobayashi, Toshimi Kobayashi, Akira Kudo, Mikio Kuwayama, Claudio Maggi, Alberto Medina, Ivan Mertens, Ariaky Nagasawa, Nobuaki Nagasawa, Yuji Nemoto, Ricardo Norambuena, Hector Novoa, Masato Ohira, Nelson Perez, Luis Pichott, Mario Puchi, Ricardo Rodriguez, Marcela Rojas, Mitsuo Sakai, Hidemitsu Sakurai, Teiji Sakurai, Toru Shionoya, Kojiro Suzuki, Andreas Takamiya, Eiichiro Uchida, Takayuki Uchida, Juan Carlos Uribe, Alfredo Valenzuela, Antonio Velez, Mario Vargas, and Francisco Vasquez.

Bibliography

Achurra, Manuel. 1995. La Experiencia de un Nuevo Producto de Exportacion: Los Salmones. In *Auge Exportador Chileno: Lecciones y Desafios Futuros*, ed. Patricio Meller and Raul Eduardo Saez, 43–71. Santiago: CIEPLAN: Dolmen Ediciones.

Aquagente. 2006a. *Historia de AquaChile: Empresa del Tercer Milenio, Parte I.* Aquagente, *AquaReportaje*, Sept–Oct.

Aquagente. 2006b. *Historia de AquaChile: Empresa del Tercer Milenio, Parte II.* Aquagente *AquaReportaje*, Nov–Dec.

Basulto Del Campo, Sergio. 2003. *El Largo Viaje de Los Salmones: Una Cronica Olvidada: Propagacion y Cultivo de Especies Acuaticos en Chile.* Santiago: Subscretaria de Pesca/ SERNAPESCA/FAO/Universidad Andres Bello/Federacion Caza y Pesca/Industrias Pesqueras.

Boston Consulting Group. 2007. *Estudio de Competitividad en Clusters de la Economia Chilena.* Santiago: Consejo Nacional de Innovación y Competitividad.

Castro, Raul D., Rauld H. Roberto, and Jun-Ichi Nakazoe. 1991. Estudio de Digestibilidad in Vivo de Harinas de Pescado. *Alimentos* 16(2): 13–16.

Cimoli, Mario, Giovanni Dosi, and Joseph E. Stiglitz (eds.). 2009. *Industrial policy and development: The political economy of capabilities accumulation.* Toronto: Oxford University Press.

Claude, Marcel, and Jorge Oporto (eds.). 2003. *La Ineficiencia de la Salmonicultura en Chile: Aspectos Sociales, Economicas y Ambientales.* Santiago: Corporación Terra Australes/ Fundación Terram.

CORFO. 2007. *70 Casos de Innovacion Apoyados por INNOVA Chile de CORFO entre 2000 y 2006.* Santiago: Editorial Valente Ltda.

Correa, Felipe, Mauricio Garcia, and Sebastian Melo. 2003. *Distantes Isla Chaullin (Pelicula),* Fundación para la Superacion de Pobreza, Programa Servicio Pais.

Departamento de Ingeneria Industrial, Universidad de Chile. 2008. *Informe de Caracterizacion: Agenda y Planes de Mejoramiento de la Competitividad en la XI Region, La Industria de Salmon,* Universidad de Chile.

Diaz Andrade, Estrella. 2003. *Transnacionalizacion de la Industria Salmonera: Aspectos Socio-Laborales de un Proceso en Curso.* Santiago: Hexagrama Consultoras.

Editorial Committee of the Centenary Celebration of the Friendship Treaty Between Japan and Chile. 1997. *Nihon Chile kouryu shi* [History of Japan-Chile relations]. Tokyo: Japan Association of Latin America and the Caribbean.

Fazio, Hugo. 2002. *La Transnacionalizacion de la Economia Chilena: Mapa de la Extrema Riqueza en el ano 2000.* Santiago: LOM Ediciones.

Fazio, Hugo. 2006. *Los 30 Anos de Fundación Chile: Visualizando y Construyendo Futuro,* Fundación Chile.

Furukawa, H. 1987. Mayoeru Sake: Aru Kaigaikyouryoku no 15 nennkan [Lost Salmon: 15 Years of an International Cooperation]. *Yomiuri Shimbun.* 18–23 May 1987.

Hosono, Akio. 2010. *Nambei Chile wo Sake Yushutu Taikoku ni Kaeta Nihonjintachi* [The Japanese who Changed Chile into a Great Salmon-Exporting Country]. Tokyo: Diamond, Inc.

Huss, Torben. 1991. Transferencia de tecnologia: el caso de Fundación Chile. *CEPAL Review* 43: 99–120.
Iizuka, Michiko. 2006. *'Low tech' industry: A new path for development? The case of salmon farming industry in Chile.*. Paper submitted for 4th Globelics Conference in India.
Iizuka, Michiko. 2008. *Global Standards and Local Producers: Knowledge Governance and the Rise of the Chilean Salmon Industry.* DPhil thesis SPRU, University of Sussex, June 2007.
Instituto de Fomento Pesquero (IFOP). 1989. *National Salmoniculture Program: Report of the present situation and scope of a post Chile-Japan agreement.* Valparaiso: IFOP.
Instituto de Fomento Pesquero (IFOP). 1998. *Estado de Situacion y Perspectivas de la Acuicultura en Chile.* Valparaiso: IFOP.
Instituto de Fomento Pesquero (IFOP). 2003. *Indicadores Economicos y Sociales de la Acuicultura en Chile.* Valparaiso: IFOP.
Japan International Cooperation Agency (JICA). 1984. *Chile Suisan Youshoku project evaluation team report. [Report of evaluation team on aquaculture project in Chile].* Tokyo: JICA.
JICA/JBIC. 2008. *Report of the stocktaking work on the economic development in Africa and the Asian growth experience.* Tokyo: JICA.
Katz, Jorge. 2005. Salmon farming in Chile. In *Technology, adaptation and exports: How some developing countries got it right*, ed. Chandra Vandana. Washington, DC: World Bank.
KMT Consultores. 2007. *Estudio para la Determinacion de la Linea Base de la Industria del Salmon en la XI Region de Aisen: Salmon Aysen, Programa Territorial Integrado.* Place? KMT Consultores.
Kudo, Akira. 2008. *Chunambei ga Nihon wo Oinuku Hi: Mitsubishi Shouji Chuzaiin no Me* [The day Latin America left behind Japan: From the perspective of Mitsubishi Corporation's Resident Representative]. Tokyo: Asahi Sensho.
Kuwayama, Mikio, and José E. Durán Lima. 2003. *La Calidad de la Inserción Internacional de América Latina y el Caribe en el Comercio Mundial.* Santiago: CEPAL.
Lin, Justin Yifu. 2012a. *New structural economics: A framework for rethinking development and policy.* Washington, DC: World Bank.
Lin, Justin Yifu. 2012b. *The quest for prosperity: How developing economies can take off.* New Jersey: Princeton University Press.
Lin, Justin Yifu, and Ha-Joon Chang. 2009. Should industrial policy in developing countries conform to comparative advantage or defy it? A debate between Justin Lin and Ha-Joon Chang. *Developing Policy Review* 27(5): 483–502.
Lindbergh, Jon M., Richard E. Noble, and Kenneth Blackburn. 1981. Salmon Ranching in Chile: The Private Sector. *ICLARM Newsletter*, October.
Maggi Campos, Claudio. 2006. The salmon farming and processing cluster in Southern Chile. In *Upgrading to compete: Global value chains, clusters, and SMEs in Latin America*, ed. Carlo Pietrobelli and Roberta Rabellotti, 109–142. New York: Inter-American Development Bank.
Meller, Patricio, and Raul Saez. 1995a. *Lecciones y Desafios Futuros del Auge Exportador Chileno.* Santiago: CIEPLAN: Dolmen Ediciones.
Meller, Patricio, and Raul Saez. 1995b. *Auge Exportador Chileno: Lecciones y Desafios Futuros.* Santiago: CIEPLAN: Dolmen Ediciones.
Mendez, Ricardo, and Clara Munita. 1989. *La Salmonicultura en Chile.* Santiago: Fundación Chile.
Moguillansky, Graciera.1999. *La Inversion en Chile: ?El Fin de un Ciclo en Expansion?* CEPAL/ Fondo de Cultura Economica.
Montero, Cecilia. 2003. *La Revolucion Empresarial Chilena.* Santiago: CIEPLAN: Dolmen Ediciones.
Montero, Cecilia. 2004. *Formacion y Desarrollo de un Cluster Globalizado: El Caso de la Industria del Salmon en Chile*, Serie Desarrollo Productivo 145. Santiago: CEPAL.
Nagasawa, Aliaky. 1981. Salmon ranching in Chile: The Japanese project. *ICLARM Newsletter*, October.

Nemoto, Yuji. 2002. Chile no Sake Masu Youshoku no Saishin Jijyou [Recent trends of salmon and trout culture in Chile].*Aqua-net,* January.
Norman, Akbar, and Joseph Stiglitz. 2012. Strategies for African development. In *Good growth and governance in Africa: Rethinking development strategies in Africa*, ed. Akbar Norman, Kwesi Botchway, Howard Stein, and Joseph Stiglitz. Oxford: Oxford University.
Phyne, John, and Jorge Mansilla. 2003. Foreign linkages in the commodity chain: The case of the Chilean Salmon Farming Industry, 1987–2001. *Sociologia Ruralis* 43(2): 108–127.
Politzer, Patricia. 2006. *Chile: ¿De Que Estamos Hablando? Retrato de una Transformación Asombrosa*. Santiago: Editorial Sudamericana.
Rodrik, Dani. 2007. *One economics many recipes: Globalization, institutions, and economic growth*. Princeton: Princeton University Press.
Sakai, Mitsuo. 1999. *Chile ni Okeru Sake Ishoku to Youshoku Keikaku Oyobi IFOP Shiraishi Hakushi Fukajyo no Katsudo Jyoukyou* [Salmon introduction and aquaculture project in Chile and activities of the Dr. Shiraishi Hatchery of IFOP]. Tokyo: JICA.
Sakai, Mitsuo, and Ishida Ken-ichi. 2002. The pacific salmon ranching in the Southern Chile: Evaluation of a project-type technical cooperation by JICA. *Fisheries Science* 68(Supp. II): 1552–1555.
Sakurai, Teiji. 1995. *Chile Koku Santiago Chuzai no Ki* [Record of activities in Santiago, Chile]. Tokyo: JETRO.
Servicio Nacional de Pesca (SERNAPESCA). 2008. *Proyecto de introduccion de Salmon Pacifico en la Region de Aisen por JICA: Antecedentes Historicos*.
Shiraishi, Yoshikazu. 1973. *Misuumi no Sakana* [Fishes of lakes]. Tokyo: Iwanami.
Soms Garcia, Esteban. 2006. *Estrategias y Planes Regionles,* MIDEPLAN.
Stiglitz, Joseph, and Bruce Greenwald. 2014. *Creating a learning society: A new approach to growth, development, and social progress*. New York: Columbia University Press.
Subsecretaria de Pesca, ProChile and Chilean Fisheries Association (SONAPESCA). 2006, *Chile Azul: Main Fisheries and Aquaculture Resources,* Subsecretaria de Pesca, ProChile and Chilean Fisheries Association (SONAPESCA).
TechnoPress. 2007a. *Pioneros en Chile: Con la Acuicultura en las Venas.*
TechnoPress. 2007b. *Aqua: La Revista de la Acuicultura, Edicion Conmemorativa de 20 Anos, Diciembre*. Santiago: TechnoPress.
TechnoPress and SalmonChile. 2003a. *Aquiculture in Chile*. Santiago: TechnoPress.
TechnoPress and SalmonChile. 2003b. *La Acuicultura en Chile*. Santiago: TechnoPress.
UNCTAD. 2006. *A case study of the salmon industry in Chile*. New York: United Nations Conference on Trade and Development.
Villaroel, Arias, and Jaime Esteban. 2003. *Analisis de la Competitividad de la Industria del Salmon en Chile*. Santiago: Estudio de Titulo, Universidad Catolica de Chile.
World Bank. 1993. *The east Asian miracle: Economic growth and public policy*. New York: Oxford University Press.
World Bank. 2005. *Technology and growth series: Chilean salmon exports. PREM Notes, No.103*. Washington, DC: World Bank.
Wurmann, Carlos F. 2007. Salmon farming in Chile: History, policies and development strategies. In *Species and system selection for sustainable aquaculture*, ed. PingSun Leung, Cheng-Sheng Lee, and Patricia J. O'Bryen, 415–444. Ames: Blackwell Publishing.

Chapter 3
The Chilean Salmon Industry Takes Off: From the Commercialization to the Early Development Phase

Akio Hosono

1 Introduction: Building a Knowledge Base to Entice Entrepreneurs

Norman and Stiglitz (2012, 7) emphasize that the long-term success of economic development rests on the ability of societies to learn "new technologies, new ways of doing business, new ways of managing the economy, new ways of dealing with other countries." Related to this notion of a "learning society" is the view of Cimoli et al. (2009, 2) that great industrial transformation "entails a major process of accumulation of knowledge and capabilities, at the level of both *individuals* and *organizations*."[1]

The next difficult stage of industrial development, after building an adequate knowledge base, is how to entice entrepreneurs to venture into the emerging businesses, which are highly risky, yet potentially profitable. No industry can take off without the presence of entrepreneurs willing to take risks to 'discover' market niches and opportunities. These so-called pioneering entrepreneurs, or the 'first movers', are crucial in establishing new industries, and therefore Rodrik (2007) emphasizes the need to compensate them for the information externalities generated by the pioneer firms. At the early phase of industrial development—creation of a sound knowledge base, promotion of 'soft and hard infrastructure' (Lin 2012, 28), and the presence of entrepreneurs willing to take risks—are considered essential.

This chapter focuses on the following points: (1) the technological knowledge and capabilities that were incrementally accumulated in the case of the Chilean salmon industry, (2) ways in which new industries such as this can be scaled up,

[1] Emphasis in original.

A. Hosono (✉)
Japan International Cooperation Agency Research Institute (JICA-RI), Tokyo, Japan
e-mail: hosono.akio@jica.go.jp

A. Hosono et al. (eds.), *Chile's Salmon Industry*,
DOI 10.1007/978-4-431-55766-1_3

(3) the kind of drivers (driving forces) that maintain the momentum towards transformation, and (4) the policies and institutions that facilitated the process. This chapter will analyze the above points to discuss the Chilean salmon industry, which had to overcome several challenges during its early development phase, especially in building sufficient capacity to penetrate global markets.

2 Salmones Antártica, a Filial of Fundación Chile: A Pioneer in Full-Fledged Commercial Production

Fundación Chile[2] was a semi-governmental corporation that functioned as a kind of industrial and technology development organization. The organization provided the technological assistance necessary for the establishment of new promising industries and to set up businesses, and then sold successful ones to the private sector for profit. Fundación Chile played a crucial role in bringing salmon farming to a stage sufficient for take off, and in linking it to commercial interests.

In 1981, Fundación Chile acquired the facilities that Domsea Pesquera, the firm owned by Campbell's Soup Co., located in Curaco de Vélez in Chiloé Island. This was the starting point for Fundación Chile to enter into the salmon industry (Mendez and Munita 1989, 108). One year after the acquisition, Fundación Chile changed the name of the firm from Domsea Pesquera to Salmones Antártica (Spanish for "Antarctic Salmon"). At the time of purchase, Domsea Pezquera's operation was still at the pilot stage.[3] Hence it was Fundación Chile that provided technological transfer and market research to bring the firm to commercially viable level.

2.1 Investing in a New Industry and Securing Entrepreneurial Experimentation

Knowledge, in its pure form, has the features of being a public good; the costs of efforts to develop or create a good are substantially higher than that of making it

[2] Fundación Chile was created as a result of compensation consultations that the Chilean government undertook with an American multinational corporation, the International Telephone and Telegraph Corporation (ITT). During the Allende Administration, Chilean Telephone Company, owned mostly by ITT, was nationalized. The post-coup administration of General Pinochet compensated ITT for its losses caused by the nationalization. As part of the compensation, both parties agreed to establish Fundación Chile, half-owned by the Chilean government and ITT, with the aim of developing technologies needed for industrial development in Chile.

[3] This company had not yet sold salmon—Union Carbide had stepped out of the salmon project and Campbell's Soup was not interested in the salmon business (from the interview with Ricardo Rodríguez in 2008).

available to many users, and once it is available to the public, knowledge is essentially a non-rival and non-excludable good. These features of knowledge mean that market forces cannot work perfectly to invest at the optimal level for the development of knowledge, making policy intervention necessary to stimulate investment towards its creation.

In developed countries, such sizable investments in new technologies have been undertaken through government-led research or research consortiums (such as in the case of environmental and medical technologies, or agricultural sciences). Alternatively, private firms may invest in the purchase of already available technology or develop their own technology if they consider that such technology/ knowledge would make them more competitive in the market. Under such conditions, firms would endeavor to obtain a patent for an advanced technology that would bring about novel products so as to preclude copycat products by competitors. In other words, patents protect companies that have made investments and successfully developed novel technologies or products, preventing imitators from entering the competition for a certain period to avoid the risk of losing the initial investors' profits. This also means that access to knowledge and technology is restricted from use by other potential 'followers' and is unlikely to be diffused widely. While the above remains true, unless there is a certain amount of diffusion of new technologies and knowledge by entrepreneurs, dynamics will remain weak and new industries will not emerge.

2.2 "Market Failure" Averted by Fundación Chile

In the case of the Chilean salmon industry, "market failure" in knowledge creation and diffusion was averted by Fundación Chile. First, Fundación Chile demonstrated the commercial profitability of sea farming as a pioneer in this business. Second, Fundación Chile provided information and knowledge on salmon farming to the wider public. It did not treat the acquired knowledge on farming techniques as an exclusive good but freely diffused it to other potential entrepreneurs interested in venturing into this business. The fact that Fundación Chile owned a successful business, Salmones Antártica, also contributed positively to the diffusion process. Due to the role played by Fundación Chile, many companies were able to invest in the salmon farming industry with access to knowledge without having to make a sizable investment into research and development. This allowed the entry of a number of nascent firms into the industry.

It is important to remember that there were also knowledge spillovers during that time among actors located in geographical proximity. Between 1982 and 1983, Fundación Chile continued salmon stocking operations that had been conducted by Domsea Pesquera[4] after its purchase. At the same time, Fundación Chile began

[4] To be precise, Domsea Pesquera Chile Ltda.

cage farming in Ensenada Baja near Puerto Chacabuco in the Aisén Region. This place was very near to the site where the Japan-Chile Salmon Project (SERNAP and JICA) had been conducting mariculture (sea farming) operations ahead of Fundación Chile. The Japan-Chile Salmon Project not only accumulated technical experience in sea farming, seed production and fry farming in fresh water but was also equipped with a number of laboratories, egg incubators, and culture facilities as well as a feed factory. This constituted the most modern and largest aquaculture center in Chile at that time with two sites of experimentation, Coihaique and Ensenada Baja in the Aisén Region, not to mention that top-notch scientists on fish disease and feed were working there as part of the Japan-Chile Salmon Project. This will be explored in more detail later.

2.3 Fundación Chile's Initiative for Mariculture

In 1984, Fundación Chile started the sea cage farming of coho salmon in earnest at two locations: Changuitad on Chiloé Island (across the water from Curaco de Vélez) and Puerto Chacabuco in the Aisén Region.[5] At that time, Fundación Chile needed to make sea farming commercially viable and thus demonstrate the feasibility of salmon farming as a new industry. This was the first major project for Fundación Chile. Its performance in mariculture was a critical test to determine whether the Fundación would be able to demonstrate its significance to the public at large.

2.3.1 The Encounter Between Fundación Chile and the Japan-Chile Salmon Project

Fundación Chile's aim was to make a major investment in sea farming so that salmon farming would become a viable industry in Chile. The first step the foundation took toward this end was to cultivate, on an experimental basis under different conditions (including on a farming scale), various salmonid species to find ways to make salmon farming profitable and identify the conditions for maximizing profitability. At this time, the salmon project of Salmones Antártica, a company under the umbrella of Fundación Chile, came into contact through informal networks with the Japan-Chile Salmon Project of JICA and SERNAP (the National Fisheries Service).

It all came about as a result of a coincidence: Mr. Pablo Aguilera, one of the original counterparts and project leader for the JICA-SERNAP project, and José Miguel Hernández, one of the key players in Fundación Chile's salmon project,

[5] The first sea cage in Puerto Chacabuco was the one that Ricardo Rodríguez built in Dalcahue, Chiloé Island. This cage was moved to Puerto Chacabuco (Mendez and Munita 1989, 95).

were classmates at Universidad Católica de Valparaíso (Catholic University of Valparaiso). This allowed the Fundación Chile to have access to already accumulated knowledge on adaptation of salmonoid by the JICA-SERNAP project as well as its hatchery in Ensenada Baja near Puerto Chacabuco and its sea-farming site. Furthermore, to cultivate salmon, Fundación Chile used both feed that had been produced by the Japan-Chile Salmon Project and dry pellets that the Fundación had started to produce.

In 1980, Fundación Chile proposed a research project on the feasibility of salmon sea farming to the Regional Secretary for Planning and Coordination (SERPLAC) in the Aisén Region. In 1981, SERPLAC approved the project and agreed to finance it.[6] Then, Fundación Chile sent José Miguel Hernandez to Coihaique, where he met Pablo Aguilera. Fundación Chile and the Aisén regional office of the National Fisheries Service (SERNAP) reached an understanding on partnership. According to Mendez and Munita (1989, 95) and an interview with Hernández in 2008, the purpose of this project was to establish the technical feasibility of producing Pacific and Atlantic salmon and to define which was the most advisable species to begin exploitation in bio-economic terms. The alevins used for this experiment were obtained from the National Fisheries Service (SERNAP), which under an agreement with Fundación Chile would provide the *juveniles* from the Ensenada Baja facilities.

To identify the most suitable salmonoid species, Fundación Chile decided to focus on six species. The selected species were: coho and chinook salmon (king salmon) that Fundación Chile had been raising in Los Lagos Region; rainbow trout in Pucón, the Araucania Region; chum and cherry salmon that the Japan-Chile Salmon Project had been rearing; and brown trout. In order for Fundación Chile to decide to start salmon mariculture on a large scale, it was necessary to collect data to evaluate commercial viability and to demonstrate its feasibility.

The experimentation was conducted in the Aisén Region. This process is described in *La Salmonicultura en Chile (Salmon Farming in Chile)* a voluminous book published by Fundación Chile, as follows:

> The feasibility of this type of culture had been demonstrated in 1980 to 1984, with the project undertaken jointly by the Fundación and the Regional Secretary for Planning and Coordination (SERPLAC) in the 11th Region [the Aisén Region]. The project included different salmonoid species and was developed for both large and small scale operators, and was, without doubt, important in the "go-ahead" decision process of this new venture which we now view as a milestone in the development of industrial scale salmon farming in Chile. The project was carried out with support provided by staff and by the use of equipment that was in the hands of SERNAP, 11th Region.[7]

---

[6] The contract between SERPLAC and Fundación Chile was signed in 1982 (Mendez and Munita 1989, 95).

[7] Here, "staff" and "equipment" of "SERNAP, 11th Region" [the Aisén regional office of SERNAP] refers to staff and equipment of the Japan-Chile Salmon Project by SERNAP and JICA. The director of the regional office at that time was Mr. Pablo Aguilera (Mendez and Munita 1989, 110 and 206).

Fundación Chile's foothold in the Aisén Region was in Puerto Chacabuco, which is just a stone's throw from Ensenada Baja and also near Coihaique, two main sites of the Japan-Chile (JICA-SERNAP) Salmon project. The Fundación team benefited from this project in terms of access to its laboratories and feed. These laboratories were helpful in analyzing water properties. The Fundación team received advice from Japanese experts regarding BKD (bacterial kidney disease) and other bacterial infections, which were common to salmon in captivity, because cage nets at that time had knots, making the salmon vulnerable to skin injuries.[8]

At the same time, Nichiro's success in pioneering mariculture and its commercialization in Chile had a great impact on Fundación Chile; it preceded the success of the semi-governmental corporation. Nichiro's chronicle says: "Fundación Chile of the Republic of Chile had been keeping an eye on our progress in coho salmon mariculture. Upon learning about our success, the Fundación wasted no time in launching feasibility studies on sea farming." The above accounts suggest that Fundación Chile started feasibility studies after verifying Nichiro's success and that the JICA-SERNAP project facilitated the Fundación in conducting these studies. Here, Fundación Chile acted as the local knowledge mediators.

Fundación Chile's biggest goal was to create a commercially viable salmon industry. The Japan-Chile (JICA-SERNAP) Salmon Project aimed at scientifically exploring the possibility of a salmon industry in Chile. Nichiro was the foreign company with advanced techniques on salmon farming. Fundación Chile obtained the information through observations of the actual technology accumulated by the JICA-SERNAP project and scaled it up to a commercial level. Therefore, Fundación Chile was situated in a conducive environment where the key actors could complement each other to produce synergic effects.

2.4 Chilean Entrepreneurial Investment Prompted by a Commercialization Model and Diffusion Efforts

Fundación Chile made the three most important contributions toward the development of the salmon farming industry in Chile. First, it successfully put its salmon mariculture project on a commercially viable footing with an annual production volume of 1000 tons. Second, the Fundación, based on this business model, offered consulting services, including a comprehensive business package, to companies wishing to invest in similar activities. Third, Fundación Chile organized a salmon industrial association in Chile.[9]

---

[8] From an interview with Ricardo Rodríguez in 2008.

[9] The salmon industrial association was called "Association of Salmon and Trout Producers" at the beginning, and later, the name was changed to "SalmonChile" as we see today. The contribution that Fundación Chile made for organizing the industrial association was emphasized in Mendez and Munita (1989, 110).

In 1986, in an aim to diffuse their consultancy services, Fundación Chile featured salmon farming in a TV broadcast. This program was produced by Cristián Olguín, a popular news anchor on Channel 13 at that time. Many Chilean entrepreneurs who watched the program made inquiries to the TV station about salmon farming and some of them later ventured into the industry. Among such entrepreneurs were the Errázuriz family led by one of the most influential entrepreneurs in Chile, Francisco Javier Errázuriz; the Echeverría family; and the Fullman family. They set up salmon farming companies: Salmones Unimarc, Salmones Aucar, and Mainstream, respectively. These entrepreneurs originally had little knowledge about salmon. Fundación Chile provided necessary services for them in such areas of obtaining a mariculture license, producing wooden fish cages, and providing smolts and feed.[10]

It was around that time that the Chilean private sector entered the salmon farming industry in earnest. Fundación Chile supported projects by seven private companies including the three mentioned above.[11] With the income generated from such support, Fundación Chile invested in Salmones Antártica with the aim of building new feed mills. These newcomers started production in the late 1980s.[12] In November 1987, the Japan-Chile Salmon Project moved from the phase of JICA-SERNAP partnership to a follow-up phase with the Fisheries Development Institute (IFOP) and JICA. By this stage, many Chilean counterparts who were involved in JICA-SERNAP project had been recruited by several private aquaculture companies as experts in salmon farming, taking advantage of their experiences and skills accumulated over the years of involvement with the project. The details will be discussed later in this chapter.

Even after the entry of numerous firms, Salmones Antártica, Mares Australes (Mytilus), and Nichiro remained as the top three salmon farming companies in Chile throughout the late 1980s (TechnoPress and SalmonChile 2003a, b, 31).

2.5 *Fundación Chile's Production Reaches 1000 Tons in 1988*

Despite being a latecomer following the trailblazing Nichiro and the second-comer Mytilus (latter-day "Mares Australes"), Fundación Chile's Salmones Antártica successfully put larger-scale salmon mariculture on track. In contrast, Nichiro and

[10] From the interview with Ricardo Rodríguez in 2008.

[11] From the interview with Ricardo Rodríguez in 2008.

[12] Fundación Chile making a 25 % investment, Salmone Huillinco Ltda was established as the first private enterprises to farm Atlantic salmon in 1987. In the same year, Finamar Ltda, a smoked salmon processing company, was built in Santiago, and Salmtec Ltda was established in 1988 aiming for establishing farm technology research. Moreover, Fischer brothers built Salmones Pacifico Sur Ltda, merging it with Salmones Huillinco Ltda. Pacific Star Ltda and Friosur Ltda were also established.

Mytilus, which started mariculture earlier, fell short of Fundación Chile in terms of production scale. For the 1987/1988 production period, Fundación Chile produced some 1,000 tons of salmon (250 tons in Chiloé and 700 tons in Puerto Chacabuco), as against 300 tons for Mares Australes and 100 tons for Nichiro (Mendez and Munita 1989, 165). It should be added, however, that the latter two companies reached the 1,000-ton level during the 1990s.

A number of factors enabled Salmones Antártica to increase its production so rapidly. One of the most significant reasons was the ability to mobilize ample risk capital. Originally designed to encourage venture businesses, Fundación Chile was in a better position to promote salmon farming than private companies in general. Following its feasibility studies and pilot projects on mariculture in the Aisén Region, Fundación Chile in 1984 started the sea cage farming of coho salmon on a major scale at two locations: Changuitad in Chiloé, Los Lagos Region; and Puerto Chacabuco, Aisén Region. Between 1984 and 1985, Fundación Chile expanded its dry feed pellet mill and decided to build a moist pellet plant and a salmon processing plant in Dalcahue, Chiloé Island. These two facilities commenced operations in 1986.

Fundación Chile's salmon business was launched under its subsidiary Salmones Antártica as a one-thousand-ton program. As a result, Salmones Antártica experienced rapid growth over a short period of time. In 1985, the company had a staff of 200, including 15 technicians. By 1988, the staff had increased to 600, 30 of whom were technicians, and production reached 1,000 tons. This made Salmones Antártica the largest salmon farming company in Chile. The remarkable success of Fundación Chile was achieved only in 4 years after the start of coho salmon mariculture on a major scale (Mendez and Munita 1989, 96). The success story became widely known and was lavishly praised at home and abroad.[13] Figure 3.1 shows changes in salmon exports from the establishment (commercialization) phase to the early growth phase of the Chilean salmon industry.

[13] According to TechnoPress and SalmonChile (2003a, b, 17), many publications about the aquaculture industry in Chile pointed to the contribution of Fundación Chile as follows. "Fundación Chile greatly contributed to our economies through adding new economic activities by introducing new technologies from abroad and applying the results obtained from R&D in Chile. The development of salmon farming industry would be the typical case of their contribution..." This document, beginning with a message from President Lagos, is one of the most important documents about the Chilean aquaculture industry, especially salmon farming. In addition, the document is one of the few documents translated into English, and it seems to have been widely read around the world. The English version (2003a) is slightly different from the original document in Spanish (2003b); therefore, upon writing this book, the original document is referenced. TechnoPress is an affiliated company of Fundación Chile.

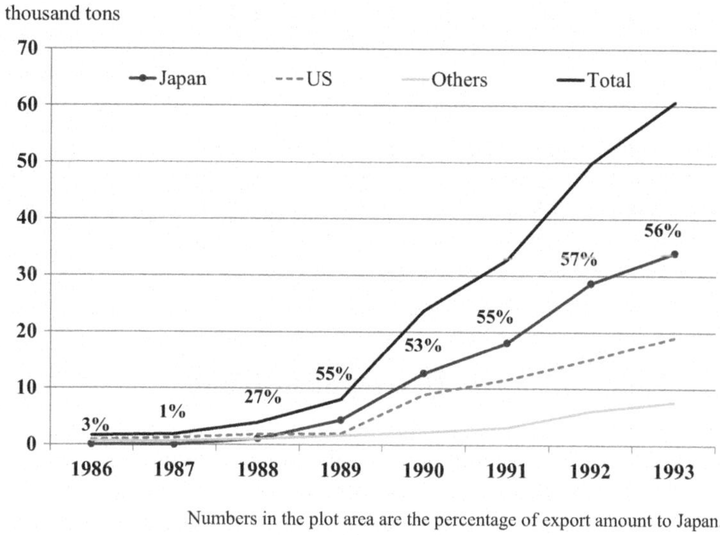

Fig. 3.1 Chilean exports of salmon by market from 1986 to 1993 (*Source*: Created by the author based on Achurra (1995), Cuadro N°2.5, 53)

2.6 Fundación Chile Sold Salmones Antártica

Fundación Chile terminated its salmon business with the successful achievement of the 1,000-ton program and decided to sell its company, Sarmones Antártica off to a private company. An international bidding process took place in 1988, with many companies participating. Nippon Suisan Kaisha (present-day Nissui), one of the major fisheries in Japan and also operating in Chile at that time, won the bid. As a result, Salmones Antártica became a subsidiary of Nippon Suisan Kaisha.[14] This was a timely boon to the Japanese fishery, which had been looking for an appropriate site for its own aquaculture.

Nippon Suisan Kaisha had been conducting a salmon and trout business in the North Pacific Ocean since before the WWII. With its advanced technical capabilities, the long-established Japanese fishery began a coho salmon farming business in Onagawa, Miyagi Prefecture in Japan in the mid 1980s. In Onagawa, Nippon Suisan Kaisha outsourced aquaculture operations per se to local fisheries cooperatives, while it selected fry, provided feed, and distributed adult fish. This form of business was established because the right to use coastal waters precluded private companies from engaging in aquaculture in Japan.[15]

[14] Ricardo Rodríguez who had played an important role at Salmones Antártica retired after the acquisition. He started a new company, Seafine Salmon, producing 2500 tons at maximum, with production continuing until the year 2000.

[15] The story of Nippon Suisan Kaisha looking for a new site to apply experiences in Onagawa, Miyagi is in *Nissui Frontier* 18 (www.nissui.co.jp/corporate/frontier).

The successful sale of Salmones Antártica by Fundación Chile also made it widely known to the world that the salmon business was commercially viable in Chile. This provided a critical history-making springboard for the development of the salmon business as a new industry in Chile. As a result, quite a few private companies in Chile came to show greater interest in salmon farming, with some even commencing investments in it. Against this background, the Undersecretariat of Fisheries of the Chilean government conducted a study to assess the potential of selected sites as a salmon farming ground in 1984, with funds coming from the government and the Canadian International Development Agency (CIDA).[16]

3 After Take-Off: Early Development Phase

Fundación Chile had successfully put its salmon aquaculture business on a commercial footing. The aquaculture business created by the Fundación Chile was sold to a company from Japan, of which markets became the largest export destination for salmon farmed in Chile. These developments now set the stage for the Chilean salmon farming industry to take off to self-sustained development. Salmones Antártica became a wholly private-owned company, which achieved self-sustained management based on salmon production of more than 1,000 tons. Other pioneering private companies also expanded their production.

For an industry to establish itself and develop in earnest, it is crucial both to secure capital, labor, technology, and human resources that support it (industrial personnel training) on the supply side, and to cultivate markets on the demand side. Chile had sufficient capital and labor. Southern Chile provided a relatively abundant source of labor. Technology was gradually being accumulated through the developments discussed above. Industrial personnel were being trained, as will be detailed later. Entrepreneurs ready to invest in promising businesses existed. Capital (in the form of bank loans) was readily available. Yet for entrepreneurs to invest and banks to finance them, it was necessary to demonstrate that salmon farming was commercially viable—and Fundación Chile proved it in a crystal clear manner. Then Nippon Suisan Kaisha, which was headquartered in Japan, then the largest market for exports of salmon farmed in Chile, especially coho salmon, won a tender to acquire Fundación Chile's aquaculture business as the highest bidder. This highlighted the potential of aquaculture in Chile at home and abroad. Figure 2.1 in Chap. 2 summarizes the supply-side requirements for the establishment and growth of the salmon farming in Chile. It shows that technology development

[16] This study was conducted by the Canadian consulting firm Hatfield Consultants, Inc., which selected the Rio Negro River in Hornopirén as the most appropriate site from ten candidate locations. In addition, the consulting firm offered advice for salmon farming projects planned by private companies. It also built and managed some hatcheries on behalf of such companies. The Canadian firm set up a joint consulting firm specializing in salmon farming with Chilean entrepreneur José Puga (TechnoPress and SalmonChile 2003a, b).

and industrial personnel training were the keys for success, given the availability of capital and labor as well as favorable natural conditions.

In this way, the Chilean salmon farming industry shifted to the phase of self-sustained growth driven by the private sector. However, this did not guarantee sustained development. In the early growth phase, companies had to address a number of challenges.

3.1 Three Challenges in the Early Development Phase

In the early development phase, the Chilean salmon industry faced following three challenges. First, at times, market cultivation was no easy task. Efforts were required in relation to conducting market research, catering to market preferences, and securing distribution channels. Second, the provision of one of the most important elements—that is, safe seeds, especially disease-free, domestically produced eggs, as well as good-quality feed—was essential for the self-sustained, private sector-driven development of this industry. Third, it was also crucial to establish a regulatory framework for many aspects of the Chilean farming salmon industry, especially quality standards for the aquaculture industry. In other words, what was needed was so-called "institutional infrastructure," including laws, regulations, and quality standards. Failure to address these challenges successfully in the early growth phase could have inhibited the sustenance, much less the development, of the Chilean salmon industry. This represented the first hurdle to be overcome for the Chilean salmon industry, which had shifted to the private sector-driven phase.[17]

Among the three challenges, market research was particularly important. Of vital importance was the Japanese market, as it had clear dominance (50–60 %) of Chilean exports of farmed salmon. Chile was able to overcome the market cultivation challenge via various information sources on the market. First, Nippon Suisan, which acquired Salmones Antártica, was perfectly familiar with the Japanese market. Also of significance were contributions made by Nichiro, which had already begun commercial production, though on a smaller scale, and the role played by Japanese buyers who had been in Chile to purchase farmed salmon. Japan External Trade Organization (JETRO) and the Export Promotion Bureau of the Chilean government (ProChile) all supported the export of Chilean salmon to Japan. Regarding the second challenge, follow-up technical cooperation under the Japan-Chile Salmon Project by the Fisheries Development Institute (IFOP) and

[17] To discuss challenges related to market and process technology of early growth phase, this chapter mainly focuses on those related to Japanese market, because more than half of Chilean salmon was exported to Japan during this phase. With regard to challenges in other main markets as well as the anti-dumping issue in the United States, see TechnoPress and SalmonChile (2003a, b).

JICA played a pioneering role in producing and providing safe, domestically produced eggs and good-quality feed.

The third challenge was related to institutional infrastructure, and to meet it the Undersecretariat of Fisheries of the Ministry of Economy and the National Fisheries Service (SERNAP) promoted the establishment and implementation of a legal framework and regulations. In the legislative process, they put the knowledge gained from the Japan-Chile Salmon Project to good use wherever necessary. Generally speaking, quality standards are established by an industrial association and complied with by its member companies. In the case of the Chilean salmon industry, a pivotal role was played by the Chilean Association of Salmon and Trout Producers (present-day SalmónChile), which had earlier recognized the importance of quality standards, and Fundación Chile, as it had formulated such standards. Fundación Chile became the first organization in Chile to provide quality certification services for farmed salmon (TechnoPress and SalmonChile 2003a, b, 17).

The above suggests that in the early stages of the growth phase of the Chilean salmon farming industry, significant contributions were made by a combination of various organizations including Fundación Chile, the Chilean government such as the Undersecretariat of Fisheries, National Fisheries Service, Pro-Chile, the Japanese public and private sectors via JICA-IFOP project, JETRO, private firms such as Nippon Suisan Kaisha, Nichiro, and Japanese trading companies that purchased and exported Chilean farmed salmon to Japan. The Japanese public and private sectors were deeply involved in addressing the three challenges—all key factors in ensuring the self-sustained development of the Chilean salmon industry. With more than half of all farmed Chilean salmon being exported to the Japanese market at the time, this was a key factor behind this process. Among many actors, those from Japan played significant roles with respect to the cultivation of the Japanese market.

In this sense, Mr. Akira Kudo of Mitsubishi Corporation, who had long been involved in trade with Latin American countries, hit the mark when he said: "Japan has played an essential role in the process of the Chilean salmon industry standing on its own. It all started with JICA's assistance in salmon incubation and stocking, launched in 1969. Since then, Japan's support involving both the public and private sectors has greatly helped Chile to build foundations for this industry" (Kudo 2008, 42).

3.2 Cultivation of the Japanese Market by Salmones Antártica

Salmones Antártica, a subsidiary of Nippon Suisan Kaisha, was then the largest salmon-farming firm in Chile, having achieved steady growth as a pioneer in this field. It was therefore not a coincidence that the timely introduction of quality assurance and processing techniques for Japanese market was made by this firm. A significant contribution was also made by four Japanese purchasing companies that stationed residential staff in Chile and Japanese importers that dispatched their employees to these companies, especially in the areas of freshness preservation and processing technology.[18]

Japan dominated the export market of coho salmon. For one thing, coho salmon closely resembles sockeye salmon, a popular salmonid species among the Japanese. For another, coho salmon from Chile appeared on the Japanese market when sockeye salmon was off-season, as the seasons are reversed in Chile. Due in part to these advantages, the price of coho salmon was generally linked to that of sockeye salmon produced in Alaska, although lower. This trend continued until the late 1990s.[19]

The methods that Chilean salmon industry used to gain competitiveness in its export markets, particularly in Japanese market at the early growth phase, held the key to its further development.

It is worth repeating here that Japan represented some 55 % of the export market of salmon farmed in Chile from 1989 to the mid-1990s. In that respect, it was of vital importance that Nippon Suisan Kaisha, as a pioneering company in the Chilean salmon industry, bought out Salmones Antártica. Nippon Suisan Kaisha was most familiar with the Japanese market, possessed its own research institutes, and had the capacity to conduct production and exports that catered to market requirements. This buyout was also a timely event in the early development phase of the Chilean industry.

3.3 Introduction of Advanced Processing Technology

Yet such production and export that catered to market requirements for Japan did not come easily. Messrs. Yoshiomi Hoshino, Katsumi Hanamura, and Masao Tamaki needed to exert tremendous effort to relaunch Salmones Antártica after the acquisition. After acquiring Salmones Antártica, Nippon Suisan Kaisha wasted no time in starting the production of high value-added processed products. The company started off by processing coho salmon into *aramaki-jake*, a specially

[18] The concern with quality by Japanese importers and consumers is well known. For example a study, based on interviews, reported that one Japanese supermarket chain bought a Chilean firm's entire production of 3,400 tonnes of coho salmon in 1999 and that the final product was inspected during the site visits by a representative of this supermarket chain. The study concluded that, "This is a perfect example of retail chains acting as lead governors in determining the nature of the process upstream in the chain" (Phyne and Mansilla 2003, 115).

[19] This trend waned due in large part to the gradual disappearance of sockeye salmon from Alaska on the Japanese market. Sockeye salmon have not been artificially cultivated anywhere in the world.

salted salmon typically served during New Year holidays in Japan, shipping them each in a special wooden box. This was followed by the production of *sujiko,* or salted salmon roe. These two types of products became strategic goods for the Japanese market. Many Japanese processing technicians who had worked on a mother ship in the well-known salmon and trout fishing fleet that had operated in the North Pacific fisheries came to Chile to provide technical guidance. The production of evenly salted salmon began in 1992. Trout salmon was first used in 1991 for smoked salmon.

The company also contributed to the introduction of trout salmon into the Japanese market. It even invited buyers at mass retailers and chain restaurant operators in Japan to Chile, showed them around, and convinced them of the safe and stable supply of salmon farmed in Chile. These efforts by Japanese firms gradually opened up the Japanese market. The presence of these firms is likely to have created spillover effects for other Chilean salmon farming firms as well.

3.4 Establishment of the Association of Salmon and Trout Producers

The Association of Salmon and Trout Producers of Chile was established in 1986. The Association, after studying quality standards for salmon in selected countries, established its own standards, required its member companies to comply, and issued a certificate of quality accordingly (Mendez and Munita 1989, 110).

Mr. Alfredo Valenzuela, an executive at the Association at that time, who would later become president, remembered that he considered it important, from his experience in trout exports, to assure high quality at an early point, in order to establish the good reputation of Chilean farmed salmon in the export market.[20] As has been mentioned earlier, Valenzuela was the founder of Llanquihue Ltd.

3.5 Chilean Officials' Visits to Japan

Japan External Trade Organization (JETRO), a public organization for trade promotion, also played an important role in cultivating the Japanese market. Among those that JETRO invited to Japan in the late 1988, was Alfredo Valenzuela, then President of the Association of Salmon and Trout Producers of Chile.[21] Valenzuela

[20] From an interview with Mr. Valenzuela.

[21] According to Sakurai (1995). Teiji Sakurai, was then chief of the JETRO office in Chile.

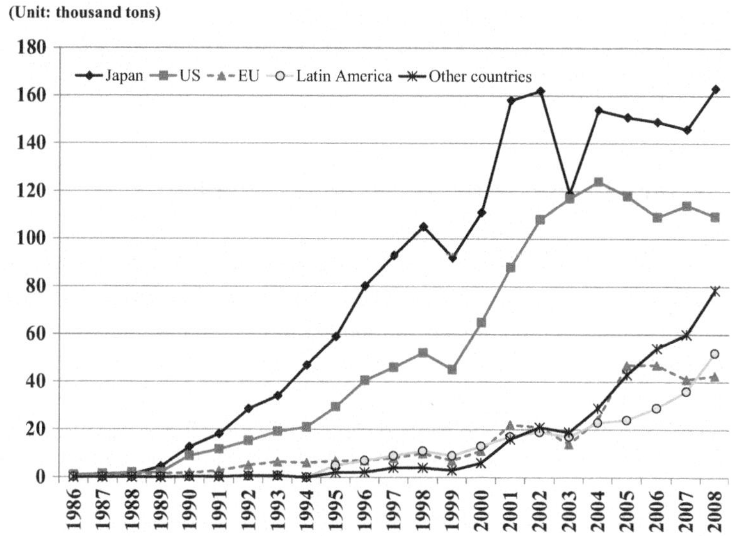

Fig. 3.2 Chilean exports of salmon by market (*Source*: Created by the author, based on Manuel Achurra (1995) for the 1986–1993 figures, TechnoPress and SalmonChile (2003a, b) for the 1994–1997 figures; figures for 1998 onward were compiled by the author from data posted on the website of SalmonChile)

recalled that he was surprised at the large scale of the Japanese market during his visit. He organized and headed a subsequent mission made up of Chilean salmon farmers to Japan in 1989, with JETRO again serving as the host organization for their visit (Sakurai 1995, 27–28). The Chilean Export Promotion Bureau (ProChile) also played an important role in cultivating the markets of Japan and other major importing countries. ProChile is an official entity similar to JETRO, which is an external organ of the Chilean Ministry of Foreign Relations. Commercial attachés in Chilean embassies in countries of the world double as ProChile representatives, engaging in market cultivation in those countries.[22]

As a result of this good collaboration between public and private organizations on both sides of the Pacific in understanding the market, Chile's salmon exports to Japan swelled from 1,100 tons (8.37 million dollars) in 1988 to 4,700 tons (30.47 million dollars) in 1989 and further to 32,000 tons (174 million dollars) in 1993, more than a sixfold increase in value terms between 1989 and 1993[23] (see Fig. 3.2).

[22] The Chilean Association of Salmon and Trout Producers noted that Mr. René Acklin was the one who contributed to the development of the market for Chile besides Salmones Antártica, Mares Australes, and Nichiro (TechnoPress and SalmonChile 2003a, b, 31).

[23] Sakurai (1995, 27). According to Chilean data, the amount of Chile's salmon exports to Japan in 1993 was 34,000 tons.

Salmon exports to Japan are continuing to be important to this day. The share of the Japanese market in Chile's total exports of salmon and trout was 49 % in 2010 and 47 % in 2013 in terms of volume.

4 Transfer of Improved Processing Technology

As shown in the previous section, Japan's public and private sectors contributed significantly to the cultivation of the Japanese market at a critical period during the establishment phase of the Chilean salmon farming industry. This was perfectly complemented by the contribution of Japanese companies in the area of processing technology.

The total cost of salmon farming business can be largely divided into four categories: cultivation, processing and packaging for shipment, transportation and distribution, and administration and finance. According to a 2003 document of the Association of Salmon and Trout Producers of Chile, cultivation topped the list in terms of share of the total cost with 54.6 %, followed by processing and packaging with 18.9 %, transportation and distribution with 18.5 %, and administration and finance with 8.0 %.[24]

While costs of cultivation are considered those of producing the raw material, costs of processing and packaging represent those of adding value to the material. The higher the added value of export goods, the greater the cost of production, and the even higher price they can fetch. In that sense, the production process and technology that supports it both play an important role in making salmon farming a higher value-added industry. Norway, the other world top exporter of salmon, is clearly different in this point. Norway's salmon exports are largely directed to the EU, which imposes high tariffs on processed goods.[25] Hence they export their product in a virtually unprocessed form and processing is usually performed in importing countries.

In contrast, Chilean salmon are highly processed for export. Salmon products include, in ascending order of degree of processing, fresh salmon (refrigerated salmon), frozen salmon, head-on salmon, and headed and gutted salmon (salmon HG). A more highly processed form is the fillet. Cross-cut slices are produced for the Japanese market and longitudinally-cut slices for the European and North American markets. Salmon slices are classified into TRIM C, D, or E. TRIM E is for *sashimi*. As we move forward through the alphabet, more parts are trimmed.

[24] The actual budget breakdown differs from case to case such as selling at FOB or CIF as well as degrees of processing (TechnoPress and SalmonChile 2003a, b, 129).

[25] Salmon processing hubs are in Poland, Denmark, and some others. France has domestic processing industry.

Products processed to a greater degree include smoked salmon and salmon for steak. The 18.9 % of total cost for processing and packaging, discussed above, represents the average cost for all these different degrees of processing (TechnoPress and SalmonChile 2003a, b, 128). The higher the degree, the higher the added value of the end product.

The document of the Association of Salmon and Trout Producers states that Chile was ahead of Norway in terms of increasing the added value of salmon export products (TechnoPress and SalmonChile 2003a, b, 250). Before its acquisition by Nippon Suisan Kaisha, Salmones Antártica outsourced processing work to Frio Sur and Pesca Chile.[26] These two companies were not established to process salmon.

The plan to build a processing plant in Aisén Region did not materialize until Nippon Suisan Kaisha (later, Nissui) acquired Salmones Antártica. Upon acquisition, Nippon Suisan Kaisha put the plan into action and constructed a state-of-the-art salmon processing plant in Puerto Aisén. This marked a significant milestone for the Chilean salmon industry, because it symbolized the introduction of processing technology that was essential for its development. The ceremony to celebrate the completion of the plant was attended even by the Chilean Minister of Economy, who had come all the way from Santiago.

It is worth mentioning that Chile exerted significant efforts to improve its processing technology as early as the nascent period of development. This contrasts sharply with the case of Norway, a rival to Chile. At that time, Norway was ahead of Chile in terms of salmon exports to Japan. Japanese companies imported frozen salmon from Norway and processed it. In contrast, Chile acquired the capacity to export processed salmon to the Japanese market.[27]

Japanese buyers attentively advised salmon farmers and exporters in Chile on the importance of freshness and other qualitative aspects that were preferred in the Japanese market. Technicians at Japanese companies visited Castro on Chiloé Island to provide technical advice. The processing technology that these Japanese companies introduced was extensive, covering the range of products from salmon slices, *sujiko* (salted salmon roe) to evenly salted fillets (salted in order to suit the Japanese tastes, and may be cut into slices later). Japanese companies made a significant contribution in teaching local producers how to prepare goods that

---

[26] As mentioned before, Salmones Antártica built a processing plant in Dalcahue, Chiloé Island and started the operation in 1986 before its acquisition by Nippon Suisan Kaisha.

[27] The situation has remained more or less the same. Norway exports salmon as semi-dressed fish (gutted only) to Europe, which accounts for some 80 % of its export market. When the infectious salmon anemia (ISA) virus broke out in Chile in 2009, Norway tried to fill the gap left by the decrease in U.S. salmon imports from Chile. Because the U.S. market does not accept semi-dressed fish, Norway tried to export salmon fillets. Due to its limited processing capacity, however, Norway's salmon exports to the U.S. fell way short of the target figure of 50,000 tons to 17,000 tons. This nevertheless represented a fourfold increase over a year earlier. While Chile exports Atlantic salmon largely in the form of unskinned fillets to the U.S., Norway does not usually perform this kind of processing.

consumers would like to buy, which helped Chilean producers in a long run to create an industry.

4.1 Higher Degrees of Processing of Salmon and Higher Added-Value Exports

Chile has been trying to increase the degree of processing and thus the added value of its exports, as it is located far from the world's major consuming markets. Another important factor behind this process is that Chile has relatively abundant labor, ensuring that the most labor-intensive part of salmon processing was competitive in Chile. This contrasts sharply with the situation of Norway, which exports unprocessed salmon.

Processing technologies have been increasingly disseminated in the Chile salmon industry since the early growth phase. The degree of processing for Chilean salmon has steadily increased during the two decades from the early growth phase to date. In 1991, Chilean exports of processed products such as fillets and smoked salmon were almost nil. In 2008, they topped 1.5 billion dollars, accounting for 63 % of total salmon exports, as against 10 % in 1992, indicating the great results of this increased degree of processing. The breakdown of salmon exports in 2008 shows frozen fillets accounting for 22 %, fresh fillets 23 %, smoked salmon 3 %, canned salmon 2 %, and other processed products 13 % (Table 3.1). The share of processed salmon was 47.4 % in volume terms and 63.0 % in value terms, suggesting that a higher degree of processing meant higher added value of export products.

The average export price of processed salmon per ton was 1.9 times that of unprocessed salmon. In other words, salmon processing almost doubled in terms of

Table 3.1 Chilean salmon exports according to degree of processing

	1998 (million dollars)	2003 (million dollars)	2008 (million dollars)	Percentage (2008)
Fillets (fresh)	198	353	544	(23 %)
Fillets (frozen)	108	217	527	(22 %)
Salted salmon	18	18	1	(0 %)
Smoked salmon	9	31	74	(3 %)
Canned salmon	7	23	42	(2 %)
Others	30	129	322	(13 %)
Total processed products	**370**	**770**	**1,510**	**(63 %)**
Unprocessed products	**344**	**377**	**882**	**(37 %)**
Total exports	**714**	**1,147**	**2,392**	**100 %**

Source: Author, based on data posted on the website of SalmonChile

the amount of export income it was able to garner. We should not neglect to consider, however, that the higher the degree of processing, the lower the volume, because unwanted parts are cut off, although the unit price is higher. For example, the weight of the whole fish (known as "round weight" in the industry) is reduced to 80 % (HG80)[28] when it is processed to a minimum degree. It is reduced to 75 % (HG75) when processed into TRIM C (unskinned fillets), and further down to 60 % (HG60) when processed into TRIM E.

Another advantage of selling products with a higher degree of processing is that they are less vulnerable to price fluctuations. Products with a low degree of processing (in a dressed form) are more vulnerable because of the presence of intermediate processing firms. In this way, they are more like trading "commodities". A higher degree of processing allows aquaculture and processing firms to increase total sales; sales of unprocessed salmon alone would not amount to much. Increased salmon exports naturally brought about changes to physical distribution and logistics. For example, a new terminal equipped with refrigeration facilities was constructed at Santiago International Airport to deal with increasing air shipments of salmon. Refrigerated container yards were built in San Antonio, Lirquen, and other major ports, which helped to increase the traffic volume, especially that of frozen cargo. Figures 2.5 and 2.6 in Chap. 2 shows the above-mentioned technological developments in the activities of different actors, including the Japan-Chile Salmon Project by JICA and the Chilean government, Fundación Chile, and private sector companies such as Nissui, Nichiro and Mytilus.

Together with the transfer of advanced processing technology, Japanese fishery companies and trading companies made far-reaching efforts to further 'cultivate' the Japanese market for Chilean salmon. This process was incremental and steady, and included the development of new niche markets for Japanese consumers, different from those attended by traditional Japanese salmon producers of Hokkaido, Tohoku and other regions. These enduring efforts gradually cultivated a stable market space for Chilean salmon, without causing extremely strong concern among Japanese traditional producers, as happened in the case of the US market during the early growth phase. Today, salmon is an affordable food in Japan. For example, meal boxes and rice balls featuring grilled salmon are readily available in "convenience stores". While such affordability would not have been possible without ample imports of farmed salmon from Chile, the above-mentioned enduring efforts as well as the new business models such as conveyor-belt sushi bars (*kaiten sushi*) and convenience store rice balls (*sake onigiri*) in Japan may have played an important role.

[28] Process yield is 80 %. HG stands for "headed and gutted."

5 A New Goal: To Develop Technologies for Domestic Seed Production

A key issue in this period, from the establishment phase to the early development phase, was to expand the domestic production of safe eggs free from pathogens to be used for mariculture. Chile was largely dependent on eggs imported from the United States for its source of seeds (eggs) for the main production species of coho salmon, which gave rise to problems including the introduction of fish diseases and the unstable supply of eggs.

The Japan-Chile Salmon Project took on the new responsibility of addressing these problems. To that end, SERNAP was replaced by IFOP as JICA's counterpart organization in 1987. In 1988, JICA and IFOP launched a joint follow-up project under the framework of Project-Type Technical Cooperation (PTTC).[29] The purpose of the JICA-IFOP project was "to develop technologies for domestic seed production for salmon farming." To verify the project performance against this purpose, two targets are introduced: (i) increasing the share of domestically produced eggs to 50 % of the demand for seeds of coho salmon; and (ii) providing seeds of cherry salmon. Mr. Mitsuo Sakai, who participated in this follow-up project as a JICA expert, said: "The developments in the PTTC project around the closing year of 1989 show that the development of technologies for the domestic production of coho salmon eggs was completed at the Dr. Shiraishi Hatchery of IFOP." He noted: "By starting technology transfer activities concerning feed development and fish disease control early, the PTTC project forestalled the problems the farming industry faced later, including concerns about the spread of salmonid bacterial kidney disease (BKD), and the paucity of feed for the salmon farming business that had traditionally used living feed rather than fish meal." He concluded by saying: "These technology transfer activities anticipated technical problems that would arise in the early stages of the development of the Chilean salmon industry, and thus devised precautionary measures, including the development of necessary technologies" (Sakai 1999, 8; Sakai and Ishida 2002). This indicates the significant contribution by the Japan-Chile Salmon Project in the area of seed production (Fig. 3.3).

[29] The project planners were divided over the role of this new project. Some argued that the stocking of chum salmon should be continued in areas south of the Aisén Region. In making a difficult decision, the project planners revisited the principle of what was really needed to establish the salmon industry. The new project consequently supported domestic production of eggs and conducted cherry salmon stocking in inland waters. JICA changed its counterpart organization from SERNAP to IFOP, an organization under the umbrella of CORFO, to allow for the sale of domestically produced eggs.

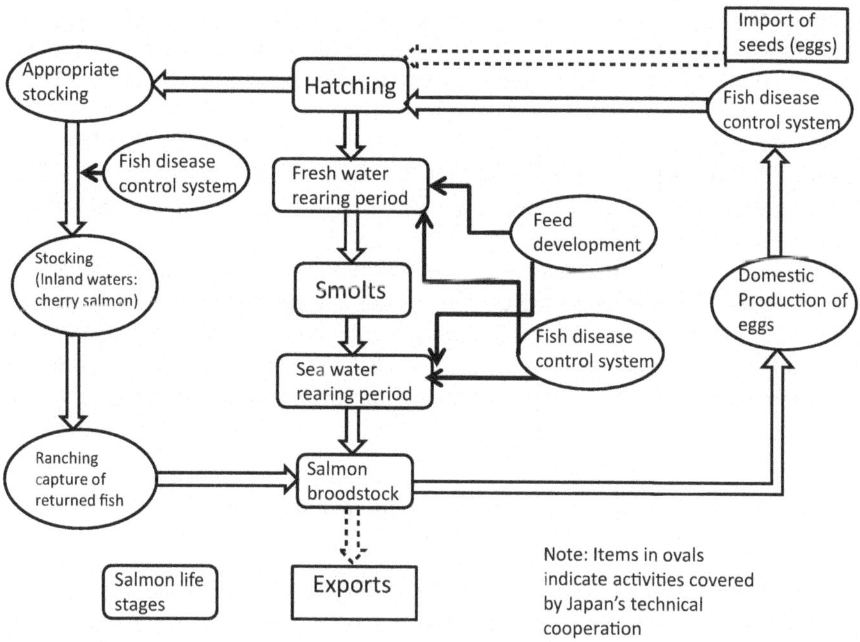

Fig. 3.3 Establishment of technology and infrastructure of domestic seed production and fish disease control system by the Japan-Chile Salmon Project (Note: Items in ovals indicate activities covered by Japan's technical cooperation. *Source*: Created by the author, based on Sakai (1999, 5))

The salmon farming business by Chilean companies, including Salmones Antártica when it was a company under the umbrella of Fundación Chile, was dependent on imported eggs even in the 1990s, not to mention the 1980s. This was because importing eggs was more expedient and less costly than making the necessary investment in domestic egg production. The Japan-Chile Salmon Project played a pioneering role by working to establish systematic seed production in advance.

Domestically produced eggs were originally used to fill the gap when imports from the Northern Hemisphere were unavailable for seasonal reasons. Salmones Antártica did not operate its processing plant in certain seasons, because trout salmon (steelhead) and coho salmon were produced in summer. To allow the plant to operate throughout the year, the company planned to produce salmon with domestically produced eggs. This was because the extraction of eggs for domestic seed production was carried out at the end of summer. Meanwhile, imported seeds (eggs) continued to be used for year-round production. Later, however, the technique of controlling the temperature and photoperiod in hatcheries in Chile made it possible to provide domestically produced seed throughout the year. This paved the way for the accumulation of salmon broodstock for reproduction.

As mentioned above, technologies for domestic seed production that had been developed from early on under the Japan-Chile Salmon Project were spread widely in Chile after many of the Chilean counterparts moved to private companies and applied these technologies there.

One such former counterpart was Mr. Mario Vargas. At Salmones Antártica, Vargas designed hatcheries and conducted salmon control for seed production, especially salmon genetic control 5 years after the completion of the Japan-Chile Salmon Project. He also planned the company's first major production of domestic seed (domestically produced eggs) together with Mr. Tatsuyoshi Hirata from Japan.

6 Feed Development and Fish Disease Control

Among the products of JICA's assistance in the area of feed development, the development of pellets for fry is well known. Fry pellets (crumbles) are produced when pellet-shaped feed is crushed into fine pieces using a fine mesh with its stable nutritional value intact. They are small enough for young fish to eat. Dr. Masaaki Takeuchi and Mr. Shunji Toshida, both JICA experts, provided technical guidance for the development of this kind of feed. This resulted in the construction of a pilot plant furnished with state-of-the-art equipment, and later on, the spread of the technology to Chile (Fig. 3.4).

In terms of fish disease control, Dr. Takeshi Hara, who participated in the Japan-Chile Salmon Project as a JICA expert, conducted pioneering research in the development of disease control technologies by capitalizing on the findings of Japan's advanced research on BKD. JICA's technical cooperation in the areas of feed development and fish disease control contributed to the development of the Chilean salmon industry. Moreover, IFOP, the Chilean counterpart organization, continued to produce seeds free from pathogens at the Dr. Shiraishi Hatchery and supply them to salmon farmers even after the termination of JICA's cooperation project, contributing to the development of the salmon farming industry in Chile, especially the Aisén Region.

At the request of salmon farmers, the Dr. Shiraishi Hatchery of IFOP "began to sell eyed eggs and fry of coho salmon and cherry salmon fry. IFOP's consulting services, including feed analysis, together with its proprietary fry pellets, is highly appreciated"[30]

[30] The Editorial Committee of the Centenary Celebration of the establishment of diplomatic relations between Japan and Chile (1997).

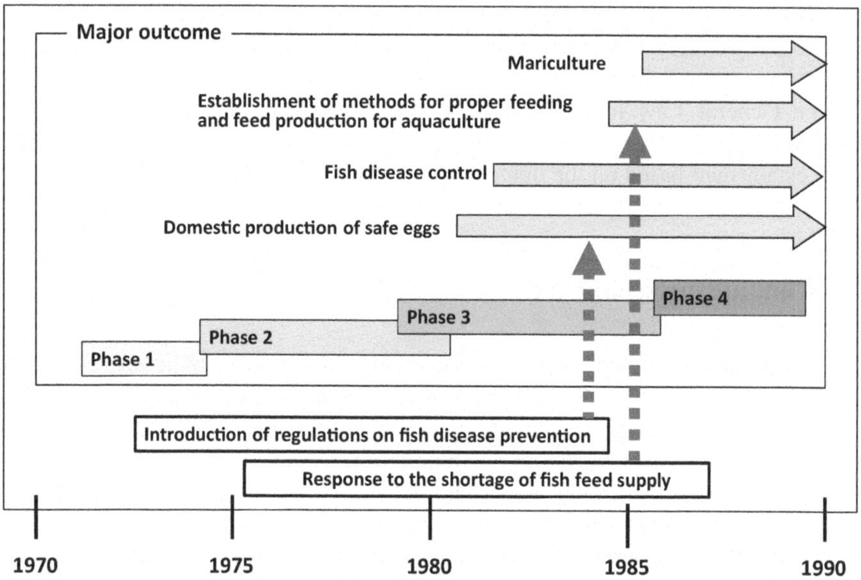

Fig. 3.4 A chronology of major outcomes of the Japan-Chile Salmon Project. Note: Phases 1–4 in the chart roughly indicate the phases of JICA's cooperation. Phases 1–2 and Phases 3–4 correspond to the preparatory and establishment phases, respectively, of the Chilean salmon industry (*Source*: Created by the author based on Sakai and Ishida 2002, 1554, Fig. 4)

7 Development of Legal Infrastructure

As noted earlier, the development of any new industry calls for the development of laws and regulations; that is, legal infrastructure for that particular industry as an enabling factor. The General Law for Fisheries and Aquaculture, which was established in 1991 by revising the existing fisheries law, provides an important legal framework for the salmon farming industry in Chile. It is interesting to note that the foundations of this legal infrastructure were developed in the establishment phase of the Chilean salmon farming industry.

The Undersecretariat of Fisheries (SubPesca), created in 1978, played the pivotal role in establishing relevant laws and regulations. SERNAP assumed the responsibility for their enforcement. Each of these two organizations served as the counterpart organization of JICA. SERNAP, the Chilean counterpart organization for the Japan-Chile Salmon Project until 1987, has put many of the project's outcomes to good use in establishing laws and regulations concerning the aquaculture industry in Chile.

For example, technical cooperation in the area of fishery disease control has resulted in the development of regulations on the prevention of infectious disease epidemics associated with salmon and trout farming (Sakai 1999, 8). Likewise, the Chilean Ministry of Economy's ordinance No. 162 of 1985 imposed controls on imported salmon eggs (Achurra 1995, 63). This ordinance included provisions for the disinfection of hatcheries and other control measures, including the introduction of veterinary checks of farmed salmon, making the ordinance the starting point for salmonid infectious disease control in Chile.

The General Law for Fisheries and Aquaculture, established in 1991 after completion of the JICA project, builds on the previous laws and regulations that were established based on the outcomes of Japan-Chile Salmon Project.

8 Concluding Remarks

As explained above, it was important to demonstrate that the salmon business was a promising and commercially viable business in order to kick start a new industry such as this. This point was made clear by conducting feasibility studies and investing in the salmon business. An important role was played by the Fundación Chile as a knowledge broker in creating networks of diverse actors, contributing greatly to the establishment of the Chilean salmon industry. Together with technological development, training of industrial personnel was an important activity in the early phase.

The Chilean government, SERNAP and IFOP, independently or through the Japan-Chile Salmon Project, also served as a catalyst and played a facilitating role, contributing to technological development and formation of specialized industrial personnel. Furthermore, the Japan-Chile Salmon Project contributed a great deal to the establishment of a legal framework based on scientific evidence. The Undersecretariat of Fisheries (SubPesca), established in 1978, played the pivotal role in establishing relevant laws and regulations. SERNAP assumed the responsibility for their enforcement.

The full-fledged growth of the Chilean salmon industry was triggered by the successful production at scale of Salmones Antártica of Fundación Chile, and thereafter, the private sector started to play the major role in industrial development. Nevertheless, the industry faced several challenges, such as commercialization, especially how it should be positioned in major salmon markets and explore new markets, meet quality standards and increase the value added through processing.[31] Public entities supported private companies' efforts to cultivate external markets. It deserves mentioning that some future oriented/long-term knowledge and technology enhancement in areas such as safe natural egg production, control of diseases, etc. was led by Japan-Chile Salmon Project. These are strategic areas for the future needs, that may not attract sufficient investment from the private sector. It is important that investments in strategic areas, requiring long term/risky investment, are dealt with at early stage (i.e. in the case of the salmon industry, in the 1980s) because this would increase the resilience within the

[31] As mentioned above, this chapter has mainly focused on issues related to the Japanese market, because more than half of Chilean salmon was exported to Japan during this phase.

Fig. 3.B1 Twelve pioneers in aquaculture in Chile

industry against future shocks or threats. For instance, as is discussed in Chaps. 4 and 5, the creation of effective feed becomes instrumental in enhancing competitiveness of the salmon production, and, regarding disease control, ability to create domestic eggs becomes a key to control sanitation by avoiding infected imported eggs (Table 3.2).

Twelve Pioneers in Aquaculture in Chile

The Chilean fishery journal *AQUA* highlighted the roles of people who had been involved in salmon farming in Chile when it issued a 20th anniversary special issue in December 2007. The article on the aquaculture pioneers in Chile carried pictures of many faces familiar to those who had worked in the industry for more than two decades (Fig. 3.B1).

For many people in the industry in Chile and abroad, the year 1988 highlighted the Chilean salmon farming industry's transition to a growth phase, as that was the year that Fundación Chile sold Salmones Antártica to Nippon Suisan Kaisha. The following year, the publishing house TechnoPress, an affiliate of Fundación Chile, launched *AQUA*. Carried in the 20th anniversary special edition were 12 pictures of these pioneers. The picture of Mr. Pablo Aguilera attracts initial attention (upper left).[32] Aguilera was one of the central figures and original members of the Japan-Chile Salmon Project. Four decades ago, in 1970, he came to a hatchery in Nakashibetsu on the northern island of Hokkaido, Japan, for training. He

(continued)

[32] Photographs show (from upper left to right) Pablo Aguilera, Adolfo Alvial, Gustavo Araya, Rodrigo Balart, Boris Cotreras, and Oscar Gárate; (from lower left to right) José Miguel Hernández, Rodrigo Infante, Hector Novoa, Vjekoslav Rafaeli, Mario Puchi, and Alfredo Valenzuela (from the feature story of *AQUA*, December 2007 issue).

met Mr. Ariaky Nagasawa there. Aguilera is now respected as the pioneer of the pioneers in the salmon farming industry in Chile.

Aguilera is not alone. Eleven of the 12 pioneers have been engaged mainly in salmon farming, including Mr. Alfredo Valenzuela, who was responsible for the management of a local hatchery as a technician at the Agricultural and Livestock Service (SAG) of the Chilean government. He said in an interview: "I had the chance to go to Japan for study. That determined my future life, and I devoted my life to salmon farming. I was blessed with the opportunities to learn from great teachers, including Dr. Yoshikazu Shiraishi" (Technopress 2007). He later served as President of the Chilean Association of Salmon and Trout Producers (now known as SalmonChile). Other Chileans who had a chance of learning in Japan included Mr. Gustavo Araya, Mr. Hector Novoa, and Mr. Mario Puchi, all of whom took part in the Japan-Chile Salmon Project early on, as well as Mr. Boris Cotreras, a veterinary researcher who joined the project after he met Aguilera and Puchi.

In all, 6 out of the 11 pioneers in salmon farming in Chile had opportunities to visit and observe Japanese salmon farming and/or receive training in Japan. Of the six, five played a central role in the Japan-Chile Salmon Project over a long period.

From Fundación Chile, Mr. José Miguel Hernández, Mr. Adolfo Alvial, Mr. Rodrigo Balart, and Mr. Vjekoslav Rafaeli were selected as pioneers. Mr. Hernandez was appointed head of the Aquaculture Project of Fundación Chile. His important contribution to salmon farming is discussed in Chap. 3. He visited Japan and inspected aquaculture businesses when he was young. Mr. Alvial is known for his contribution to turbot farming. He worked for Fundación Chile and was also editor of the AQUA. He then became director of Intesal, the research institute of SalmonChile. Recently he became a technical director at Marine Harvest.

All these accounts suggest that the Japan-Chile Salmon Project and Fundación Chile served as a school that trained pioneers who later contributed to the development of the salmon farming industry in Chile. In addition to the above-mentioned pioneers, many others who built the foundations of today's Chilean salmon farming industry had acquired their skills through the Japan-Chile Salmon Project. Between 1970 and 1989, as many as 28 Chileans received training in Japan under the salmon project, which was implemented by JICA and its counterpart organizations in the Chilean government—first the National Fisheries Service (SERNAP, including its predecessor, a department of SAG), and later IFOP. These training participants to be dispatched to Japan were selected from Chilean technicians who had been assigned to the project based on an order of priority that took their assignment into consideration.

(continued)

In Japan, the technology of seed production and fry farming was advanced. According to Nagasawa, what Chilean young professionals learned in Japan later translated into specialties of their own, which in turn proved to be of great help in establishing and developing the salmon farming industry in Chile. Chilean counterparts worked with experts from Japan on the frontline of the project both before and after their training in Japan. The capacity building through this on-the-job training (OJT) greatly paid off later. "None of the trainees left the project immediately after returning home from Japan. Many of them were later headhunted by private companies, though," according to Nagasawa.[33]

Nagasawa identified "a long-term strategy and the policy of not changing Japanese experts so long as the same Chilean counterparts remained in place" as two major factors for the successful training. He said: "It is often the case with Japan's technical cooperation that experts from Japan are replaced after a certain period of time. This practice, however, could discourage the counterparts from maintaining their interest in a long-term undertaking. Once committed, you should follow through to the end. Replacing experts entails changes in approach. That means one step forward, one step back. That's not the way to go, I thought."

Many Japanese experts participated in the project. Between 1972 and 1989, Japan assigned a total of 52 Japanese experts to the project, which amounted to 498 person-months in total. Many of these experts had been conducting cutting-edge research in various fields of aquaculture. They spared time from their busy work in research projects in Japan, came all the way to Chile, and helped the technical development process in the preparatory and establishment (commercialization) phases of the Chilean salmon industry. Some of the experts who worked in Chile, after returning home, were assigned Director-General of the National Research Institute of Fisheries Science, a leading aquaculture research institution in Japan.

It is difficult to accurately assess the actual number of Chilean technicians who participated in the project with these Japanese experts and received OJT from them on the project sites and elsewhere. It is clear, however, that most of these Chilean technicians are now working in the salmon farming industry in Chile.

[33] This and other statements of Mr. Ariaky Nagasawa is from an interview with him in August 2010.

Table 3.2 Chronology of development of salmon industry in Chile (preparatory and early development phases)

	Activities of Japan-Chile Salmon project and related institutions (Governments of Chile and Japan)	Activities of Domsea farms, Fundación Chile, SalmonChile, and private firms (Nissui, Llanquihue, Nichiro, Mytilus, etc.)
69	Japan Fishery Association's first survey of aquatic organisms in rivers, lakes, and fjords in two southern regions	
70	Pablo Aguilera visits Hokkaido for training	Release of coho salmon brought from the United States in Los Lagos Region fails
71	Second survey of aquatic organisms in rivers, lakes, and fjords in two southern regions	
72	JICA experts Nagasawa and Shiraishi arrive in Chile/eyed eggs of cherry salmon arrive/ Dr. Shiraishi suddenly passes away	
73	Cherry salmon juveniles released for the first time	
74	Eyed eggs of chum salmon arrive/Chum salmon juveniles released for the first time (non-feeding)	
75		Valenzuela and Muena establish Llanquihue Ltd. for trout farming
76	Dr. Shiraishi Hatchery is built in Coyhaique	Domsea farms brings coho eggs to Lake Popetan in Chiloé, but many die due to a storm. Later, it builds a hatchery in Curaco de Vélez
77	Chum salmon released (feeding)	
78		Domsea released 200,000 coho salmon and 170,000 chinook salmon/Nichiro Chile established, begins imports of coho eggs
79	JICA's project-type technical cooperation starts. Salmon juveniles raised in ponds and sea cages in Ensenada Baja, and spring release starts in October	Domsea: 30 coho salmon return. Domsea sold to Campbell's Soup/Nichiro Chile began mariculture of salmon/Mytilus began to import coho eggs
80	Marine environment survey begins	Nichiro harvests 130 tons of first sea-farmed coho salmon/Mytilus begins mariculture
81	The hatchery built in Ensenada Baha/mariculture begins (sea cage farming)/pink salmon juveniles released for the first time	Rodriguez in Domsea purchases floating cages/Fundación Chile acquires Domsea/ Mytilus domestically produces 200,000 coho eggs for the first time in Chile
82	Chum salmon eggs collected for the first time/Chum salmon migrating in the bay return	Fundación Chile begins feasibility study on salmon mariculture (1981–1984)
83	Domestically produced coho salmon introduced/BKD (bacterial kidney disease) found, and fish disease control strengthened	

(continued)

Table 3.2 (continued)

	Activities of Japan-Chile Salmon project and related institutions (Governments of Chile and Japan)	Activities of Domsea farms, Fundación Chile, SalmonChile, and private firms (Nissui, Llanquihue, Nichiro, Mytilus, etc.)
84	JICA's project-type technical cooperation extended	Fundación Chile (Salmones Antártica) begins the operation of mariculture, expands the dry feed pellet mill, and builds a moist pellet plant
85	The operation of pilot plant for feed production begins	Chile exports 30 tons of farmed salmon to Japan/law for salmon disease control implemented
86	7 chum salmon return in Magallanes region/ production of high quality feed pellets begins	Fundación Chile (Salmones Antártica): salmon processing plant in Dalcahue begins operation/TV program featuring salmon farming broadcast/shortage of fish feed supply
87	The counterpart changed from SERNAP to IFOP/Chum salmon released for the last time	Fish disease problem is aggravated
88	The follow-up phase of the JICA's technical cooperation starts/examination of fish disease in Los Lagos and Aisén regions begins	Production of farmed salmon by Fundación Chile (Salmones Antártica) reaches 1,000 tons/Fundación Chile sold Salmones Antártica to Nippon Suisan/export of salmon to Japan reaches 1,000 tons
89	Development of domestic coho eggs production begins/large cherry salmon raised in the lake return, and profits of selling fish pellets increase/BKD-free seeds developed for the first time/follow-up phase ends	Exports to Japan increase, and Japan becomes the largest importer of Chilean salmon
90	IFOP: BKD-free egg production established	
91		The general law for fisheries and aquaculture established
92	IFOP: research on seeds and genetic selection starts/cherry salmon released for the last time	
93	IFOP: resource survey of cherry salmon begins	
94	IFOP begins production of 8 million eyed eggs of coho salmon	
95	IFOP supplies half of coho salmon seeds in Aisen Region	
96	IFOP: development project to farm sturgeon begins	
97		USA files claim against Chile for dumping

Source: Created by the author, based on Sakai (1999) and other sources

Note: Some important events relevant for salmon industry development in Chile in this period are: 1970, the Allende administration begins; 1973, coup d'etat and the Pinochet administration begins; 1982, the debt crisis in Chile; 1990, the Aylwin administration begins and Chile shifts to a civilian government; 1994, Chile joins Asia-Pacific Economic Cooperation (APEC); 1997, centenary celebration of the establishment of diplomatic relations between Japan and Chile

Acknowledgments In addition to the references listed here, the author consulted a number of articles and books listed in the bibliography of Chap. 2 and drew on approximately 80 h of interviews with Chileans and Japanese considered to be key people in the development of the Chilean salmon industry.

References

Achurra, Manuel. 1995. La Experiencia de un Nuevo Producto de Exportacion: Los Salmones. In *Auge Exportador Chileno: Lecciones y Desafios Futuros*, ed. Patricio Meller and Raul Eduardo Saez. Santiago: CIEPLAN/DOLMEN.

Cimoli, Mario, Giovanni Dosi, and Joseph E. Stiglitz (eds.). 2009. *Industrial policy and development: The political economy of capabilities accumulation.* Toronto: Oxford University Press.

Editorial Committee of the Centenary Celebration of the Friendship Treaty between Japan and Chile. 1997. *Nihon Chile Kouryu Shi* [History of Japan-Chile relations]. Tokyo: Japan Association of Latin America and the Caribbean.

Kudo, Akira. 2008. *Chunambei ga Nihon wo Oinuku hi: Mitsubishi Shouji Chuzaiin no Me* [The day Latin America left behind Japan: From the perspective of a Mitsubishi Corporation resident representative]. Tokyo: Asahi Sensho.

Lin, Justin Yifu. 2012. *The quest for prosperity: How developing economies can take off.* Princeton: Princeton University Press.

Mendez, Ricardo Z., and Clara O. Munita. 1989. *La Salmonicultura en Chile.* Santiago: Fundación Chile.

Norman, Akbar, and Joseph E. Stiglitz. 2012. Strategies for African development. In *Good growth and governance in Africa: Rethinking development strategies in Africa*, ed. Akbar Norman, Kwesi Botchway, Howard Stein, and Joseph E. Stiglitz. Oxford: Oxford University Press.

Phyne, John, and Jorge Mansilla. 2003. Foreign linkages in the commodity chain: The case of the Chilean salmon farming industry, 1987–2001. *Sociologia Ruralis* 43(2): 108–127.

Rodrik, Dani. 2007. *One economics, many recipes: Globalization, institutions, and economic growth.* Princeton: Princeton University Press.

Sakai, Mitsuo. 1999. *Chile ni Okeru Sake Ishoku to Youshoku Keikaku Oyobi IFOP Shiraishi Hakushi Fukajyo no Katsudo Jyoukyou* [Salmon introduction and aquaculture project in Chile and the activities of the Dr. Shiraishi Hatchery of IFOP]. Tokyo: JICA.

Sakai, Mitsuo, and Kenichi Ishida. 2002. The pacific salmon ranching in the southern Chile: Evaluation of a project-type technical cooperation by JICA. *Fisheries Science* 68(Supplement II): 1552–1555.

Sakurai, Teiji. 1995. *Chile Koku Santiago Chuzai no Ki* [Record of activities in Santiago, Chile]. Tokyo: Japan External Trade Organization (JETRO).

TechnoPress. 2007. Pioneros en Chile: Con la Acuicultura en las Venas. TechnoPress (2007), *AQUA: La Revista de la Acuicultura*, Edicion Conmemorativa de 20 Años, (Diciembre 2007), Santiago: TechnoPress.

TechnoPress, and SalmonChile. 2003a. *Aquiculture in Chile.* Santiago: TechnoPress/SalmonChile.

TechnoPress, and SalmonChile. 2003b. *La Acuicultura en Chile.* Santiago: TechnoPress/SalmonChile (Spanish version of TechnoPress and SalmonChile 2003).

Chapter 4
The Development of Salmon Aquaculture in Chile into an Internationally Competitive Industry: 1985–2007

Michiko Iizuka, Pedro Roje, and Valentina Vera

1 Introduction

Since the mid-1980s, the Chilean salmon industry has steadily increased its annual production, propelled by a rapidly growing world demand for seafood (Montero 2004).[1] The rapid expansion in production volume came hand in hand with the development of new institutions and new forms of social interaction among industry associations, universities, research institutions and other bodies. However, we can also observe that even at this incipient stage, there were already some imbalances in the co-evolutionary process. Chile achieved a successful 'catch up' in terms of nearing the production capacity of Norway (the largest exporter of salmon in the world) at the beginning of the first decade of the 2000s. However, this catch up was not comprehensive in all areas, particularly when we consider the aspects of innovation, development of local technological capabilities, sustainable production via monitoring of sanitation and environmental conditions, and overall institutions in general. Thus the process of industrial growth might not have been as successful as first impressions would suggest.

In order to understand how such imbalances may have played out in the rush to catch up, this chapter discussed the early period of industrial development from 1985 leading up to the sanitary crisis in 2007. Our focus is on understanding the process of industrial development from different perspectives, including

---

[1] Topics covered in the previous chapter.

M. Iizuka (✉)
Maastricht Economic and Social Research and Training Center for Innovation and Technology (UNU-MERIT), United Nations University, Maastrciht, The Netherlands
e-mail: iizuka@merit.unu.edu

P. Roje • V. Vera
Departamento de Ingeniería Industrial, División de Proyectos Externos, Universidad de Chile, Santiago, Chile

A. Hosono et al. (eds.), *Chile's Salmon Industry*,
DOI 10.1007/978-4-431-55766-1_4

organizational development, production capability and formation of industrial clusters. The aim of this chapter is to provide a wide historical picture that will illustrate and assess how the industry grew to become a global player through learning and acquiring capabilities. We do this by first, observing the general growth in exports and industrial dynamics; second, we look at the historical development of the industry; third, we look at the challenges that the industry faced and overcame; and fourth, we examine technological upgrading achieved by the industry in course of the knowledge-building process. In an attempt to understand the above achievements, the fifth and sixth sections of this chapter look at the evolution of institutional support and capacity building in terms of both human resources and research. The final section offers some conclusions based on the above observations and analysis.

2 Overview of Chilean Salmon Industry: Growth of Exports and Contribution to the National and Regional Economy

The Chilean salmon industry grew exponentially between 1985 and 2007. The volume of production increased by 20 times – from 3000 tons in the 1980s to 600,835 tons in 2007. In 2007 world production of farmed salmon was 1,768,000 tons, with Chile accounting for 34 % of the total, making it the second-largest producer in the world after Norway (Fig. 4.1). This demonstrates that Chile had caught up quite successfully, becoming one of the largest producers/exporters, surpassing Canada and the UK.

The rapid growth of exports from this sector contributed significantly to the Chilean economy. The growth of salmon and trout exports from 1996 to 2007 was higher than the other core export products from Chile – that is, agricultural products, extractive fishery, copper and forestry. Furthermore, the industry was said to have created an important source of employment,[2] from 8000 direct jobs and 2200 indirect jobs in 1992 to 38,400 direct jobs and 15,000 indirect jobs in 2004 (Fig. 4.2).

Until the late 1990s, the industry was located mainly in the Los Lagos region (10th region; see Fig. 4.3), as this region had by far the most suitable natural conditions for salmon farming, such as fjords, rivers and lakes. Only since the late 1990s has salmon farming started to move southwards into the region of Aysen and Magallanes (11th and 12th regions). This process of southwards expansion will

[2] Direct employment is employment generated directly by the industry. Indirect employment is employment generated by supporting or related industries.

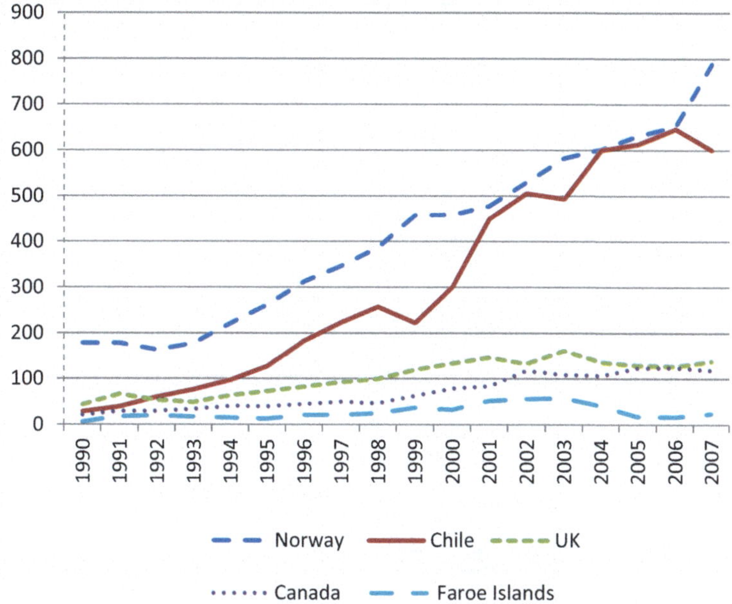

Fig. 4.1 'Catch up' of the Chilean salmon industry: export volume (thousand tons) (*Source*: SalmonChile 2009)

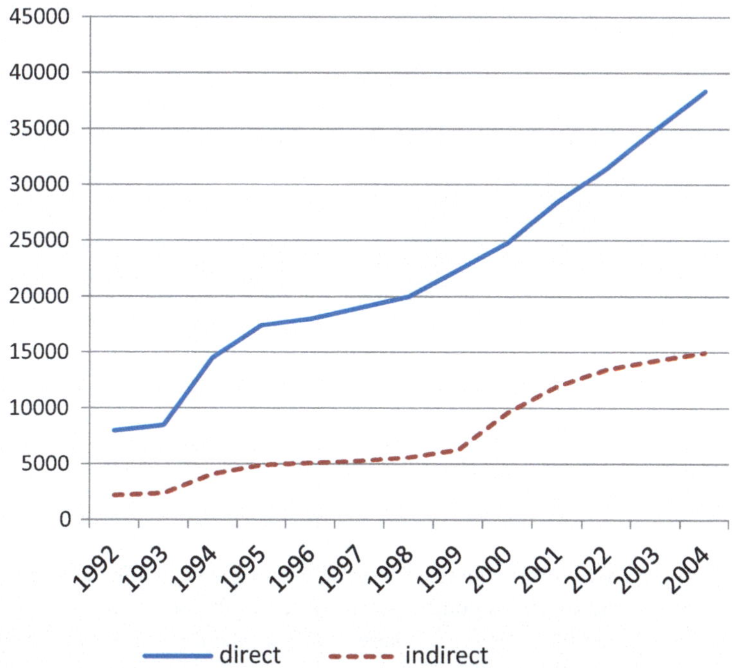

Fig. 4.2 Employment created in the salmon industry in Chile (number of jobs) (*Source*: SalmonChile 2009)

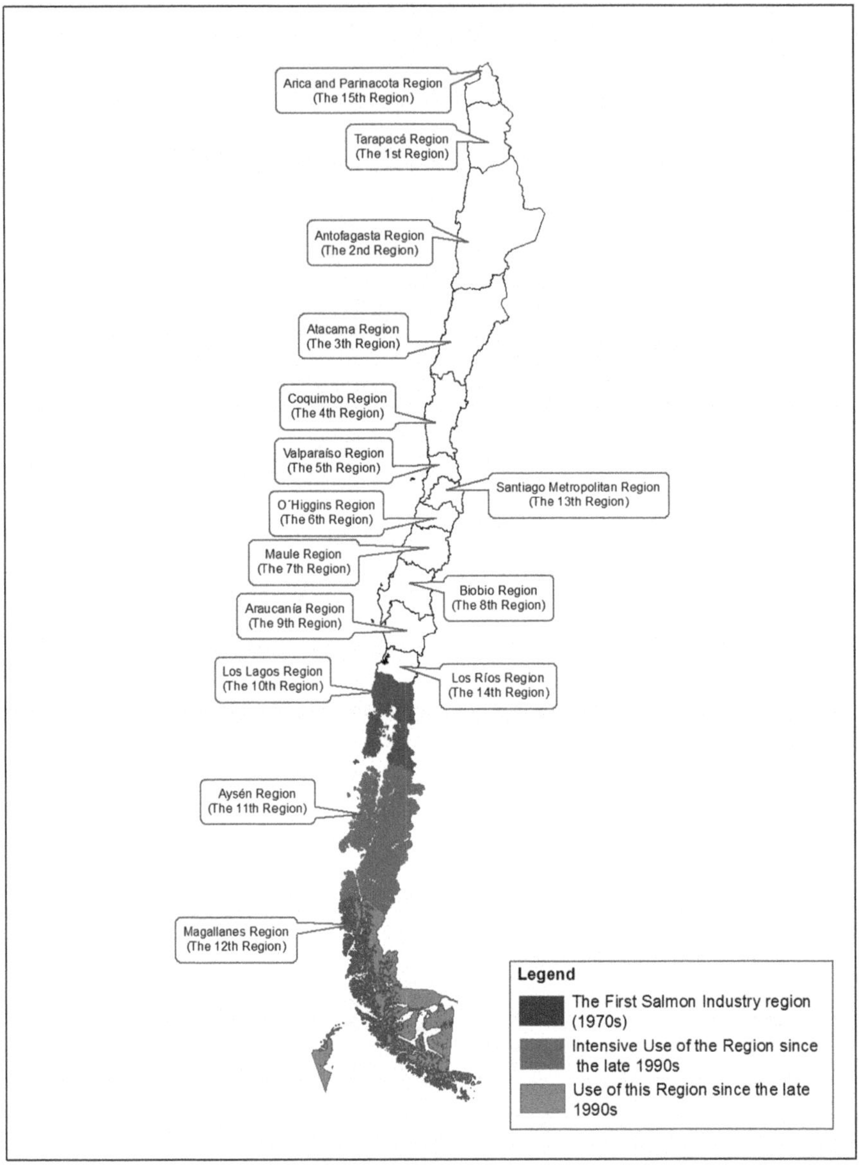

Fig. 4.3 Geographical distribution of the salmon industry over time (*Source*: University of Chile)

be examined in detail in Chaps. 5 and 6. This occurred due to the lack of space in the Los Lagos region to accommodate new salmon farming sites, while the rising prices of salmon at the end of 1990s compensated for the high operation costs in the far southern regions due to a lack of infrastructure and insufficient human resources.

Apart from the southern regions, there are new developments in other regions, such as Araucania (9th region) and Los Rios (14th region).[3]

3 Evolution of Chilean Salmon Industry: 1985–2007

The period between 1985 and 2007 can be divided into two distinctive phases (Montero 2004; Iizuka 2007; UNCTAD 2006; Maggi 2007; Katz et al. 2011). These are: (1) a growth phase (1985–1995) and (2) a globalization phase (1996–2007).

The **growth phase (1985–1995)** demonstrated consolidation of the production system with an increase in production volume, making Chile one of the leading salmon producers at the global level. During this period the government started to provide multiple forms of support, mostly in the form of competitive grants, thereby contributing to the industry's development and improved productivity. In this period, we can also observe consolidation of firms as an industry or 'salmon cluster' with the emergence of groups of input and service providers as well as the establishment of an industrial association, the Association of Salmon and Trout Producers of Chile (APSTC).

The second **globalization phase (1995–2007)** is characterized by increasing global insertion. The salmon industry became well established as an important economic sector within Chile and as a leading global supplier of farmed salmon internationally. During this phase, production volume was still growing quite strongly, although at a slower pace than in the previous phase, and by 2007 exports came close to annual production of half a million tons. The industry and related stakeholders were quickly incorporated into the global environment and came under the scrutiny of international standards and regulations, as well as being the subject of mergers and acquisitions (M&A) by the global players.

3.1 Rapid Increase in Number, Size and Concentration of Firms: 1985–2007

Dramatic changes took place in firm demography between 1985 and 2007. In the growth phase (1985–1995), the number of firms increased substantially. This increase parallels the increase in exports. As Fig. 4.4 demonstrates, the number of firms increased almost seven times, from 36 in 1985 to 219 in 1997, while exports in value terms increased on an even larger scale, from US$1.1 million to US$201.5 million. The increases in the number of firms and value of production were

[3] There are some important players in these regions. In Valdivia (capital of Los Rios, 14th region), there is an important producer of wellboats, used to transport live fish. In the Bio-Bio region (the 8th region) there is a salmon food plant (Ewos, the global fish feed firm).

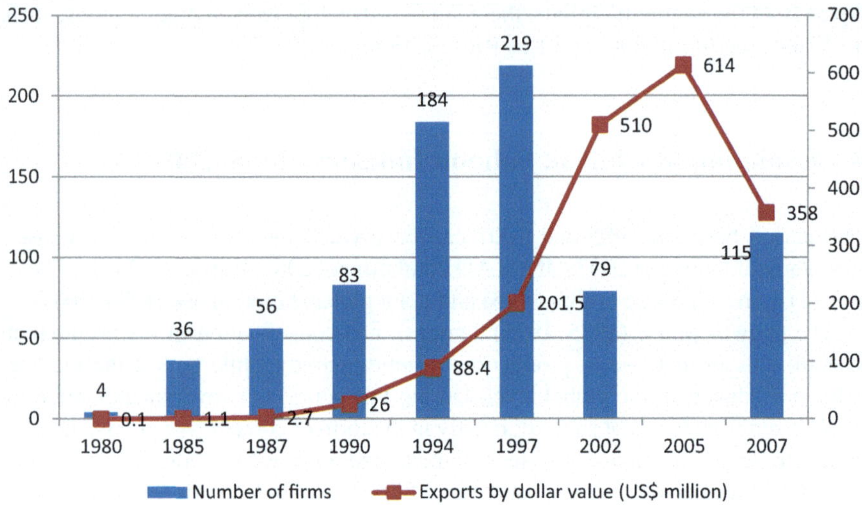

Fig. 4.4 Changes in number of firms and amount of exports by value: 1980–2007 (*Source*: Based on SalmonChile 2009; Iizuka and Gebreeyesus 2012)

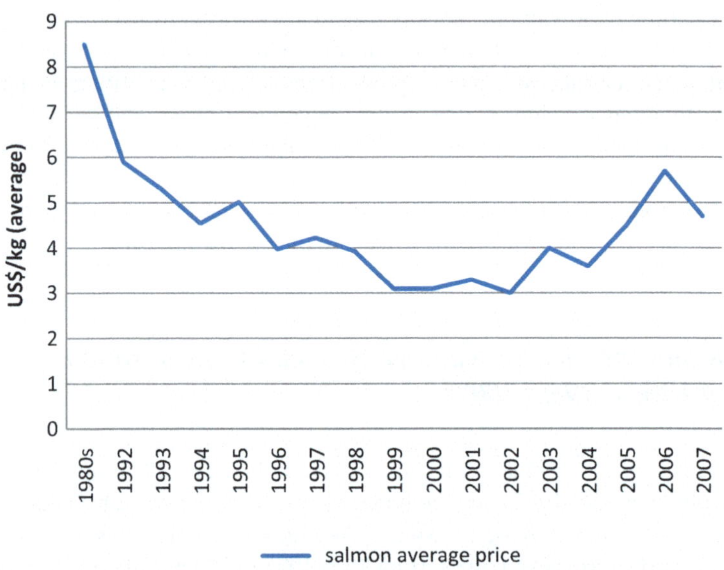

Fig. 4.5 Price of salmon per kg: 1980s–2007 (*Source*: Based on *RevistaAqua* (various years))

supported by the high demand and high price of salmon, which remained above US $5.00 per kg until 1995 (see Fig. 4.5).

In the following phase (1996–2007), these companies faced fierce competition due to the increased number of firms and the declining average price of salmon, which reached its lowest point at US$3.00 per kg in 2002. To confront this fierce competition, mergers and acquisitions (M&A) took place in order to: (1) increase the scale of production to lower the unit cost; and (2) secure inputs and services through vertical integration (including fish feed, egg and smolt production (pisciculture), salmon rearing phase and processing).

By the early 2000s three types of firms had emerged in the Chilean salmon industry (Montero 2004; Maggi 2007). The first group included six large companies with a significant foreign presence, and sales exceeding US$50 million each annually. These were fully integrated companies that incorporated all three main components of production (pisciculture, farming, processing[4]) and carried out some kind of in-house R&D. The second group, mostly national and somewhat smaller firms, attained sales in the order of US$20–40 million annually each, ensuring sufficient capital of their own to be able to start new investment projects. The third group consisted of smaller companies, mostly family-owned and lacking adequate capital of their own to expand their activities. Table 4.1 depicts some of the typical firms belonging to each of the three groups. It illustrates the nationality of owners, degree of vertical integration and value of exports circa 2001.[5]

The composition of the above three groups changed completely due to the rapid M&A process that continued throughout the 2000s. The M&A was mostly comprised of first-tier firms buying up the second and third-tier firms, or between the first-tier firms to increase production capacity and integrate productive activities. For instance, the leading Chilean firm, AquaChile, merged with Salmon Pacific Star in 1999, acquired Best Salmon in 2003, picked up Salmon Chiloe, Salmon Cailin, Salmon Maulin and Aquas Claras in 2005, and then went into the fish feed business with another firm, BioMar, as Alitec in 2006. In other words, through M&A, AquaChile became a fully integrated company, from fish feed and eggs to processing plants, with numerous cultivation sites. Another leading salmon-producing firm, Marine Harvest, originally a Scottish firm, was acquired by the Dutch animal feed company Nutreco in 1999. Nutreco also acquired Stolt Seafarm, the pisciculture firm, in 2005 converting the company into a fully integrated firm, from pisiculture, cultivation center, processing plant and feed industry. Nutreco, however, later on in 2005 sold the company to Norwegian firm Panfish, which had already purchased Fjordo Seafood Chile. Fjordo Seafood, purchased by Panfish, was also the result of a merger between Salmon America, Salmones Linao and Salmones Tecmar in 1999. As can be seen from some of the representative cases, repeated M&A among firms reduced the number of actors significantly, from 219 in 1997 to 79 in 2002. The production in value terms, however, continued to increase, from US$201.5 million in 1997 to US$614.0 million in 2005.

[4] The freshwater phase produces smolt, the fry; the seawater phase fattens the fry to mature salmon; and the processing phase slaughters and processes the salmon.

[5] The industrial structure has gone through various changes since then. This is just to illustrate how complex and diverse the types of firms were at one point in time.

Table 4.1 Some representative firms of the Chilean salmon cluster (2001)

Group	Name of firm	Value of exports (US $ million)	Nuclear production phases	Origin of capital
First group	Marine Harvest	115	Pisciculture, farming and processing	The Netherlands
	AquaChile	84	Pisciculture, farming and processing	Chile
	Camanchaca	76	Pisciculture, farming and processing	Chile
	Multiexport	64	Pisciculture, farming and processing	Chile
	Mainstream	60	Pisciculture, farming and processing	Norway
	Fjord Seafood	54	Pisciculture, farming and processing	Norway
Second group	Salmones Antártica	45	Farming and processing	Japan
	Cultivos Marinos Chiloe	40	Pisciculture, farming and processing	Chile
	Aguas Claras	38	Pisciculture, farming and processing	Chile
	Invertec	29	Pisciculture, farming and processing	Chile
	Salmones Pacific Star	25	Farming and processing	Chile
	Salmopesnac	24	Farming and processing	Chile
Third group	Ventisqueros	17	Pisciculture, farming and processing	Chile
	Robinson Crusoe	15	n/i	Chile
	Cultivos Yadrán	15	Pisciculture, farming and processing	Chile
	Trusal	8	Pisciculture, farming and processing	Chile
	Fiordo Blanco	6	n/i	Canada

Source: Authors' elaboration based on information from Montero (2004) and Maggi (2007)
n/i means No information

The consolidation of the industry through repeated M&A had increased the scale of production and transformed the industrial structure into a mature monopoly by the mid-2000s where the five largest exporting firms had a combined share of 52.2 %, the highest proportion of exports ever, while the five second-largest exporting firms declined to a share of 20.8 %. This period, from 2000 to 2006, coincided with a period of increase in the price of salmon (see Fig. 4.5) from US$3 per kg in 2000 to US$5.70 per kg in 2006. The rising price of salmon encouraged the firms to invest further in increasing their production capacity.

Table 4.2 New market entrants in the late 2010s

Name of firm	Year of entry	Production capacity (in 1000 tons)	Region of operation	Main activity of the firm	Origin of capital
Salmones El Golfo	2005	20	XI	Extractive fishery	Chile
Salmones Humboldt	2006	20	X	Extractive fishery	Chile
Salmones Itata	2006	30	XI	Extractive fishery	Chile
Salmones Cupquelan	2004/2008	40	XI	Global sea-food business	Iceland/Canada
Salmones Aysen	2007	25	XI	Extractive fishery	Chile/USA
Provi. Fish Farms	2006	3	XI	Extractive fishery	Chile
RiverFish	2007	18	XII	Investing firm	Chile
Tornegaleones		20	XII	Investor in salmon farming	Chile
FoodCorp SA/Pacific seafood	2008		XI	Global sea-food business	Norway
Acuimag SA	2007	–	XII	Investing firm	Chile

Source: Katz et al. (2011)

In addition to increased investment by the existing salmon firms, the rising price of salmon in the middle of the first decade of the 2000s attracted new entrants to the industry. The new entrants came from different businesses seeking strategic investments. Table 4.2 lists 11 representative cases of new entrants, which were reported in secondary sources (mentioned in the *RevistaAqua* (http://www.revistaaqua.com/) and others). The table demonstrates that most of the new entrants came from the extractive fishery[6] business into salmon farming with the aim of diversifying their business portfolios and improving on the declining returns from extractive fishery. Other new owners were investors of various kinds. The entry of these firms, although "small" in terms of production capacity (ranging from 30,000 to 40,000 tons) transformed the dynamics of the salmon industry. In fact, Fig. 4.4 demonstrates an increase in number of firms from 79 in 2002 to 115 in 2007. These firms located their cultivation sites in the 11th and 12th regions, due to the

[6] Of course, not all of these actors were new in the salmon industry. In fact, various active salmon farms originated from extractive fishery, such as Camanchaca (which commenced salmon farming in 1987), Pesquera Friosur (Salmones Friosur 1987). Of foreign firms, Cermaq of Norway has a seafood business, and so has Nihonsuisan (Salmones Antartica 1986), with other extractive fishery activities in Chile (Endepes). Invertec, owned by a family of investors (the Montenari family), is run by a holding firm with investments in agribusiness and real-estate. However, these firms were in a minority in the group of large exporters compared to the recent trends (based on Iizuka 2007).

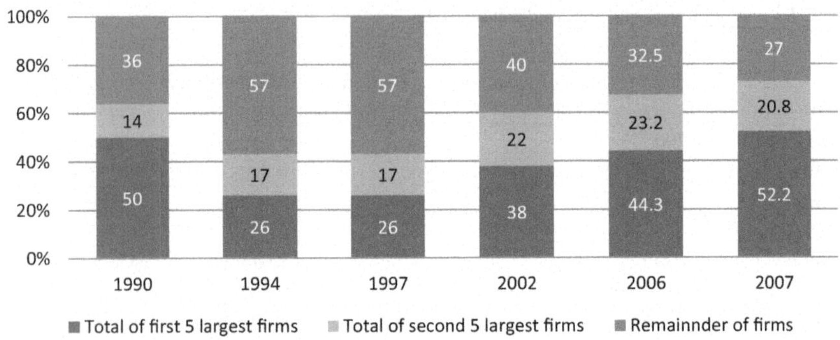

Fig. 4.6 Share (%) of export value by firm size (*Source*: Iizuka 2007)

Table 4.3 Number of supplier firms

Years	National total	Of which foreign	Of which are region X	% foreign	% region X
1993	75	20	14	26.7	18.7
1998	240	35	119	14.6	49.6
2003	461	96	228	20.8	49.5

Source: Iizuka (2007)
Note: Region X denotes those firms with legal residence in region X

unavailability of concessions in the more favorable 10th region. It is our view that these new entrants, coming from different backgrounds and characteristics, created a new dynamic in the industry as a whole (Fig. 4.6).

3.2 The Expansion of Intermediate Inputs and Services Suppliers

In the 1990s, the suppliers for the salmon industry also increased significantly. Salmon-producing firms, faced with increased competition, started to concentrate on their core activities – salmon rearing – and started to outsource other activities to third parties. There are no official statistics for the supplier firms in the salmon industry; however, the annual directory of the salmon industry includes a list of supplier firms. The number of supplier firms in the directory increased dramatically from 75 in 1993 to 461 in 2003 (Table 4.3). The number of suppliers in the tenth region, where the headquarters of the salmon producing firms were located, increased rapidly from the late 1990s onwards.

The suppliers for the salmon industry include many diversified inputs and services. In each phase of production – freshwater, seawater and processing – numerous services and inputs are needed and are provided by specialized firms (see Table 4.4).

Table 4.4 Types of goods and services required in each phase of production

	Fresh water phase		Seawater phase		Processing phase	
	Goods	Services	Goods	Services	Goods	Services
Domestic	Fish feed, tanks, nets, buoy, cage, egg, iodine, some simple machinery	Maritime and land transport (trucks, tractors and ships), maintenance of cages and nets, veterinary services	Fish feed, cage and buoy, nets, medicines (vaccine, antibiotics, immune depressors), pigments, smolts, ultrasonic, iodine	Maritime transport (trucks, tractors, ship and well boat), maintenance of cage, nets, harvesting services, veterinary services (vaccine), pathology consultants	Salmon and trout, packaging materials (plastic bags, aluminum coated trays, polyethylene trays etc.), salt, sugar, detergents, iodized soaps, charcoal	Transport (trucks, ship, air), traders, clearing services
Imported	Automatic feeders, computers, oxygen system, machine to count the eggs and alevines	Genetic services,	Automatic feeders, computers, sensors, underwater cameras. nets (for some), pigments and medicine (vaccines)	Laboratory services	Cutting machinery, skinning machine, smoking machine replacement knives, parts, detergents, injectors	Transport, trading, marketing, retailing

Source: Montero (2004)

The increasing specialization of suppliers in the 1990s can also be confirmed by some examples of key suppliers. For example, salmon feed was originally made 'in house' by salmon producers; however, it became increasingly specialized with the growing size of the industry. For instance, it is possible to see the consolidation and specialization of feed firms, from numerous locally owned companies to more specialized foreign-owned firms from 1992 to 2002.

A similar trend can also be observed in the specialized net workshop firms catering for the salmon industry. These firms started to become established between the 1990s and the first decade of the 2000s. It was revealed that the service evolved to become a specialized industry from 'artisan-like' activities (Iizuka 2007). Unlike the feed industry, net workshop firms remained mostly small- to medium-scale family-owned business throughout the first decade of the 2000s.

Another good example of the development of the specialized service supplier is the wellboats industry. ASENAV (a firm located in Valdivia, Los Rios region), a manufacturer of marine vessels, undertook the production of wellboats with up to 800-ton capacity for the transport of salmon. Designs for these products are produced by both local and Norwegian firms (UNCTAD 2006).[7]

As demonstrated in the examples above, specialized suppliers for the salmon industry emerged and expanded their activities in specific areas: salmon food, nets and wellboats. The increase in suppliers is the 'scale effect' of the salmon farming industry. The industrial clustering was triggered by the salmon farming industries starting to outsource their services to lower their unit cost of production. Nevertheless, the input and service suppliers, with increased specialization, gradually started to have their own dynamics.

4 Tackling the Global Challenges

As the industry expanded exports, firms started to face numerous challenges from external sources. In this section, we review the challenges encountered by the industry during the growth phase (1985–1995) and globalization phase (1996–2007) in order to explore the reasons behind the structural changes within the salmon industry in Chile.

[7] It is worth noting that the Universidad Austral de Valdivia in Chile is possibly the only university with a course in naval engineering is. This seems to show a connection between the requirements of the ASENAV and the university.

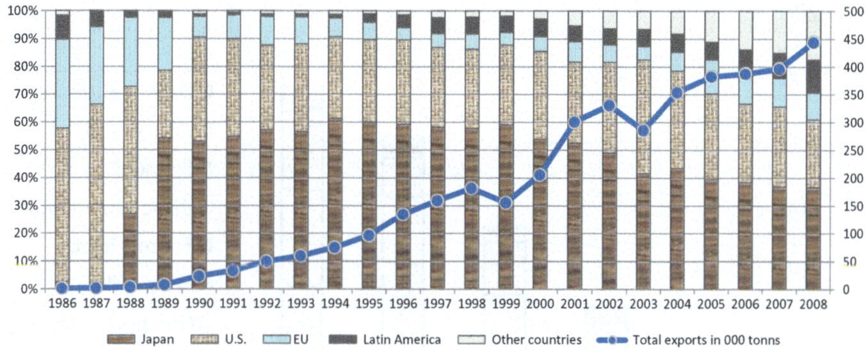

Fig. 4.7 Transition of destination market for Chilean salmon exports in % and exports by volume (thousand tons) (*Source*: Based on Achurra 1995; SalmonChile 2009)

4.1 Diversification of the Market

During the growth phase (1985–1995), firms were required to search for alternative markets because the growing volume of production induced a decrease in price, as the industry was dependent upon great two large markets – Japan and the United States (Fig. 4.7).

Figure 4.7 demonstrates the share of export destinations throughout the growth and globalization phases (1985–2007) and the overall increase in the volume of exports. The share of destination markets during the growth phase, particularly in the late 1980s, was dominated by the US and Japan.[8] The proportion of the Japanese market gradually increased from the latter part of the 1980s. The proportion of the two markets combined – Japan and the USA – amounted to around 90 % during the 1990s.

Dependence on two markets obviously created vulnerability when firms needed to negotiate prices in a situation of excess supply. The firms tried to resolve this issue by searching for alternative markets. As this interest was shared by several firms, some of them got together and created an organization (a short lived organization called Salmoncorp and later, a more formal association called the Association of Producers of Salmon and Trout in Chile, APSTC) to find new export markets. These attempts gradually increased the number of destinations, as the increase in the proportion of European, Latin American and other markets was observed during the globalization phase. Nevertheless, it must also be noted that even in 2007, more than half of Chilean salmon in volume was still exported to the USA and Japan.

[8] At this stage, the production size was very small and hence the only major markets were Japan and the USA until 1989.

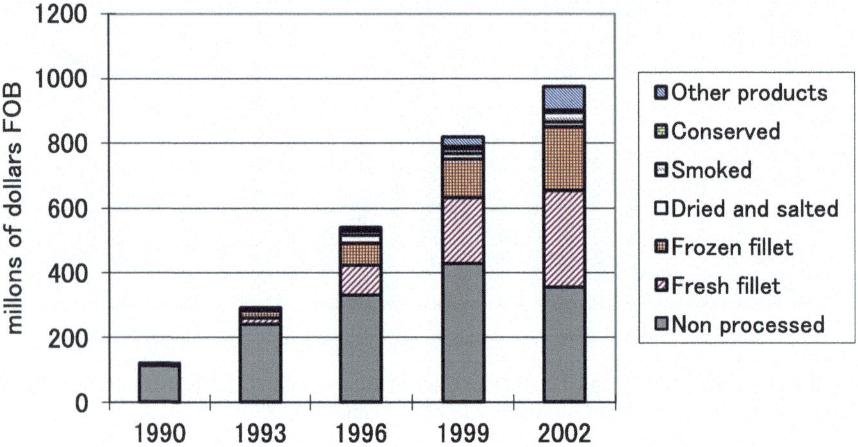

Fig. 4.8 Proportion of processed salmon for export (*Source*: Achurra 1995)

4.2 Increasing Added Value and Differentiation of Exports

Throughout the 1980s and for much of the 1990s, Chilean salmon exports were dominated by a non-processed product called salmon HG (head and gut out). From the 1990s, the firms started to expand the processed component into fillet, salt, preserving and smoking with the aim of generating more added value. As a result, by 2002, the proportion of non-HG products increased to about 40 % of total production (see Fig. 4.8).

The share of processed products in salmon exports increased further during the globalization phase. However, non-processed products still dominated in terms of exports. This was due to the fact that processed salmon does not always return a higher price. Instead, non-processed fresh salmon is often preferred by the buyers. In some cases, the price of fresh unprocessed products is higher than that of frozen products due to difficulties in transportation and cold chain management. Some producers also expressed concern that the more enhanced the product, the more it is targeted to a specific market, placing it at greater risk when there is insufficient demand in the target market. This suggests that added enhancement does not always create additional value unless the producers are well integrated into global value chains. The issue of adding elaboration for value became less a cause of debate in the first debates of the 2000s.

During the growth phase, Atlantic salmon (or salmon salar) replaced coho as the most commonly exported species of salmon. As shown in Table 4.5, salmon coho maintained a high share among exports until the late 1980s. However, exports of Atlantic salmon (salmon salar) began to dominate after that date due to the stronger profit margins resulting from the higher unit prices for Atlantic salmon. Furthermore, Atlantic salmon was the preferred species for the growing US market as well as for the European market. The other important export species was trout, which

Table 4.5 Exports of Chilean salmon and trout species (tons)

Species	1986	1987	1988	1989	1990	1991	1992	1993
Coho salmon	892	1,188	2,936	4,740	9,995	14,108	17,565	17,960
King salmon			2	9	246	496	612	400
Atlantic salmon		36	145	1,437	9,529	12,496	19,964	24,833
Sakura salmon					23	60	90	0
Trout	753	635	888	1,864	4,020	5,527	11,114	16,670
Salmon s/spec.						118	526	865
Total	1,645	1,859	3,971	8,050	23,813	32,805	49,871	60,728

Source: Achurra (1995)

began to gain prominence during the early 1990s. At present, the percentage share of each species remains similar to those seen in 1992 and 1993 (Achurra 1995). The change of species also required adapting to different production methods from the existing ones. The transition from the familiar rearing technique of coho salmon to Atlantic salmon required a learning process, this time involving different stakeholders from countries such as Norway.

5 Technological Upgrading in the Salmon Industry

During the early stage of growth (1985–1990) Chilean salmon farming firms were mainly family-owned enterprises, highly artisanal in their model of production organization and with important in-house efforts devoted to the development of firm-specific technological knowledge and production routines. In this phase, all processes of production were done in house, as there were no specialized service suppliers. The small scale of production made it infeasible for specialized services and products to emerge. Hence each salmon farming firm designed and built its own cultivation tanks, mostly employing local carpenters and regional raw materials, produced its own salmon food daily with fresh fish, developed its own routines to deal with fish mortality in the cultivation tanks, learned how to deal with predators such as seals, and much more (Katz et al. 2011). As can be seen from these experiences, during this phase, technological progress was mainly 'incremental' learning involving a trial-and-error process. A great deal of tacit knowledge was generated in the process, obtainable only from in-house cumulative efforts at solving emerging new problems and production difficulties. Under such circumstances, knowledge creation tended to be highly experimental at the firm level. The presence of organizations such as Fundación Chile and the Association of Producers of Salmon and Trout in Chile: APSTC established in 1986, helped firms to overcome issues related to productivity growth by providing the space for frequent exchange of knowledge among pioneers in the early phase.

This 'incremental' form of technological upgrading changed with the industrial transformation – increase in firm size; increase of the number of firms within the industry; presence of foreign capital and the formation of specialized suppliers – that happened after the 1990s and with escalating speed in the first decade of the 2000s. The increase in scale resulting from mergers and acquisitions induced various changes with regard to acquisition of technology. These firms started to equip themselves with highly specialized equipment, automation process machinery and scientific food formulae, among others, all purchased from abroad. The technology used in this phase was quite different from the more artisanal technologies and tools used in the early 1980s. With increasing access to frontier technology in terms of intermediate inputs, the technological gap between local practice and the international state of the art methods and technology gradually became smaller, at least for the large firms in the industry.

Although this technological gap was reduced through the introduction of new machinery and equipment, the gap did not completely disappear. Many of the Chilean firms, in particular the smaller firms, did not have sufficient resources to close the technological gap by purchasing a more updated inputs, machinery and equipment. For example, in 2003, the use of vaccines was close to 100 % in Norway for different diseases, while in Chile the coverage against yersiniosis (a bacterial disease) of salmon was only 68 %, 78 % against infectious pancreatic necrosis (IPN: severe viral disease for salmonoid fish affects mainly young fish), and less than 17 % against Salmon Rickettsial Syndrome (SRS: another bacterial disease common in Chilean salmon) (Katz et al. 2011, 31). The same trend of lagging behind the advanced technology can be seen with the use of wellboats, ships that can transport live salmon and reduce the risk of spreading pathogens. By the early 2000s, 99 % of Norwegian firms used wellboats while only 20 % used them in Chile (Montero 2004, 36). In a broader sense, in the industry as a whole, there was sporadic adaptation of high technology; implemented in leading firms during the latter period while the remaining firms continued to innovate incrementally.

Furthermore, due to increases in firm size, the organizational setting within firms became more hierarchical and complex, with differentiated levels of responsibility within the company organizational structure. In other words, firms became more specialized and the division of labor intensified, but this also developed into a bureaucratic 'culture' of dealing with problems. The board members of the firms became more professional and incorporated many economists and MBAs, so that the self-awareness of being the business of 'rearing fish in natural environment' was gradually abandoned and the industry became more routinized resembling the manufacturing sector. This trend can easily be observed in the large firms but less so in the smaller firms.

The following sections examine an important segment of production in the salmon industry as a means of illustrating the technological upgrades that contributed to improving productivity. It is important to note that each segment of production had a different pattern of upgrading.

5.1 Egg Production

An important technological upgrading in the Chilean model of salmon farming has been associated with the expansion of the domestic salmon egg sector. Salmon eggs have been imported from various salmon-producing countries, such as Ireland, Scotland, the USA, Denmark, Sweden, Norway, Finland and Canada. The importation of eggs declined as the industry obtained sufficient capacity to produce eggs domestically and these became competitive with foreign suppliers. Egg production has been a sensitive issue because it not only determines the growth and quality of fish but also market access and prices. The importation of eggs from abroad involves the risk of transmitting fish diseases, because it is still technologically difficult to detect the presence of viruses in eggs.

As demonstrated in Fig. 4.9, egg imports rose with the increase in export volume of salmon during the growth phase (1985–1995); however, the domestic production of eggs picked up towards the end of the 1990s, reaching a peak in 2006. Various factors influenced this shift from imported to domestic eggs. The first were the regulatory measures introduced by the public sector to restrict egg imports as a reaction to the increasing outbreak of fish diseases in the early 2000s. This increased the demand for domestic eggs, with the result that various forms of pisciculture were established in Chile during the early 2000s by both domestic and foreign firms. There are no official statistics for domestic egg production from the 1990s as this was not a significant activity at the time; however, available information of different sources indicates that domestic production increased from the 2000s with improvements in quality (see Fig. 4.9).

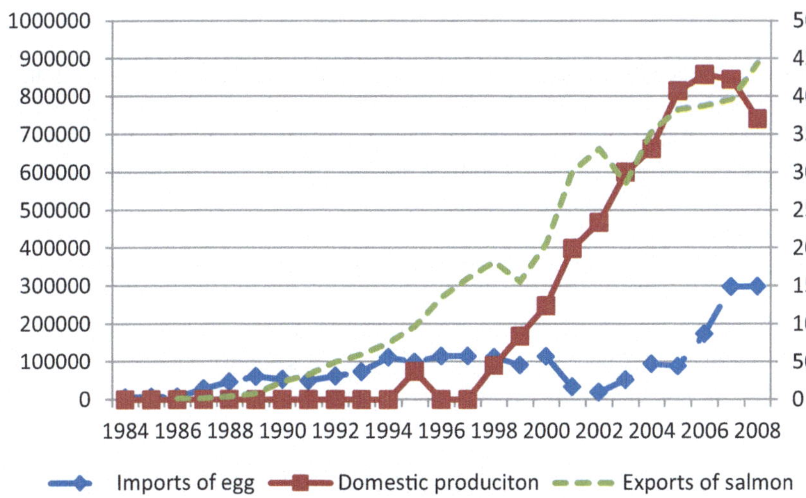

Fig. 4.9 Transition of salmon egg production in millions of units and salmon production volume in thousand tons (*Source*: Iizuka 2007). Note: Eggs are in millions of units; salmon exports are in thousand tons

Other reasons for increased domestic production of salmon eggs were, according to Edardo Salvador, general manager of Gentech S.A.: "(1) technology had reached a certain level in Chile, meaning that there were little or no differences between the domestic and imported eggs; (2) the domestic eggs may sometimes be preferred over imported ones since the salmon producers can have direct information about the fish, production sites and people to guarantee the quality, especially being free from infectious diseases; (3) the price of domestic eggs had fallen substantially due to competition coming from abroad". Furthermore, due to the changes in production methods, domestic producers were now able to produce eggs all year around, whereas before it was only possible to produce them for a limited time period after which time, egg imports would once again be necessary (interview with Edardo Salvador, in Iizuka 2007).

Although some progress in domestic egg production has taken place, the main challenge for future development is said to lie in scaling up R&D efforts in search for better quality genes. In Chile there are many small projects for improvement of genes; however, these are not big enough to create any real impacts (Svein Sorvick, interview; in Iizuka 2007). In fact, in 2004, the firm was importing top-quality genes from Norway to produce eggs in Chile using the facilities of large Chilean firms through collaboration schemes. As stated above, firm-level efforts for R&D are present and interaction with foreign firms – Norwegian in particular – could result in technological upgrading; however, dispersed R&D efforts at the individual firm level may not be enough to bring about substantial changes in productivity and quality of eggs.

5.2 Fish Feed

Another important example of technological upgrading occurred in fish feed. Feed accounted for 30 % of the cost of production in salmon farming in 2003 (Iizuka 2007) (Table 4.6). This was the single most expensive item of expenditure, and means that the efficiency of fish feed production can have a substantial impact on the overall productivity of the firm.

The productivity of fish feed is measured by an indicator called the 'conversion factor rate'.[9] This rate is calculated by measuring the amount of fish feed necessary to produce 1 kg of salmon. When the salmon industry started, fish feed was made in an artisan way; hence the conversion rate of feed was very low at a rate of 4 (i.e. 4 kg of feed is necessary to produce 1 kg of salmon). The conversion rate improved significantly during the early growth period (1985–1990) with

[9] There are two types of 'conversion rates' in salmon feed. One is the 'biological factor conversion rate', which measures the amount of feed for 1 kg of salmon. The other is the 'economic factor conversion rate', which is the conversion rate from 1 kg of feed to 1 kg of salmon adjusting for other economic factors. Usually the economic factor conversion rate is lower than the biological rate.

Table 4.6 Cost structures of salmon farming firm (%)

Production of smolts	3.0
Farming operation	
Feed	30.0
Pigments	6.0
Annual labor	6.0
External services	4.8
Other costs	4.6
Other costs of grow-out	0.2
Subtotal	51.6
Processing Plant	
Manual labour	12.0
Packaging material	4.0
Energy	0.9
Maintenance and other costs	2.0
Subtotal	18.9
Transport and sales	
Ground freight	1.5
International airfreight	13.0
International ocean freight	3.0
Cool and frozen storage	0.5
Sales costs	0.5
Sub total	18.5
Administrative and financing costs	8.0
Total costs	100.0

Source: Iizuka (2007)

introduction of wet feed. In the latter half of the growth phase (1991–1995), the introduction of dry pellets improved the conversion rate from 2.8 to 1.7. In the globalization phase, extruded pellets were introduced to further improve efficiency: these products improved the conversion rate to 1.3 and 1.25 respectively (Fig. 4.10).

5.3 Net Workshop

In salmon farming, fish are artificially kept in a net cage stationed along the coast during their rearing period. The net workshop provides a crucial service to salmon farming by maintaining the cleanliness of the net in which firms keep their fish. The net workshop manages the whole package of net maintenance services (including cleaning and repairs)[10] as well as designing nets to fit the topography of various cultivation sites. Hence, although the simple manual task of cleaning the net seems

[10] This involves knowing crucial firm-level secrets about fish density per m^2, feeding times and production schedule, because each of these variables determine the frequency of net cleaning.

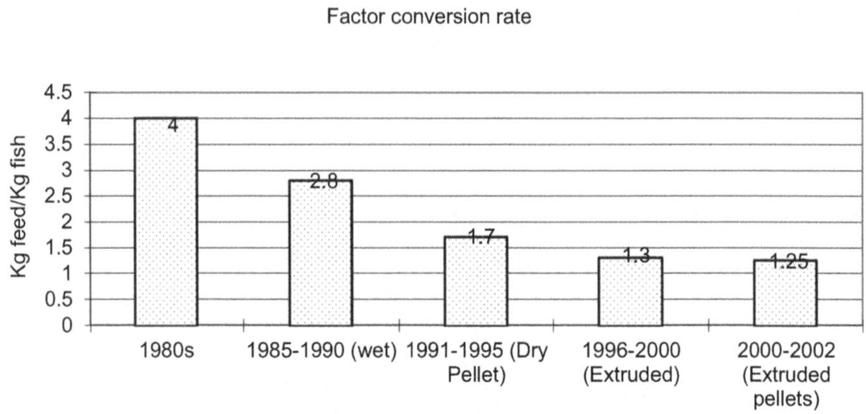

Fig. 4.10 Conversion rate of feed: 1980s–2002 (*Source*: Iizuka 2007)

straightforward, certain aspects of the service are very technical and specialized, requiring experience and knowledge of fish rearing.

The first generation of net workshops emerged in the late 1980s. Before that period, this service was kept in house in the salmon farming firms. As the size and number of salmon farming firms increased, outsourcing of this as a specialized service became feasible. In the 1990s, specialization and outsourcing of this service became more and more prevalent, contributing to an increase in net workshops. The increase in firm size and efforts to increase productivity led to an increased scale of production by enlarging the size of nets in salmon farming firms. The increased net size required more specialized techniques of fabrication, cleaning and maintenance, as well as specialized equipment and infrastructure (e.g. cranes, washing facilities etc.). This change promoted further specialization and intensification of technology. For instance, with the increase in the size of the net, the use of antifouling substances (chemicals that prevent organic materials from adhering to the net) increased, indicating some cumulative improvement of technology (Table 4.7).

As can be seen from the above examples, the change in scale and number of salmon farming firms transformed the nature of productive challenges at each stage of production. The measures taken at each stage of production contributed to increases in productivity. Most of these increases during this period were generated by adaptation of an embodied form of technology (i.e. purchase of equipment), increasing economies of scale, organizational changes through outsourcing to specialized suppliers and incremental improvement in a trial-and-error manner. These efforts to increase productivity gradually shaped the industry during the growth and globalization phase (1985–2007). However, higher productivity was accompanied by certain risks and imbalances. Increasing firm size required a more hierarchical structure of management; formation of specialized supplier firms allowed firms to concentrate on and specialize in fewer stages of salmon production, but at the same time, they lost a view of the industry as a whole; and transition from an industrial structure consisting of numerous small firms to a state of

Table 4.7 Change of net size and use of antifouling

Year	Size of net (m × m × m)	Use of antifouling	No of firms
1981–1983	7 × 7 × 7	No	
1983–1987	10 × 10 × 10	No	
1987–1990	15 × 15 × 15	No	
1990–	20 × 20 × 20	Yes	50
2000–	34 × 34 × 34	Yes	20–30

Source: Iizuka (2007)

oligopoly of large firms reduced the collaborative interaction among firms. Economies of scale and better access to foreign technology offered a relatively easy and quick short-term solution to firms' productivity problems. In the face of cutthroat competition at the global level, very few of these firms invested in research envisioning long-term sustainability.

When we look back, with knowledge about the ISA sanitary crisis in 2007, the efforts made to adapt foreign technology and knowledge to increase productivity have been insufficient over time to establish sustainable economic activities and sanitary conditions at the local environmental level. Norwegian or Scottish technological knowledge and blueprints provide insufficient knowledge about Chilean oceanographic currents, the specificity of the local carrying capacity of water resources, and so on; some of these issues had not been much studied prior to the arrival of the ISA virus (Katz et al. 2011). This aspect of local environmental knowledge marks a clear difference in the learning and technology upgrading process in a natural-resource-based industry from that of manufacturing. As will be discussed later, the allocation of resources for the creation of country- specific knowledge and know-how has been insufficient at the growth and globalization phase.

6 Evolution of the Institution Supporting the Salmon Industry

6.1 Institution and Political and Economic Sentiments

With the growth of the salmon industry, institutions gradually began to take shape. During the period between 1985 and 2007, important changes in attitude on the part of the public sector can be seen *compared to* the years before 1985, when the role of the government was more passive in the areas of regulation and prioritizing growth. While the state has continued to support the industry through various measures such as grants from the Chilean Economic Development Agency, CORFO, and the Export Promotion Agency, ProChile (Maggi 2007), it has also explicitly tried to leave space for the private sector to take initiatives (Katz et al. 2011).

Regulations concerning aquaculture emerged slowly. In the 1980s, the presence of the industry was not considered substantial enough for the public sector to control the activity. Later, in the 1990s, some regulations appeared in the fisheries sector but these were aimed at the public sector to coordinate fish farming operations efficiently and to avoid conflict with extractive fisheries by providing a basic legal framework (especially for granting concessions and use of coastal areas). From the late 1990s and 2000s, the regulations gradually became more sector specific and the element of control increased to meet global standards, particularly when Chile was making bilateral free trade agreements.

While clearer regulations were being established for fish farming in the 2000s, a strong enforcement mechanism was absent due to the pro-growth and pro-export sentiments in the government at that time. Also, the public sector budget was not adequate to ensure the enforcement of regulations. To make up for the lack of regulatory measures to control the firms' behaviors in a pro-business environment, the public sector encouraged voluntary self-regulation by the firms. A similar approach was taken with financing for R&D, where the government provided a financial scheme on a competitive basis and let firms to take initiative. In so doing the government insisted on preserving principles of neutrality and horizontality in the use of resources (Katz et al. 2011). This only changed briefly with the establishment of the National Innovation Council for Competitiveness, CNIC, in 2005. The CNIC proposed the prioritization of 11 sectors, in which aquaculture was selected as one of the targeted areas for investment. This attempt was short lived, as the activity was discontinued after 2010 due to a change of government.

6.2 Creation of Laws and Regulations and Public Support from the State

From 1985 to 1990, the private sector developed new initiatives to enhance export competitiveness, and the public sector brought forward several regulations in an attempt to catch up with the speed of advances made by the private sector (Iizuka 2007). In 1991, the new General Law for Fisheries and Aquaculture (LGPA in Spanish, No. 18892) was created to consolidate, coordinate and systematize the numerous pieces of legislation governing aquaculture activities in the country (Katz et al. 2011; see also Chap. 3).

Despite the size of the salmon farming industry being considered "not significant" (interview with Ms. Saa, Chap. 6) during the 1990s, several pieces of legislation with relevance to aquaculture were implemented to set up the principal regulatory framework in the 1990s, in addition to those established earlier (see Chap. 3). For instance, a system of authorizing concessions to conduct aquaculture, with rules for the leasing and transferring of concessions (Supreme Decree (DS) No. 290), was created in 1993; a national policy for the use of Chile's coastline (Supreme Decree No. 475) was issued in 1994; a system to register aquaculture activities (DS No. 499) was issued in 1994; and rules for the disclosure of information on aquaculture activities (Regulation on Information of Fishery and Aquaculture activities: DS No. 464) was established in 1995. Parallel to the above, the Basic Environmental Law (LBMA) took effect in 1994 (Law No. 19300), and after this date, aquaculture plans were required to go through the Environmental Impact Assessment System (SEIA) (Iizuka 2007).

Chile was trying to enter the global economy in the latter half of the 1990s with increased exports, foreign direct investments and bilateral trade agreements. These, particularly the bilateral trade agreements, increased pressure to create sector-specific regulations for aquaculture in the 2000s. As a result, Environmental Regulations for Aquaculture (RAMA: DS No. 320) were issued in 2001 to ensure environmentally sustainable development for aquaculture, followed by Sanitation Regulation (RESA), which included measures for prevention, control and eradication of diseases of high risk for hydrobiological species in 2002 (Iizuka 2007).

Throughout this period, an extensive legal and regulatory repertoire of laws and resolutions concerning issues of biosecurity, environmental management and more came into being. However, much of this legal framework was restricted by at least two types of problems. First of all, almost from the beginning of the implementation, there has been weak enforcement capacity on the part of the government. The National Fisheries Service (SERNAPESCA) had limited resources to monitor enforcement (Katz et al. 2011); this was true until the outbreak of the sanitary crisis in 2007 (which will be discussed in detail in Chap. 5). Under the pro-growth and pro-export policy, the Chilean government believed that the private sector should not be burdened with 'excess audits' and that control via regulation would stop the momentum of expansion the industry was exhibiting. Second, the regulatory system, in many cases, was not based on strong scientific criteria, showing that there was a lack of understanding of the relationship between sanitary and environmental conditions and long-term industry sustainability (Buschmann et al. 2009).

Apart from regulations, sector-specific policies and institutions were created in the 2000s. In 2003, the National Commission of Aquaculture was created by law. Its function has been to advise the president on the formulation and evaluation of the actions and programs required to implement a National Aquaculture Policy (PNA) (Katz et al. 2011). The commission created a space for the industry to express its interests via representation through associations. As Iizuka (2004, 6) points out, "The original purpose of this policy was to promote growth within the context of sustainable development and equal opportunity. Its main aim is to harmonize future directions as between public and private policy". However, the only clear target recognized in the PNA was to double the value of export of salmon in 10 years from US$1200 million in 2004 to US$2400 million by 2014 (interview with Mr Norambuena 2011, and Mr Felipe Sandoval 2011, in Chap. 6). This confirms the presence of strong pro-growth sentiments in the government at that time and limited concern for impacts on the environment.

6.3 *Financial Mechanisms to Support Innovation by the Public Sector*

In the 1990s, several financial mechanisms were put in place to support industrial development. The Scientific and Technological Development Fund (FONDEF), the Fisheries Research Fund (FIP) and the National Fund for Technological and Productive Development (FONTEC) were all established in 1991, and the Development and Innovation Fund (FID) in 1995. These mechanisms are, in fact, used by firms and universities for research activities. The private innovation funds managed by CORFO were mainly used to solve short-term productive issues (Bravo et al. 2007). The OECD Review of Innovation Policy: Chile indicated that precompetitive schemes to encourage innovation remain fragmented and fell short of meeting the needs of the economy (OECD 2007).

The National Innovation Council for Competitiveness (CNIC in Spanish) was established in November 2005. This institution aimed to promote long-term innovation for competitiveness in the economy (CNIC 2006) by implementing sector-specific vertical industrial policies. After careful investigation, CNIC chose 11 sectors with the greatest potential for growth. One of these was aquaculture, a sector in which salmon farming carried substantial weight. All these lines of action involved much stronger bonds of public–private cooperation. Much of the above attempt was discontinued after the 2010 elections. A step back has been taken, returning to more neutral policies. Thus, in 2011, the CNIC decided to end its cluster policies, primarily because of their lack of neutrality.

6.4 *Private Sector Institutions and Collective Action*

Several private or non-public institutions have come into existence with close associations with the sector. These institutions' roles have changed significantly through time, reflecting the stages of industrial transformation.

6.4.1 Fundación Chile

Fundación Chile played a crucial role at the incipient phase of this industry. It had an important role in diffusing the technical know-how to pioneers in the salmon industry in various areas from trout pathology to cultivation tank construction (see Chap. 2). It also played a role as a 'technological antenna', dispatching foreign and Chilean technical consultants in order to improve access to technical and commercial knowledge in an aim to improve Chilean salmon production and competitiveness (Katz et al. 2011). Furthermore, at a time when the industry did not have important standing in the Chilean economy, Fundación Chile lobbied for the industry to raise awareness among different groups of the population and government spheres (Iizuka 2007). These activities continued throughout the rest of the 1980s.

In the period of globalization, with the salmon farming industry already an important part of the Chilean economy, Fundación Chile's role gradually diminished in comparison to the earlier period. Its strategy became 'technological consultancy' when its endowment funds were substantially reduced in around the early 1990s. With the provision of government financial mechanisms for technological improvement and its accumulated expertise in the aquaculture sector, Fundación Chile continued to play an important role as a 'technological antenna' in the industry; however, acquired technology was often exclusively used for individual client and only on a fee paying basis. This slowed down the diffusion of technical knowledge at the industry level. Hence, Fundación Chile's impact has been significantly reduced to the firm level and no longer extends beyond this to the industry level.

6.4.2 Association of the Chilean Salmon Industry

The gradual decline of the role played by Fundación Chile contrasts with the gradual emergence of an industrial association for the Chilean salmon industry. In 1986, the Association of Salmon and Trout Producers (APSTC in Spanish, later becoming SalmonChile) was created among 17 salmon producers in Chile (Achurra 1995; Iizuka 2007). The association was established to meet industry-wide problems such as quality standards and marketing at the industry level. The quality standards established in the 1990s by the Association were designed to standardize quality within the Chilean salmon industry and enabled it to position itself in the market as 'Chilean Salmon'. Pre-dating the association, there was a joint venture called Salmocoop[11] to find new markets for the exportation of salmon from 13 salmon firms.

The main challenge at that time was to find alternative markets to the USA and Japan. Confronted with this challenge, Chilean companies felt that only if they acted together could they achieve success on this front (Achurra 1995). Some of the other objectives of the association were to implement a program of technical seminars related to the spread of new aquaculture techniques such as quality control routines, as well as overall management of public relations with government agencies as an industry (Achurra 1995).

In 1995, the APSTC created the Salmon Technology Institute (INTESAL). This institute aimed to increase production efficiency and was concerned with the sanitary, environmental and personnel training aspects of the cluster, areas that

[11] The efforts made by Salmocoop can be seen in Fig. 4.8, which shows diversification of markets. The following new markets were opened: in the Latin American region: Argentina (1991), Mexico (1992), Venezuela (1995), Colombia (1996); in the Asian region, Taiwan (1994), Thailand (1994), Singapore (1995), China (1997) (Iizuka 2007).

involved common interests. For the establishment of INTESAL, the association obtained financial support from CORFO (Iizuka 2007; UNCTAD 2006). The Institute has worked more as a training center than as a source of innovation activities for the industry (Vera Garnica 2009). INTESAL was accredited by SENCE (Servicio Nacional de Capacitacion y Empleo) as a part of the governments' tax exemption scheme. This greatly facilitated training in the industry and the diffusion of production knowledge.

In 1997, the Chilean salmon industry was accused of dumping by the US salmon producers, and APSTC, in conjunction with the Chilean public sector, played an important role in resolving this issue (Vera Bahamonde 2010). Having successfully resolved the problem by representing the industry, APSTC had gained much respect and an improved reputation from both member and non-member firms in the industry. Following this, in the first decade of the 2000s, APSTC tried to adapt its image to meet the challenges of the globalization of the salmon industry. First, it removed the restriction of only representing 'salmon producers' and opened up its membership to any firms within the industry, including service and input providers. As a result, APSTC changed its name to SalmonChile in 2002. It also made alliances with US and Canadian salmon farmers in the hope of finding a stronger consensus among salmon farming industries at the global level. By this time, SalmonChile was in a good position to communicate and negotiate with governments and international stakeholders to protect the interests of the salmon farming industry against external (external to industry, country etc.) threats.

For instance, SalmonChile negotiated with the public sector in relation to changes to the system of concessions, the promotion of voluntary agreements and the diffusion of – with limited success – 'mandatory' health and environmental regulations for its members (e.g. a manual on biosafety[12]). The association had the foresight to engage with environmental and sanitary issues; however, by the nature of its existence, control and monitoring followed 'auto regulation' and had limited control and authority over their member firms.

6.4.3 Collective Action

Early attempts toward collective action involved jointly finding new export markets as well as marketing campaigns, market research, quality certification,

[12] Vera Bahamonde (2010) explains that this manual was not respected by many of the member companies of SalmonChile. In general, this entity did not achieve adequate enforcement of its provisions, which was supposed to come from a common understanding by the vast majority of member companies. At the same time, this was inevitable because SalmonChile, as an industrial association, does not have the legal authority to intervene in the management strategy of member firms.

negotiations with international brokers and more (Achurra 1995; Iizuka 2007). There was also collective action undertaken to acquire advanced production technology through INTESAL. Later in the first decade of the 2000s, SalmonChile started to take on the role of intermediary between the private and public sector so that the public sector could support the private sector more effectively by understanding its sectoral needs. The sectoral needs were mainly to confront external-competitive threats at that time. Even though many small and medium-sized firms were not members of SalmonChile, they also benefited from SalmonChile's representation.

The type of collaboration changed significantly with the evolution of the industry. During the inception period, the first type of collaboration was to deal with technological learning. This later became more specific, leading to the commercialization of products (standardization and marketing). Later on, the reason for collective action became more political, involving much negotiations with non-industry actors (be it NGO, foreign countries, or the public sector) to protect the interests of the industry as a whole. Despite such evolutional development of 'collective action', the available evidence (such as Vignolo et al. 2007) suggests that the industry has failed to generate strong bonds of trust (social capital) and cooperation among firms.

7 Education and Research Institutions to Enhance Productivity

7.1 Education and Training

In the late 1980s, institutions of higher education began to train professionals and technicians for the salmon farming industry. The University of Austral created a campus in Puerto Montt in 1989, focused mainly on marine sciences and issues related to aquaculture. By 1992 a school of aquaculture was opened at the Catholic University of Temuco. Other institutions of higher education in the region followed suit. The creation of INTESAL in 1995 also helped to develop the skills that the salmon farming industry needed (UNCTAD 2006).

The process of human capital training improved steadily through the early 2000s, reflecting the demand from large-scale, hierarchical firms that required a more specialized labor force. A horizontal policy of subsidizing all training expenses for workers in Chilean firms (via SENCE: Servicio Nacional de Capacitacion y Empleo, National Training Service and Employment) also reached the salmon-farming sector, inducing firms to take action on this front. By 2005, there were a total of 1866 training programs in the sector, accounting for a total – public and private – investment in the order of $1.8 million in the salmon-farming industry alone (Vera Garnica 2009). A significant part of that sum involved expenses aiming at helping unskilled workers to complete their primary schooling.

As a result, throughout this period we observe a steady expansion in the upgrading of labor skills. A survey carried out by the University of Austral in the early 2000s showed that 67 % of the controller of cultivation center and 83 % of supervisors or managers of production activities had a professional degree, while skilled workers remained in short supply (Montero 2004, 26), while at the same time, there was also a relative abundance of cheap unskilled labor. This condition favored labor-intensive specialization (high value-added) such as production of boneless salmon fillets in which unskilled laborers remove all the bones by hand for special markets (Montero 2004, 40).

In comparison to technical skills, higher education with a scientific base for this sector had a slow start.

However, by 2010, the education sector offered 8 doctorate and 13 master's degree courses related to aquaculture. Despite such efforts and an actual expansion of specialization in the salmon farming sector, absolute numbers of doctorate degree holders in this sector in Chile are very small when compared to its competitor, Norway.

7.2 Research

The public sector began to allocate some resources for R&D activities at the end of the 1980s. However, much of the knowledge generation process at the individual firm level involved incremental efforts carried out with the purpose of gradually solving production organization problems (Vignolo et al. 2007). Fundación Chile played a major role on this front, helping firms to introduce new technologies (see Chap. 2; Achurra 1995; Katz et al. 2011; Iizuka 2007).

In the 1990s, when the salmon cluster was being formed by suppliers, innovation efforts by individual firms intensified, reaching, in some large firms, 'state-of-the-art' frontiers. Table 4.8 and Fig. 4.11 show the growing importance of R&D in salmon farming by amount of government funding for research in this sector between 1987 and 2008 (Bravo 2009). Many competitive government grants were introduced in 1991 by organizations such as the National Commission for Scientific and Technological Research (CONICYT), CORFO (the Chilean Economic Development Agency), and the Undersecretary of Fisheries. CONICYT financed a scheme called the 'National Fund for Scientific and Technological Development' (FONDECYT) targeted at university collaboration with industry for applied research. CORFO had a scheme called the 'National Fund for Technological and Productive Development' (FONTEC) and the 'Development and Innovation Fund' (FDI). The Undersecretary of Fisheries had a financial line called the 'Fisheries Research Fund' (FIP). In addition to the above, some additional sources of funding exist in regional governments for

Table 4.8 Research in the salmon farming sector financed by government funding: 1987–2008

Thematic areas	No. of projects	%	000 Chilean pesos	%
Pathology and sanitary management	77	26.8	12,140,701	28.9
Genetics and reproduction	38	13.2	7,752,516	18.4
Nutrition and food	29	10.1	6,327,948	15.1
Environment and clean production	33	11.5	3,842,839	9.1
Technology centers	5	1.7	3,736,752	8.9
Engineering and technology	44	15.3	3,489,769	8.3
Cultivation and production	14	4.9	1,573,375	3.7
Training and transfer of technology	18	6.3	1,026,484	2.4
Processing and quality control	13	4.5	877,022	2.1
Recreational fishery	10	3.5	829,549	2.0
Administration and regulation	4	1.4	346,458	0.8
Small-scale aquaculture	1	0.3	46,874	0.1
Biology and ecology	1	0.3	43,043	0.1
Total	287	100.0	42,033,330	100.0

Source: Bravo (2009)

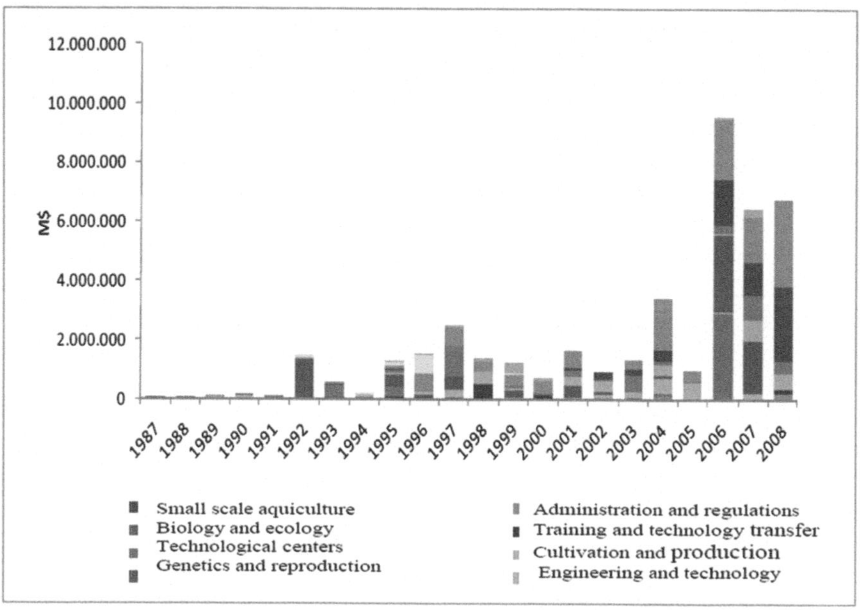

Fig. 4.11 Trends shown by projects, funded in salmonids (M$) (*Source*: Bravo et al. 2007. Note: Values are expressed in Chilean pesos. As an approximation, 500 Chilean pesos = US$1 dollar (as of Feb. 2013))

regional development, the 'Regional Development Fund' (FNDR), which was also used for the salmon sector. There were also funds coming from 'Foundacion para la Innovacion Agraia' (FIA). In 2006, the existing two channels of funding by CORFO were combined as the 'Fund for Innovation' (INNOVACHILE) (Bravo et al. 2007)[13] and the amount of funding was increased substantially.

The aggregate amount of government financial schemes from 1987 to 2008 was $42 million Chilean pesos. This was allocated through the following financial schemes: INNOVACHILE 32.4 %, FONTEC 24.7 %, FONDEF 17.1 %, FONDECYT 12.5 %, FIP 5.2 %, FDI 4.2 %, FNDR 3.1 % and FIA 0.2 %. Even though INNOVACHILE existed only during 2006–2008, this financial scheme had a large share, indicating a substantial increase in the government's investment in more recent years.

Within the first line of finance, such as pathology and sanitary management, the majority (58 %) of investments were made in vaccines and medicines for salmon. As for genetics and reproduction, the majority of financing (70 %) went toward the improvement of genes.

Summing up the various sources of finance, we can conclude that between 1990 and 2006 total R&D expenses in the cluster came close to US$76 million. A total of 49.8 % was provided by the public sector, 43 % by industry and 7 % by INTESAL (part of which does not necessarily involve R&D activities, *stricto sensu*) (Quiroz 2006; Vera Garnica 2009). We might be underestimating company expenditure in knowledge generation activities, as in many cases firms do not undertake 'formal' R&D projects, but they nonetheless make incremental adjustments to their production routines involving knowledge-generation efforts (Bravo 2009).

Assuming that our previous estimate of R&D expenditure by the industry is not too far off the mark, we can now extract a few conclusions from the evidence presented so far. First, the government has been playing a major role in financing R&D activities in this field of economic activity. Second, a wide variety of scientific and technological areas is being explored. Third, given that salmon exports come close to US$2,500 million annually, and that the private contribution to total R&D efforts in the sector is quite low, we are bound to conclude that a large window of opportunity exists in this respect if the current restructuring of the industry is to progress towards a more knowledge-intensive model (Katz et al. 2011).[14]

Finally, it is important to think about the potential contribution of higher education institutions in Chile in conducting additional scientific research in the field of the salmon industry. Many universities in the country, especially the ones near the geographical area where the salmon cluster is located, have institutes and university departments working in the field. However, when it comes to high-

[13] The typical *modus operandi* of competitive grant programs is as follows: an institution (e.g. a private company, university, research institute etc.) presents a research or innovation project in a given program (e.g. FONDECYT). Later, the organization must wait a certain time, perhaps 6 months with FONDECYT, to see if its project is approved or not. If it is approved, the program usually funds a certain percentage of the project, while the accepted institution, probably with the help of a third organization, puts up the remainder of the money.

[14] We can also use the argument that many OECD countries spend around 2 % of GDP on innovation with substantial part financed by the private sector.

impact scientific publications (ISI category) produced by these local universities, Chile's outcome is poorly ranked, even though the outcomes of such research may have enormous relevance for this industry and for the local economy. For instance, between 1988 and 2008, less than 4 % of the worldwide relevant papers in the field came from Chile (Buschmann et al. 2009). The potential roles of local universities can be further strengthened with targeted funding and strategic selection of research themes covering basic to applied areas. Currently some useful research projects are being conducted but they are not considered to have significant academic impact at the global level. It is important to strengthen this area while maintaining the current levels of applied research.

8 Conclusion

To fully take advantage of globalization, any emerging country (industry) needs to be equipped with indigenous capability as well as possessing sufficient capacity to adapt available knowhow to the local context, and thereby work more effectively. Indigenous capability is also necessary in foreseeing the future development of the industry, and investments are required with long-term vision. Managing this process is often very difficult, particularly when industry is graduating from an incipient phase and growth, because this means that public policy should identify the right time and methods to swiftly shift from its role of promoting development to regulating interventions.

The salmon farming industry in Chile managed to expand from a few thousand tons of production in the 1980s to around half a million tons by the middle of the first decade of the 2000s, second in the world to Norway. In this chapter, we have analyzed how the salmon industry became a successful export industry, paying attention to the transition of exports (destination, species of salmon, level of elaboration), industrial dynamics (number and size of firms, supplier firms) and development of institutions that support the industry in becoming competitive in the global market (i.e. education and human resources, industry-specific organization, government financial schemes and regulation) to overcome several challenges as the industry integrated into the global market. Our qualitative observations indicate that the above-mentioned elements co-evolved with each other, giving shape to the salmon industry before the crisis of 2007.

Undoubtedly the dramatic increase in exports of salmon from Chile was underpinned by the overall increase in productivity, with a range of factors potentially having contributed to these productivity gains. The circumstantial evidence we have obtained indicates that productivity gains were achieved through: (1) incremental innovation and learning; (2) purchase of embodied technology and knowledge (such as machinery, inputs and services) from abroad; (3) increasing economies of scale through M&A; (4) specialization and clustering via development of suppliers; (5) collective action for common interests; (6) governmental financial support for finding productive solutions for firms; (7) change in the institutional setting; (8) increase in human resources via training of personnel; and to some degree, (9) scientific research at universities and research institutions and within firms.

It is not possible to measure the exact impact or relative contribution of each factor mentioned above; however, if we compare Chile with Norway, much of the productivity gain in Chile was not obtained from long-term stable sources. Chile's rapid catch up in productive capacity may have had much to do with leapfrogging by imitating the forerunners; however, Chile as yet has not paid sufficient attention to environmental sustainability and the role of ecology. For example, in the years analyzed in this chapter, government financial schemes supported research which was directly linked to productivity – or provided short-term solutions to the productivity problem – but did not aim at finding ways to make this industry sustainable in the long term nor to ensuring that the environment was protected. Educational institutions were established but still were not able to develop a major scientific impact in this field, despite the increasing importance of this sector in the Chilean economy as well as in the global market. Furthermore, the public sector was not capable of developing suitable norms, regulations and audit systems for the sector at local settings during the period. A relatively low amount – for the industry's global standing – invested in R&D in this industry may provide some answers to the above. In hindsight, understanding how the industry was shaped up to the crisis in 2007 shed some light on knowing what needs to be done in the future. The forthcoming chapters in the book will examine these aspects.

References

Achurra, M. 1995. La Experiencia de un Nuevo Producto de Exportación: Los Salmones. In *Auge Exportador Chileno. Lecciones y Desafíos Futures*, ed. P. Meller and R.E. Sáez, 43–72. Santiago de Chile: CIEPLAN/Dolmen.

Bravo, Sandra. 2009. *Investigacion sobre Salmonicultura en Chile*. Paper presented at XIII Jornadas sobre Pesquerias y Acicultura en Chile: Desafios y Oportunidades Septiembre 2009. Vina del Mar, Chile.

Bravo, S., M.T. Silva, and C. Lagos. 2007. *Diagnostico de la Proyección de la Investigación en Ciencia y Tecnología de la Acuicultura Chilena*. Mimeo: FIP.

Buschmann, A., F. Cabello, K. Young, J. Carvajal, D.A. Varela, and L. Henriquez. 2009. Salmon aquaculture and coastal ecosystem health in Chile: Analysis of regulations, environmental impacts and bioremediation systems. *Ocean & Coastal Management* 52: 243–249.

CNIC (Consejo Nacional de Innovacion para la Desarrollo). 2006. *Primer Informe*. Santiago, Chile

Iizuka, M. 2004. Organizational capability and export performance: The salmon industry in Chile. Paper presented at the 2004 DRUID Winter Conference, University of Aalborg, January 22–24, 2004, Aalborg, Denmark.

Iizuka, M. 2007. *Global standards and local producers: Knowledge governance and the rise of the Chilean Salmon Industry*. PhD thesis, SPRU, University of Sussex.

Iizuka, M., and M. Gebreeyesus. 2012. *A systemic perspective in understanding the successful emergence of non-traditional exports: Two cases from Africa and Latin America*. UNU-MERIT Working Paper 2012-052. Maastricht: UNU-MERIT.

Katz, J., M. Iizuka, and S. Munoz. 2011. *Cresiendo en base a los Recursos Naturals, 'Tragedias de los Communes' y el Future de la Industria Salmonera Chilena*. Serie desarrollo productive 191. Division de Desarrollo Productivo y Empresarial, Santiago de Chile: United Nations Economic Commission for Latin America and Caribbean (ECLAC).

Maggi, C. 2007. The salmon farming and processing cluster in Southern Chile. In *Upgrading and governance in clusters and value chains in Latin America*, ed. C. Pietrobelli and R. Rabellotti. Boston: Harvard University Press.

Montero, C. 2004. *Formación y Desarrollo de un Clúster Globalizado: el Caso de la Industria del Salmón en Chile*. Santiago de Chile: ECLAC, United Nations.

OECD. 2007. *OECD reviews of innovation policy: Chile*. Paris: OECD.

Quiroz, Jorge. 2006. *Informe Economico Salmonicultura 2006*. Puerto Montt: SalmonChile. http://www.samonchile.cl. Accessed Jan. 2012.

SalmonChile. 2009. *Exportaciones Chilenas de Salmon y Trucha en Toneladas*. http://estadisticas.intesal.cl. Accessed Nov 2010.

UNCTAD. 2006. *A case study of the salmon industry in Chile, transfer of technology*. New York: UNCTAD, United Nations. (UNCTAD/ITE/IIT/2005/12), 35 pp.

Vera Bahamonde, H. 2010. *La Crisis del Salmon Porque Fallo el Tercer Motor de la Economia Chilena?* Santiago de Chile: Ril ediciones.

Vera Garnica, J. 2009. Cluster del Salmon en Chile: Analisis de los Factores de Competitividad a Escala International. *Revista Venezolana de Gerencia* 14(47): 342–369.

Vignolo, C., G. Held, and J. P. Zanlungo. 2007. *Strategic management of clusters: The case of the Chilean Salmon Industry*, Documentos de Trabajo Serie de Gestion no. 83. Centro de Gestion (CEGES). Departmento de Ingenieria Industrial, Santiago de Chile: Universidad de Chile.

Chapter 5
Environmental Collapse and Institutional Restructuring: The Sanitary Crisis in the Chilean Salmon Industry

Michiko Iizuka and Juan Pablo Zanlungo

1 Introduction

The current export boom in natural resources is considered to be the 'new window of opportunity' for many developing countries endowed with natural resources. Recent studies (Blomström and Meller 1991; de Ferranti et al. 2002; Maloney 2002; Sinnoit et al. 2010; Perez et al. 2009; Iizuka and Soete 2011) indicate that natural resource-based activities can be knowledge intensive, which contrary to earlier understandings, would lead them to productivity-led development pathways.

This positive feature of natural resource-based activities has some serious drawbacks for countries not equipped with the institutions to accurately evaluate the impacts and risks, needed to ensure environmental sustainability. This aspect is of particular importance for activities that are based on interaction with the biosphere such as agriculture, fishery, and forestry. Many case studies show that the regulatory mechanism for controlling ecological sustainability has been rather slow to develop, as emerging countries make economic development their priority (Perfecto et al. 2003; Philpott et al. 2008; Fearnside 2001; Koh and Wilcove 2007; Lenzen et al. 2012). The uneven speed of development—rapid increases in the exploitation of natural resources stimulated by global market demands with slow development of local regulatory institutions—can lead to a 'tragedy of the commons' (Hardin 1968) at the local level, and trigger environmental and economic collapse in the long run.

In an attempt to avoid this future environmental crisis, experts and policy makers are working to identify possible indicators that would help them to evaluate risk. In order to achieve this, knowledge of the local biological environment must be built up and scientific methods for understanding the possibility and probability of

M. Iizuka (✉) • J.P. Zanlungo
Maastricht Economic and Social Research and Training Center for Innovation and Technology (UNU-MERIT), United Nations University, Maastrciht, The Netherlands
e-mail: iizuka@merit.unu.edu

A. Hosono et al. (eds.), *Chile's Salmon Industry*,
DOI 10.1007/978-4-431-55766-1_5

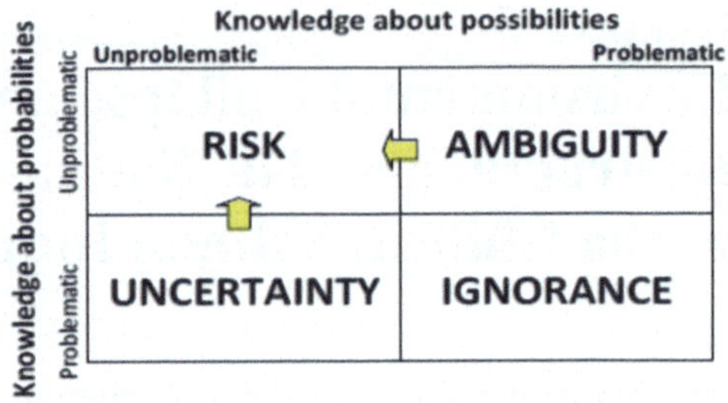

Fig. 5.1 Conceptual map of risk (*Source*: Based on Stirling (2008, 2010))

occurrences of collapse must be followed—that is, identifying the carrying capacity of the local environment. This is a cumulative learning process which converts incalculable 'uncertainty' and 'ambiguity' into a more calculable and predictable 'risk'. This process requires finding the patterns, probable causes (possibilities), and predictors (probabilities) based on information collected in a trial-and-error manner. Such exercises will eventually lead to identifying possible indicators or to a model for regulatory purposes that could prevent the worst-case scenario occurring.[1] Of course, the biological interaction in nature is dynamic and complex, making it impossible to predict all the possibilities. Stirling (2008, 2010) succinctly presents the relationships between risk, uncertainty, and ignorance in his 'Conceptual Map of Risk' (see Fig. 5.1).[2] Stirling admits that ongoing events using scientific understanding, may not fully provide for 'unknown' incidents given our current 'ignorance' (knowledge whose presence is beyond our current comprehension). Hence, there will always be some 'uncertain' elements when dealing with nature.

This chapter, using the case of the 2007 sanitary crisis in the Chilean salmon industry, seeks to explain the following: firstly, how such an environmental collapse occurred in Chile at a time when the industry was expanding so as to integrate itself into the global economy; and secondly, the ways in which the Chilean experts are currently trying to regulate this situation by identifying the indicators that can be used to prevent a crisis from happening. This study will show how natural resource processing activities need to be supported not only by advanced production technology, but also by sound scientific and technological research, which focuses on the way the local environment functions; this emerges as a *sine qua non* to regulate the use of the commons,[3] (Feeney et al. 1990; Ostrom et al. 1999).

[1] An exercise of this sort is currently being applied in an experimental preliminary phase in Chile—see Chap. 7 of this book.

[2] Stirling (2008, 2010) emphasizes the need for democratic and participatory regulatory mechanisms, especially to deal with 'ignorance'—unknown knowledge. Although we fully admit the importance and relevance of his argument, we will use his framework to focus on the areas where experts need to convert 'ambiguity' and 'uncertainty' knowledge into more calculative 'risk'.

[3] Natural resources such as air and water are typical example of commons. Commons has the properties that can have excludability (it is costly to exclude others from using the resources) and subtractability (each user is capable of subtracting from the welfare of other users).

2 The Sanitary Crisis and Its Causes

2.1 Magnitude of the Crisis

The sanitary crisis in the Chilean salmon industry started in 2007 and was due to the spread of infectious salmon anaemia ('ISA') (Sernapesca 2008). Soon after its emergence, the affected cultivation sites suspended their operations (Iizuka and Katz 2011). By 2009, close to 60 % of the cultivation centers had ceased production. In the following year, the production of salmon had fallen to around 200,000 tons from its peak of nearly 700,000 tons in 2006. The collapse of the industry due to sanitary crisis caused serious social, economic, and industrial disruptions (see Chap. 6 for more details on the industrial disruptions). In an attempt to illustrate some of the possible causes for this crisis and illustrate the actions taken to overcome it, this chapter will focus on the sanitary and environmental aspects of this crisis.

2.2 ISA Virus and Sanitary Conditions: An Ecological Triad of Illness

The ISA virus, the cause of sanitary crisis, was first believed to have originated in Norway, arriving in Chile via imported salmon eggs.[4] However, local biologists and veterinarians who have been interviewed (Bustos 2008; Nieto 2009) seem to agree that the cause of this sanitary crisis was more systemic than just the single introduction of a pathogen. According to them, 'illness' does not occur simply because of the presence of a pathogen but would require systematic collapse over a long period of time to eventually reduce the self-immunological defense capabilities of the fish and create an environment in which pathogens are able to spread quickly. In other words, the crisis should not be seen as a consequence of ISA but as the long-term, cumulative outcome of sanitary and environmental mismanagement dating back years before the outbreak.

There is no historical record of the water quality in the coastal areas of Chile where salmon is cultivated. However, veterinarians have compiled a record of sanitary incidents involving salmon in captivity. This shows that the worsening of the sanitary environment as the production volume of salmon increased started much earlier than the date of the outbreak (Fig. 5.2). The first of the major sanitary incidents—bacterial kidney disease (BKD) and caligidosis—only appeared in 1986 towards the end of the industry inception stage. The rapid growth of the industry in

[4] Many local specialists believe that a variant of the disease had for some time been present in Chile but a combination of environmental conditions triggered its mutation with a rapid spread (Bustos 2008; Nieto 2009).

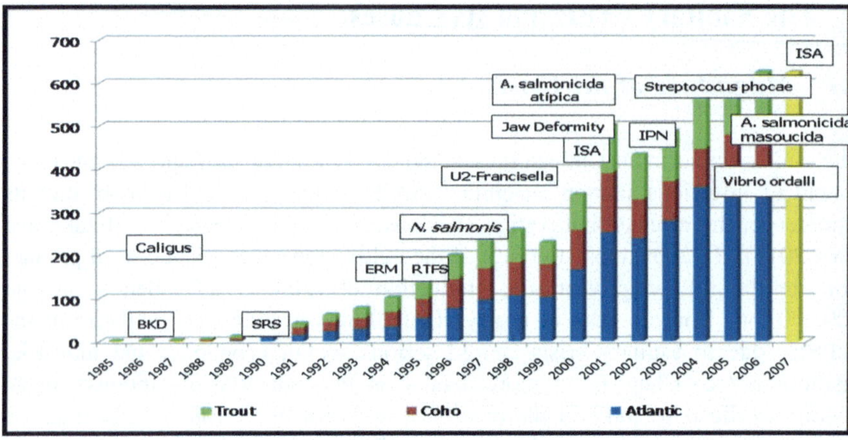

Fig. 5.2 Deterioration of sanitary conditions in salmon farming sites and increase in exports (thousand tons) (*Source*: Based on Sernapesca (2009, 2011) and Nieto (2009))

the 1990s (reaching nearly 300,000 tons by the end of the decade)—and the subsequent period of rapid growth between the 2000 and 2008—(reaching a volume of output of 500,000 tons per annum)—also seem to have coincided with the outbreak of many new diseases affecting the species. It was not only the ISA virus that causes anemia (see Box 6.1 of Chap. 6) but jaw deformation, a typical aeromonas salmonicida, infectious pancreatic necrosis (IPN), streptococcus phocae, vibrio ordalii, and aeromonas salmonicida masoucida also emerged prior to the crisis. For instance, Salmon Rickettsial Syndrome or Piscirickettsiosis (SRS), ISA, and caligidosis are the diseases that have affected the industry most recently (Fig. 5.2). The caligidosis caused by sea lice is suspected to be the vector of the ISA virus. An independent survey of the sanitary situation carried out by veterinarians also confirmed that the sanitary situation had worsened in the mid 1990s compared to the 1980s (Bustos 2008; Johnson 2007; Nieto 2009) (Table 5.1).

3 Conditions Behind the Worsening Sanitary Environment

The worsening sanitary conditions were caused by several factors. The major factor that contributed to the sanitary conditions was the activities of firms. As will be demonstrated in Chap. 6, it should not be forgotten that two important factors were behind the behavior of firms. Firstly, strong market demand and a harsh competitive global market environment forced firms to behave in a myopic, profit-driven manner (Iizuka and Katz 2011, 2012). Secondly, the regulatory system before the crisis was operated under export-oriented, strong 'pro-growth' sentiments and did not expressly control the use of resources from a sustainability perspective (as explained in Chap. 4). This was partly due to the public sector thinking it

Table 5.1 Appearance of disease: perception of local veterinarians

Disease	1980s	Mid 1990s
Bacterial kidney disease	X	X
Piscinketsiosis		X
Infectiouspancreatic necrosis	X	X
Vibriosis (v.ordeli)		X
Vibriosis (v.angillarium)		X
Ulcerative vibriosis		X
Streptococosis		X
Franciseltosis		X
Atypical furunculosis		X
Kudoa		X
Jandrice syndrome		
Nucleospondiosis	X	X
Flavovacteriosis	X	X
Columnaris	X	X
Yersimiosis	X	X
Saprolegiosis	X	X
Caligus	X	X
ISA (infectious Salmon Anemia)		X
Amoebic gill disease		X

Source: Based on survey taken in the mid-1990s (Bustos 2008)

unnecessary to regulate the salmon farming sector given its small scale during the 1980s and partly because *SalmonChile* (*Salmon Industry Association AG*), was able to exercise its power to ensure less government control over the behavior of firms in the 1990s when the industry grew substantially. As a result there was a vacuum in regulatory power, especially with regard to maintaining sustainability in economic activities involving natural resources, such as the Chilean salmon industry (for details, see Chap. 6).

3.1 *Concentration of Cultivation Sites (Cultivation Permits) in Limited Geographical Areas*

In Chile, anyone wishing to engage in aquaculture or conduct economic activities in coastal areas, rivers, and lakes needs to obtain permits (concessions) from the public authorities. The concessions are granted only after the applicants have been through several administrative clearances.

Currently, 72 % of the salmon farming concessions in Chile are located in a small territory covering no more than 300 km^2. The concentration of salmon cultivation centers in Chile is striking when compared with Norway, whose total area of cultivation is spread over 1700 km^2 (Pucchi 2009).[5] Despite the high concentration of concessions in a small territory, until 2001 there were no regulations governing the distance between salmon farming centers in Chile (currently 2.27 km).

The granting of concessions for cultivation centers in Chile increased over the period 20 years. In the late 1990s, these concessions were concentrated in the Los Lagos region (10th region). This region was by far the most suitable area for salmon farming, with natural fjords, rivers, and lakes, as well as reasonable access to physical and social infrastructure that ensured access to transportation and a labor force. From the late 1990s, as the industry ran out of space in the Los Lagos region, concessions started to move southwards—firstly to Aysen (11th region) and gradually to Magallanes (12th region) (see Chap. 6 for map and Table 5.5 for the increase in concessions). The granting of concessions also sped up from 2000 to 2005.

3.2 Fish Density Within the Cultivation Center

The production of salmon in Chile increased dramatically from 1999 onward and by 2006 it had reached an all-time historical peak of nearly 700,000 tons. The strong incentive to increase production came from the rapidly increasing global price of salmon (Table 5.3). This increase in demand—without the provision of a regulatory mechanism (for details see Chap. 6) and a collaborative mechanism among firms to control the sustainable use of resources—pushed many firms to increase production by simply adding more fish to the existing tanks and increasing cultivation sites within small geographical areas. In retrospect we now know that this caused something similar to the 'tragedy of the commons' described by Hardin (1968).[6]

The density of the fish population can be increased in various ways: firstly, by increasing the number of fish in each cultivation site and secondly, by increasing the number of cultivation sites in certain geographical areas by way of an increased number of concessions. The former is demonstrated in Table 5.2, which compares the volume of fish per cultivation center in Chile to that in Norway. The table clearly shows a larger volume of fish being cultivated at each cultivation site in Chile. The increase in the number of fish per cultivation was taking place in an already densely populated cultivation site contained within a small geographical area. This fact is confirmed by the data from EWOS—a salmon food company—which shows the increase in average numbers of fish per cultivation center (Table 5.3) from 2003 to 2007. In other words, this confirms the fact that salmon

[5] This was confirmed in the recent public lecture by Mr. Mario Pucchi, of AquaChile SA—the largest Chilean salmon farming firm. He said: 'production is 50 % larger per concession in Chile while total cultivation area is 70 % smaller' (Pucchi 2009).

[6] Hardin (1968), in explaining 'the tragedy of the commons', used a simple model of 'herder' behaviour. By putting one more cow in a limited space of land (common), the individual benefit maximization attempt—through the eventual overloading of the resource—would cause a reduction in the collective benefits to all users of the common.

Table 5.2 Average salmon weight per cultivation center: Chile and Norway

Chilean cultivation site	Average tons/center
Chiloe centro	1,136
Melinka	1,106
Chiloe sur	859
Estuario reloncavi	1,142
Aysen	757
Hornopiren	1,079
Cisnes	892
Seno reloncavi	1,076
Total	1,021
Norwegian cultivation site	Average tons/center
Finnmark	255
Troms	499
Nordland	528
Nord-trondelag	518
Sor-trondelag	522
More og fjordane	424
Hordaland	374
Rogaland	506
Ovrige fylker	689
Total	474

Source: Based on EWOS Health (2007)

Table 5.3 Key indicators for productivity in salmon firms

	2003	2004	2005	2006	2007
Kg/smolt	3.71	3.66	3.57	3.34	3.14
Kg/egg	1.3	1.28	1.25	1.17	1.1
Average weight at the harvest time	4,444	4,555	4,342	4,219	4,130
Economic factor conversion rate	1.36	1.4	1.38	1.42	1.52
Biological factor conversion rate	1.24	1.27	1.28	1.3	1.34
Days required until harvesting	487	497	484	488	543
Number of fish per cultivation center	650,000	700,000	670,000	825,000	945,000
Mortality rate (%)	16	18	17.5	20	24
Volume of production net (000) tonnes	286	355	384	387	397
Export US$ (million) FOB	1,146	1,439	1,721	2,207	2,245
Price US$ per kg	4.0	3.6	4.5	5.9	6.0

Source: Based on EWOS Health (2007) and SalmonChile (2009, 2011)

farming firms behaved quite similarly to Hardin's 'herder', who added 'one more cow' (fish) to a fixed unit of space in the commons (cultivation site, tank). The individual's maximization of benefit, in this case, is to attain higher profits from an increase in global prices for salmon. Once a given threshold of fish density at the site had been reached, increasing the density further worsened the sanitary condition of the 'common' in which the fish were being raised (Iizuka and Katz 2011).

Table 5.3 also demonstrates the decreasing trend in the productivity of firms in relation to the cost per volume of fish produced. While the total volume of salmon production increased from 2003 onwards, other indicators showed signs of deterioration. For example, the average weight per fish at the time of harvesting declined from 4.4 to 4.1 kg; the number of days required for harvesting expanded from 487 to 543 days; and the weight of salmon produced (output) per unit of input of smolt and eggs decreased from 3.7 to 3.1 kg for the former and from 1.3 to 1.1 kg for the latter. The economic and biological rate of conversion[7] deteriorated from 1.36 to 1.52 and from 1.24 to 1.34 respectively, i.e. more feed was needed to produce 1 kg of salmon. Table 5.3 also shows that the rate of fish mortality increased from 15 % in 2003 to 25 % in 2007. There must also have been an increase in sunk costs in expenditure on vaccines and antibiotics to prevent the fish from getting ill, and on the additional feed needed as a consequence of the extension of harvesting time for slower growing fish.[8]

No reliable historical data exists to indicate exactly when the deterioration of sanitary and environmental conditions started. However, a Norwegian egg-producing company located in Chile—*AquaGen*—estimated that the sanitary conditions began to worsen at the beginning of the year 2000, around the time when Chilean exports of salmon reached more than 500,000 tons. Corresponding to the growth of exports, there was a rapid increase in demand for eggs from the year 2000 onwards; however, AquaGen claims that the demand for eggs exceeded the increase of actual production of salmon, which indicates an increase in mortality rate. The company came to this conclusion by calculating the total number of eggs needed to produce 500,000 tons of salmon based on the following assumptions: that the mortality ratio of eggs to smolt is 50 %; and, that on average 3 kg of smolt is needed to produce 1 kg of salmon. Using the above assumptions, AquaGen calculated that the required number of eggs would be approximately 330 million (eyed eggs), as shown by the red line in Fig. 5.3. At the assumed level of mortality, egg input beyond that level is considered excessive. The figure demonstrates that the eggs produced grew very rapidly beyond the red line, reaching a peak in 2007—the year of the crisis. It is also noteworthy that most of the growth was accounted for by the domestic production of eggs.

[7] The economic conversion rate is the rate at which kilograms of feed are converted into 1 kg of salmon in economic value terms. The biological conversion rate is only in biological terms.

[8] One of the former directors of a salmon firm estimated the industry's total loss as a result of the ISA crisis at US$550–600 million. This included overall loss of biomass, loss of growth, loss of increased treatment costs, operational costs, and processing costs (Johnson 2007).

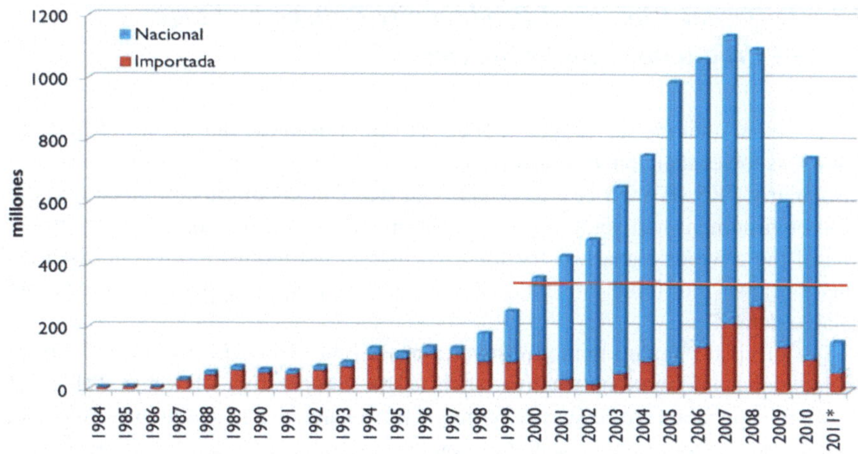

Fig. 5.3 Salmon egg production: 1984–2011 (millions of eyed eggs per year) (*Source*: Based on Dempster (2011))

Despite all the economic and biological indicators pointing to the deterioration in productivity from 2003 to 2007, exports increased substantially aided by the higher price of salmon during the same period (see the lower part of Table 5.3). Based on the above figures, we can say that the growth in profit enjoyed by most Chilean salmon firms was actually created by the rising price per unit of salmon rather than from the increase in unit productivity in biological terms. This is consistent with the claim by Katz et al. (2011a: 21) that:

> productivity gains that are achieved via economies of scale—such as larger crop tanks, various types of technological changes, process-scanning, new feeding technologies and new food formulas etc. incorporated by salmon farming companies during the course of this decade having been totally or partially annihilated by the decline in marginal efficiency of water resources, which ended affecting adversely the aggregated performance of the sector.

The increasing demand for eggs to produce the salmon—as calculated by AquaGen—suggests a high mortality rate at each stage of the rearing process: from egg to smolt and from smolt to salmon. This indirectly indicates that the amount of salmon reared in a given space of water started to exceed the local carrying capacity during the period of increasing export volume from 2000 to 2007 (see Fig. 5.2 for the volume of exports). Despite declining biological productivity, firms continued to employ unsustainable practices due to the increasing profit being generated by the higher global price for salmon (Table 5.3). It is possible to assume that this process was repeated until it reached the threshold level, causing the outbreak of the sanitary crisis in 2007.

3.3 *Different Biological Productivity Pattern by Stage of Production and by Species*

Experts claim that the survival ratio of eggs to smolt is particularly low in Chile and at 40 % is lower than that of Norway. The cause of such a high mortality is disease, particularly SRS (EWOS Health 2007). The frequent occurrence of disease in the local environment had some impact on the methods of production used by firms. One of the obvious signs was the intensive use of antibiotics to prevent diseases. This became the topic of intensive discussion despite a lack of accessible reliable data.

The survival rate during the freshwater phase (until smoltification) is influenced by locational and seasonal factors, such as the temperature of water. Table 5.4 shows the appearance of diseases by major freshwater sites: Llanquihue, Puyehue, Ranco, and Rupanco areas located in Southern regions of Chile. As can be seen in Table 5.4, despite some similarities, occurrence of diseases is quite different depending on location. This means that there are geographical differences in how nature reacts to the introduction of fish.

Moreover, there are seasonal differences in occurrences of pathogen outbreaks. This also indicates that there are seasonal differences in the pattern of their appearance (Table 5.5).

Table 5.4 Diseases diagnosed in the freshwater phase in different locations, Chile 2008

Llanquihue area	Puyehue area	Ranco area	Rupanco area
IPNv	IPNv	IPNv	IPNv
BKD	BKD	BKD	BKD
Francisella	Ichthyophthirius (Ich)	Ichthyophthirius (Ich)	Aeromonas
Fungosis	Fungosis	Flavobacteriosis	Fungosis
Yersimiosis	Yersimiosis		Yersimiosis
Aeromonas			Ichthyophthirius (Ich)

Source: Interview, Dr Nieto (2011)

Table 5.5 Seasonal changes in the spread of diseases

Pathogen	Spring	Summer	Autumn	Winter
F. columnare	x	xxx	–	–
F. psychrophilum	x	–	xxx	xxx
Aeromona	xxx	xxx	xx	xx
IPN virus	xxx	xx	xxx	xx
Fungus	xxx	–	xxx	xxx
R. Salmoninarum (BKD)	x	x	xxx	xx
Ichthyophthirius	–	xxx	–	–
Francisella	xxx	xx	x	x
Y. rucken	xxx	xx	x	–

Source: Interview, Dr. Nieto (2011)

Note: x means less frequent; xxx means more frequent

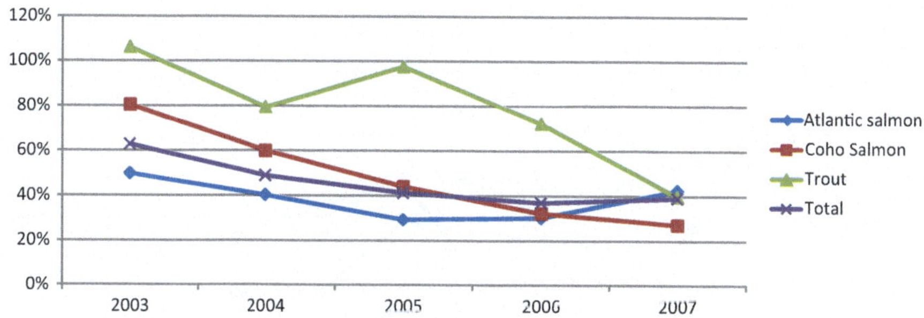

	2003	2004	2005	2006	2007
Atlantic salmon	50%	40%	29%	30%	43%
Coho Salmon	81%	60%	44%	32%	27%
Trout	106%	80%	98%	72%	40%
Total	63%	49%	41%	37%	39%

Fig. 5.4 Yield of smolt (survival rate of eggs): number of smolt (t)/number of eggs (t–2) (Note: trout in figure indicates trout salmon. *Source*: Authors)

Furthermore, the susceptibility to the disease is also different between type of salmon (Fig. 5.4). For instance, survival rate of egg to smolt is lowest for Atlantic salmon compared to Coho salmon and trout in the period from 2003 to 2007. It is also true that in 2003 Atlantic salmon had the lowest survival rate of the three. This result confirms the earlier claim by AquaGen that the worsening situation for Atlantic salmon had started earlier than 2003.

The yield of smolt compared to harvested salmon (in tons) shows different patterns by species (see Fig. 5.5). Clearly the largest decline from 2002 to 2008 was observed in Atlantic salmon due to the ISA crisis, while coho salmon and trout suffered a smaller decline. The difference in the size of the salmon species at maturation affects the pattern of growth (one grows heavier than the other as measurement is taken by the weight); hence the figures are not comparable across species in a simple manner. However, we can compare the trends from 2002 to 2008. Although coho salmon and trout were not affected by ISA, the survival rate also demonstrates a general decline. Of course, during this period, the largest decline is observed in Atlantic salmon, which started with a yield higher than the other species in 2002 and ended up with a significantly lower yield in 2008.

The above differences in yield by species are reflected by the amount of smolt sown during a similar period, as shown in Fig. 5.6. The number of Atlantic salmon smolts sown increased rapidly from 2003 to 2006, while coho stayed stable. A minor increase is also observed for trout. The circumstantial evidence above demonstrates the degrading biological productivity in the salmon industry but the impacts were felt differently by species and in localities of production.

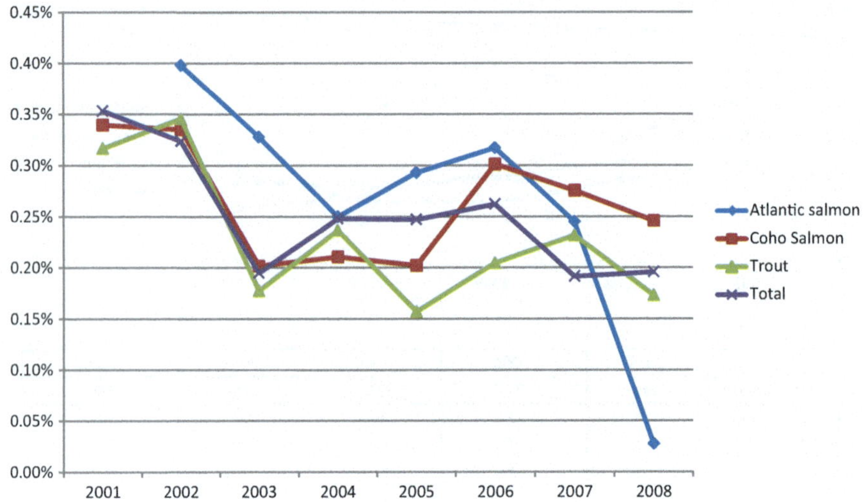

	2001	2002	2003	2004	2005	2006	2007	2008
Atlantic salmon		0.40%	0.33%	0.25%	0.29%	0.32%	0.25%	0.03%
Coho Salmon	0.34%	0.34%	0.20%	0.21%	0.20%	0.30%	0.28%	0.25%
Trout	0.32%	0.35%	0.18%	0.24%	0.16%	0.20%	0.23%	0.17%
Total	0.35%	0.32%	0.20%	0.25%	0.25%	0.26%	0.19%	0.20%

Fig. 5.5 Yield of harvested salmon (survival rate of smolt): harvested salmon (tons)/number of smolt (Note: trout in figure indicates trout salmon. *Source*: Authors)

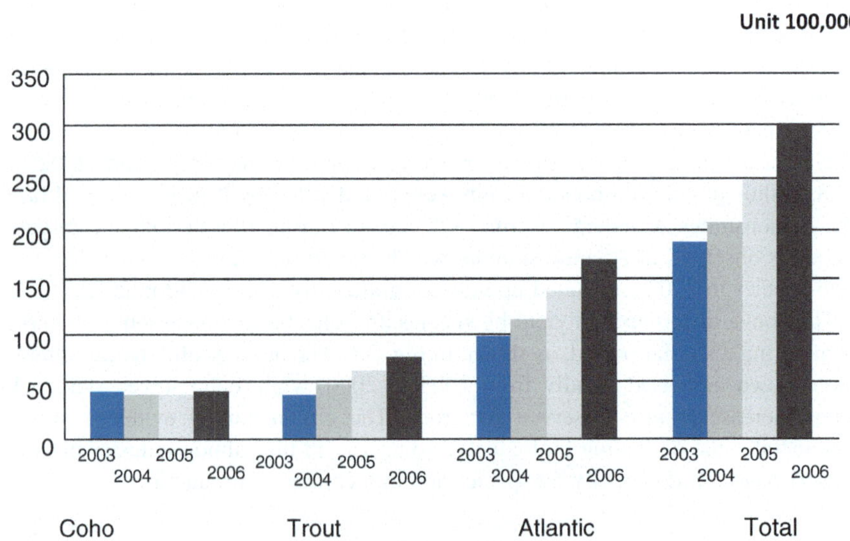

Fig. 5.6 Increasing sowing density by species: 2003–2006 (*Source*: EWOS Health (2007))

The above sanitary evidence suggests that the following factors influence the mortality rate of fish: the amount of fish introduced into the limited geographical space—the density of fish; the species of salmon; the location of cultivation sites; and the season. Accordingly, efforts to come up with effective preventive measures must include the above variables.

Thus far we have 'visited the past', looking for a better explanation of what triggered the ISA crisis. We now move to the present to examine the process involved in attempting to convert 'ambiguity' and 'uncertainty' into calculable 'risk' in a way that supports regulatory institutions and is suitable for the Chilean salmon industry. So far, several factors that may cause the difference in sanitary and environmental outcomes have been identified as: fish density; geographical locations; and the type of salmon produced. To effectively prevent the further occurrence of diseases of this nature, information from different settings must be considered.

As will be discussed in Chap. 6, since the establishment of Mesa de Salmon in 2008 attempts to recover from the ISA crisis have been well under way. The experts, public officers, and industries are trying to identify how to manage and control the situation. One of the prominent endeavors is the establishment of *barrios* and macrozones, and regulatory institutions to monitor the behavior of firms with regard to sanitary conditions. The measures that have been implemented correspond to the above findings on the salmon industry.

4 The Restructuring of the Industry into *Barrios* ('Neighbourhoods') and Macrozones

4.1 Creation of Barrios *and Macrozones*

In order to reduce the systemic risk of new diseases in the future, the National Fisheries Service (Sernapesca) required salmon farming firms to group their cultivation centers according to geographical location into *barrios* or 'neighbourhoods'. The National Fisheries Service also obliged firms operating in cultivation centers within the same *barrio* to synchronize their sowing and harvesting calendars, and provide for a 3-month resting period to allow the *barrio* to recover its biological properties after use. The coordination of the production calendar was thought to facilitate sanitary controls aimed at minimizing the transit of navigation, often instrumental in transmitting pathogens.

Figure 5.7 presents a 'stylized' description of the idea, and Fig. 5.8 shows how the idea has been implemented in southern Chile, which is highly populated with salmon farming centers.

Each macrozone houses different *barrios*, each of which is home to various cultivation centers. These cultivation centers belong to different firms. Each firm

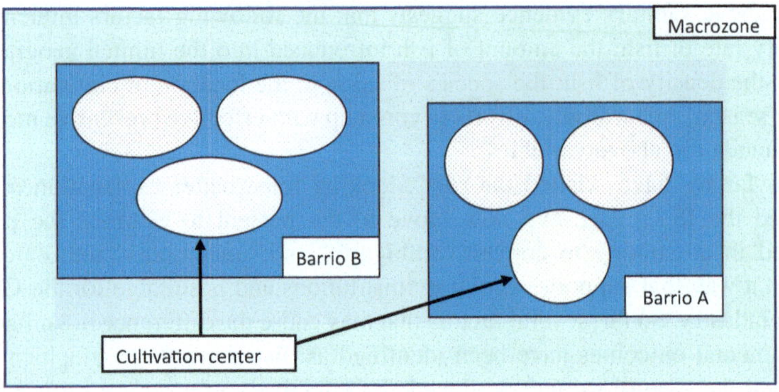

Fig. 5.7 Macrozones, neighbourhoods (*barrios*) and cultivation centers (*Source*: Authors)

has its own production strategy, organization, and 'core capabilities'. Some of them produce only Atlantic salmon (salar). Others produce coho and trout in various proportions. Coho and trout do not suffer from the ISA virus, so we have a priori expectations that large differences would prevail among firms as a result of the differences in output mix, the total amount of salmon being cultivated in the neighborhood, and the distance between cultivation centers.

In other words, differences among *barrios* and macrozones are expected to reflect not just differences in 'state conditions' (such as water quality, oceanographic conditions, ocean currents and more) but also differences in 'control variables' (such as biosecurity and environmental routines) strategically chosen by different firms. In another words, a firm's strategy for implementing preventive measures will influence greatly the degree of likelihood that they will cause a crisis—this is termed the 'risk score'.

Figure 5.8 shows the reorganization of salmon farming into *barrios* that has taken place in the regions of Los Lagos (macrozones 1, 2, 3 and 4) and Aysen (macrozones 5, 6 and 7).

4.2 Incidence of ISA Virus in Barrios[9] *from 2007 to 2011*

In the initial years of the epidemic, cultivation centers affected by the ISA virus (ISA) rose to 134 (from July 2007 to October 2008). Most of them were initially only suspected of having the virus and later developed into serious stage outbreaks. As can be seen from Fig. 5.9, the first positive cases of ISA virus were in Los Lagos

[9] There are some changes in the division of *barrios*; for details, see Chap. 6.

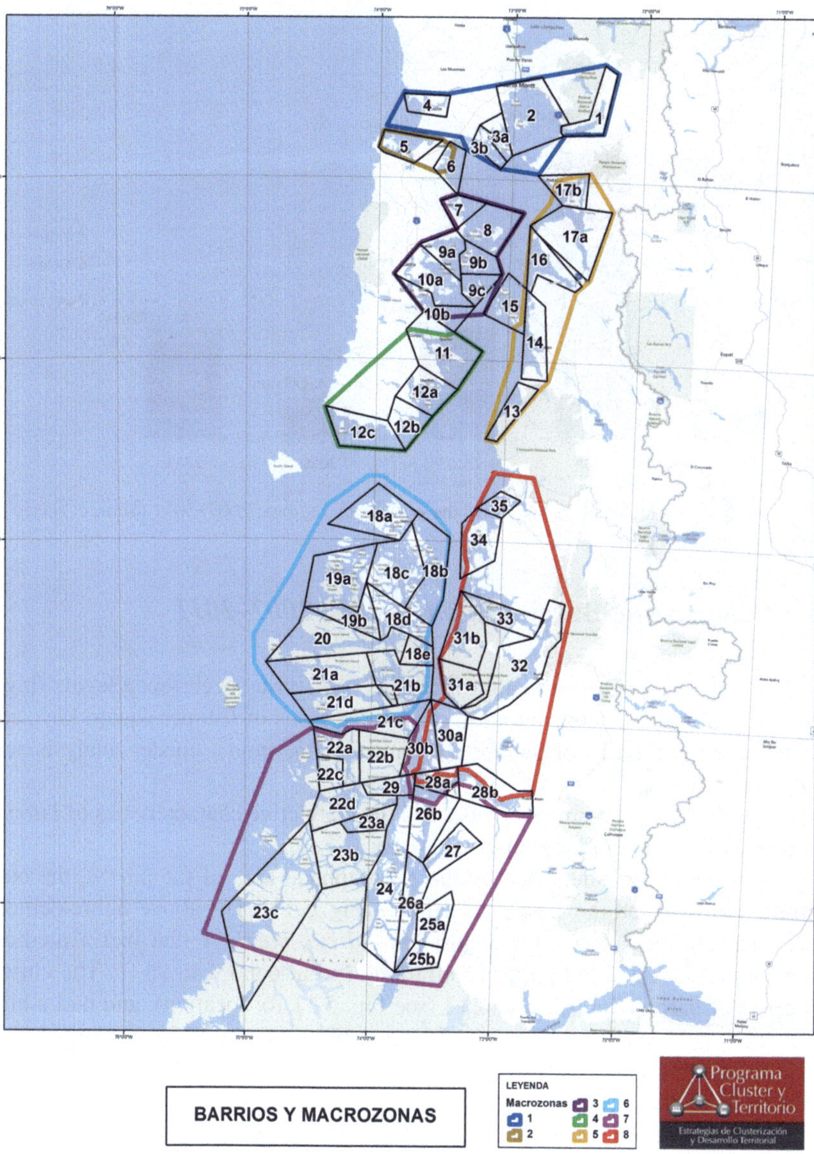

Fig. 5.8 Neighbourhoods, barrios, and macrozones in 10th and 11th regions (*Source*: Sernapesca (2010; see also Chap. 6, Fig. 6.1))

(tenth Region). The virus later spread to the Southern regions of Aysen and Magallanes. It can also be seen from Fig. 5.9 that the peak of disease detection was in 2008 and decreased significantly from 2009 to 2010, with some increase in 2011.

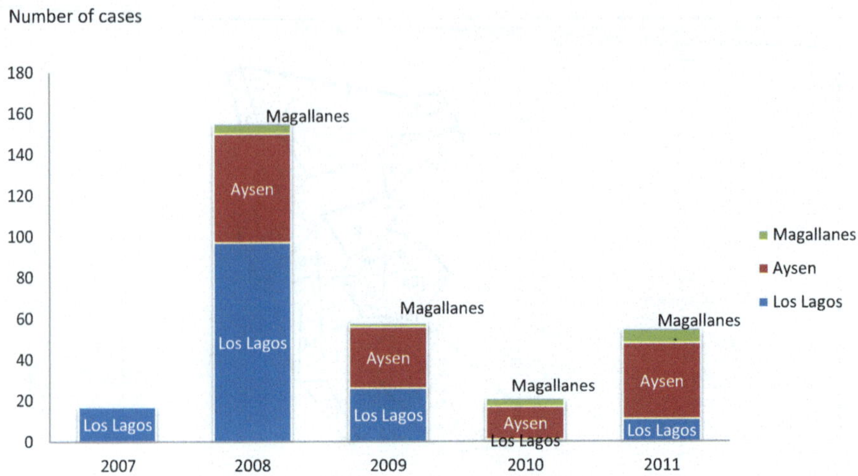

Fig. 5.9 Positive incidents of ISA virus in the *barrios* by regions: 2007–2011 (*Source*: Based on Sernapesca (2012))

4.3 Categorizing Barrios *into Clusters, 2007–2011*

Based on the available information regarding ISA, virus occurrence levels (high, medium, and low), the concentration of biomass (tons of fish per square km), and the percentage of types of salmon (Atlantic, coho, trout), cluster analysis was conducted within the *barrio*.

The results of cluster analysis separated the distinctive characteristics of *barrios* into five clusters, as can be seen in Fig. 5.10.

The clustering was identified by the geographical area of the *barrio*, the concentration of fish, and the species of salmon (Fig. 5.11). The above figure demonstrates that cluster 1 consisted of just one *barrio*, *barrio* 1 that had a medium occurrence of ISA with a high concentration of trout-coho with 94 %. The cluster 2 consists of barrios 2,3,6,7, 8 and 17 (see Fig. 5.11 for location), and had a high occurrence of ISA and a lower concentration of coho-tout of 56 % compared to Barrio 1. Cluster 3 consists of barrios 18, 19, 20, 21, 31, 33, 34, and 35, which had a medium concentration, high occurrence of ISA with a higher proportion of Atlantic salmon, 58 %. Cluster 4 consists of barrios 9, 10, 11, 12, 13, 14, 15 and 16. These barrios had a high concentration, a very high occurrence of ISA, and the proportion of trout and coho was 64 %. The last cluster 5 consists of barrios 22, 23, 24, 25, 26, 27 28, 29 and 30. The density of fish was medium, the occurrence of ISA was medium, and the trout and coho consisted of 64 %. Interestingly, the barrios clustered together were geographically located close to each other (see Fig. 5.11 for location). This suggests that the concentration of fish, the geographical location of the *barrio*, and the type of salmon (coho-trout vs atlantic) significantly influence the occurrence of ISA.

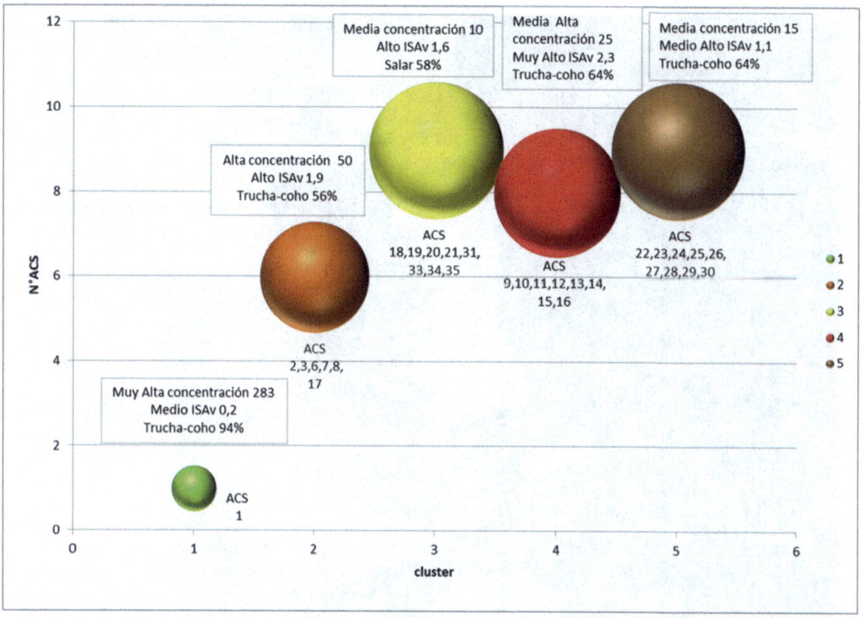

Fig. 5.10 Results of cluster analysis for grouping *barrios* in Los Lagos and Aysen by characteristics (Note: ISAv denotes ISA virus. *Source*: Authors)

Separate from the above, Vera and Zanlungo (2011) conducted correlation analysis between concentrations of fish in the area and positive cases of ISA by *barrio*. The results suggested a positive correlation between the two variables except for some anomalies found in the centers with a higher concentration of Atlantic salmon. Despite the anomalies, both analyses seem to suggest the general relationship between the concentration of fish and the occurrence of sanitary incidents, ISA.

4.4 Complex Reality Within Barrios *and Macrozones*

In order to understand the complex nature of the reality in the *barrios* and macrozones, Zanlungo and Vera (2010) took the case of macrozone 6 as an example and studied the details of how it functioned with regard to sanitary conditions. Understanding the current complexity is necessary for establishing a model for calculating risks and indicators for regulatory purposes.

Macrozone 6 has eight different *barrios*: 18A, B, C, D, 19A, B and C, and 20 (see Fig. 5.8 and Table 5.6). These *barrios* are home to 173 cultivation centers, of which only 32 are currently in operation. About half the cultivation centers produce Atlantic salmon, the species affected by ISAv. The other half of the centers

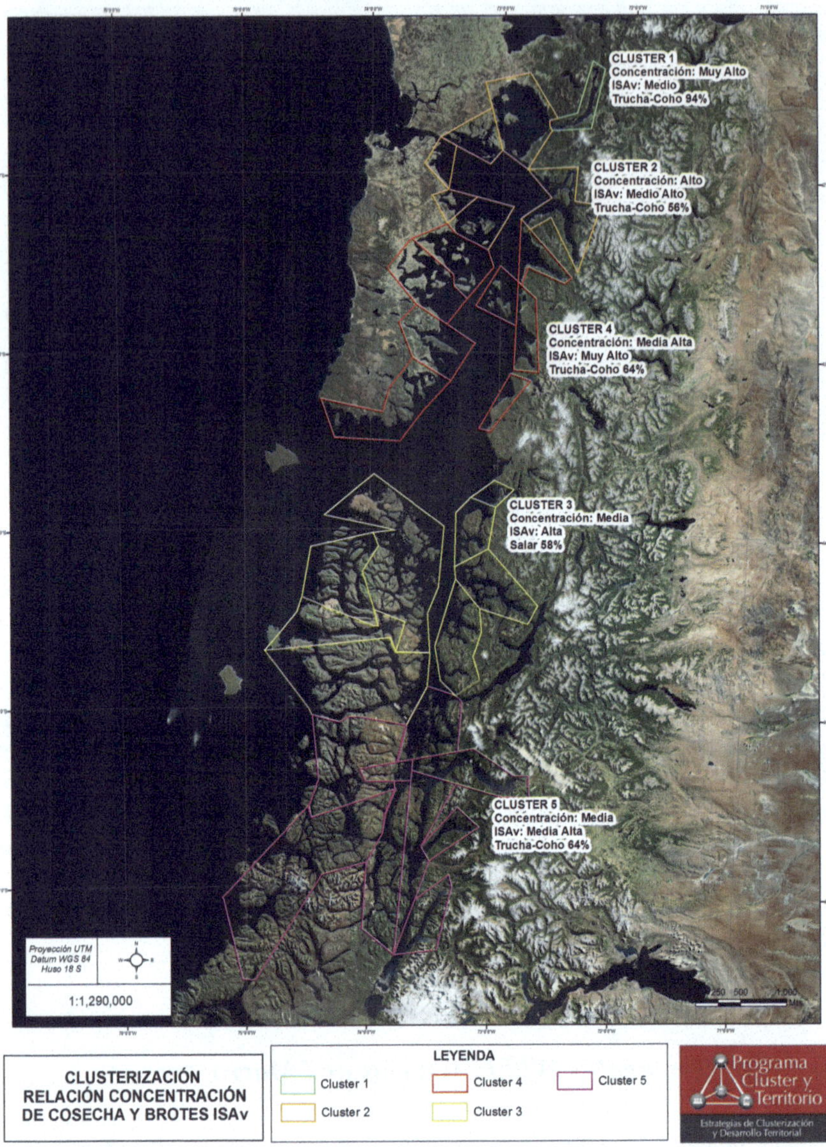

Fig. 5.11 Clusters in geographical locations (*Source*: Zanlungo (2011))

active in this macrozone produce trout and coho salmon, which do not suffer from ISA.

According to Table 5.6, the *barrio* with the most number of active cultivation centers in macrozone 6 is 18D, with 10 out of 26 centers currently in operation.

Macrozone 6's 173 cultivation centers belong to 23 different salmon farming companies (Table 5.7). Among other firms, Marine Harvest owns 35 of them and

Table 5.6 *Barrios*, cultivation centers and species cultivated by firms in macrozone 6

					Active centers producing		
Barrios	N° of firms	N° of active firms	N° of centers	N° of active centers	Coho	Trout	Atlantic
18A	4	1	15	5		5	
18B	7	2	19	2		1	1
18C	11	0	55	0			
18D	6	2	26	10	3	1	6
19A	5	2	13	3			3
19B	5	3	17	5		1	4
19C	No data						
20	6	2	28	7		2	5
Total	44	12	173	32	3	10	19

Source: Katz et al. (2011b)

Table 5.7 Firms and number of cultivation centers they own in macrozone 6

Firm	N° of centers
Marine Harvest	35
Camanchaca	29
Los Fiordos	26
Multiexport	22
Pesquera Eicosal	13
Aquachile	12
Aguas Claras	8
El Golfo	7
Chace Kehler Thomas	3
P. FishFarm	2
PacificStar	2
Ventisqueros	2
Yadrán	2
Avalos Escuderos Alfredo Julio	1
Barra Rebecco Cecilia Ximena	1
Barria Montiel, Jaime Felipe	1
Chileseafoods	1
Inversiones Chipana Limitada	1
Invertec	1
Pacheco Alvarado Luis Jorge	1
Productos del Mar Ventisqueros S.A.	1
Prov.FishFarm	1
Tornagaleones	1
Total	173

Source: Katz et al. (2011b)

Table 5.8 Firms[a] owning active centers in macrozone 6

Firms	N° of centers
Los Fiordos	12
S.Multiexport	8
Aquachile	5
Australis mar	3
El Golfo	2
Camanchaca	1
Pesquera Landes	1
Total	32

Source: Katz et al. (2011b)
[a]Ownership of cultivation centers and names of the firms are often different due to the M&A and takeovers that took place at various times in the past. The registered name is not easy to change; therefore many firms keep using the same name. Also, the registered name of the company and the name used in public can vary in some cases. Here, it was not possible to match up all the names listed in Table 5.8 with those listed in Table 5.7

therefore controls around 20 % of total installed production capacity of this macrozone. The ownership concentration of cultivation centers however, is not synonymous with having it in operation. In the particular case of Marine Harvest, in 2010 there was no active cultivation center in this macrozone. This means they have a 20 % share of the cultivation centers but 0 % are used for production.

Only seven firms have active cultivation centers in macrozone 6. Of those 7 firms, Los Fiordos is the company with the largest number—12 active centers accounting for 40 % of the total active centers (see Table 5.8).

By regulation (see Chap. 6), the rule 'one cultivation center one vote' applies when making decisions within the *barrio*. As this is not specified by the active/non active status of the cultivation center, this may not ensure the fair representation of the production structure.

5 Towards a Model for Risk Calculation[10]

Negotiations were expected to take place among actors within *barrios* and macrozones as the regulation pushed firms to come up with an agreed production calendar. The difficulties in creating a uniformed production calendar would encourage M&A (large firms acquiring smaller firms) or the relocation of cultivation sites by swapping the cultivation sites between firms in future.

[10]This section is based on Katz et al. (2011b).

Table 5.9 Risk of sanitary events in macrozones 1, 2, 3 and 4 (Los Lagos)

Macrozone	N° of risk events	N° of critical risk events	N° of high risk events
1	31	0	11
2	39	8	21
3	19	0	6
4	17	1	10

Source: Vera and Zanlungo (2011)

Katz et al. (2011b) consider that one can calculate the risk of each firm based on a mix of 'state' and 'control' variables. The state variable is the environmental/ecological factors that are essentially present with geographical location. The control variable is the firm's strategy. For instance, all the firms within a *barrio* have a similar 'state' variable because they are situated in a similar geographical location and operate under one production calendar enforced by the National Fisheries Service. Nevertheless, firms can have different 'control' variables due to different strategies chosen by the firms. If a firm follows more meticulous biosecurity and environmental practices than other firms, this firm will lower the risk. Of course, there is a collective aspect to difficulties due to the fact that firms in the same geographical area share the same bodies of water. This means if other firms in the same *barrio* 'free-ride' excessively—i.e. they do not follow regulations—on the environmental regulation, even with the strict regulatory strategy the firm can face the high risk of having environmental and sanitary crises due to lack of collective action. This feature of collective action was portrayed by Ostrom (1990).[11]

5.1 *Calculating the State Variable: Locally Specific Risk Factor*

Leaving consideration of the collective aspect of actions within the *barrio* aside, Vera and Zanlungo (2011) carried out an estimation of the imminent risk of ISA based on the four following factors that affect the state variable: (1) the type of salmon under cultivation (Atlantic salmon being more vulnerable to the risk than the other species); (2) the distance between cultivation centers (greater proximity between centers means higher risks); (3) the number of active centers in the given *barrio* (larger number of active centers means higher risk); and (4) the volume of

[11] The authors are aware that the dynamic game-theoretical notion needs to be incorporated into the model to be more realistic. However, the following section will deal only with the static model to calculate the risk. The calculation of game-theoretical interactions would require data that are not available.

production (a greater total weight of fish in the given area contributes to a higher risk). On the basis of expert opinion the risk model was specified as follows[12]:

$$Risk = 0.4{*}Specie + 0.3{*}Distance + 0.15{*}N^{\circ}Centers + 0.15{*}Production$$

Notice that the model deals only with 'state' variables, i.e. environmental/ecological variables that are supposed to be common within the same *barrio*. Here, the 'control' variable, the strategy of the firm, is not yet incorporated. Using the above equation with available data from *barrios* in the Los Lagos region (10th region), Vera and Zanlungo (2011) calculated the risk of sanitary events occurring in macrozones 1, 2, 3 and 4 (which are in the 10th region) (Table 5.9).

This simple exercise tells us that the likelihood of new critical sanitary episodes in the near future is by no means small. Differences in geographical locations—macrozones—are significant, and this should be taken into consideration by the National Fisheries Service when regulations are planned and enforced. However, given the fact that the above model estimated risk only by the differences in 'state' variables—i.e. an estimation of environmental and sanitary conditions in a certain location—it does not give a complete picture.

5.2 Calculating the Control Variable: Firm-Specific Risk Factor

We now know that different risk factors are specific to each geographical location. It is difficult, at the moment, to know a firm's strategy for implementing biosecurity. However, we can obtain evidence of the distribution of cultivation centers by the firms across *barrios* and macrozones. The available evidence shows that each firm's cultivation centers are unevenly distributed between *barrios* and macrozones. Considering Los Lagos (10th region)[13] for example, Table 5.10 shows significant inter-firm differences in the percentage of cultivation centers owned in macrozones 1 through 4.

By way of example, a firm called Caleta Bay has five cultivation centers located in macrozone 1, while Salmones Humboldt has its three cultivation centers in two different macrozones. On the other hand, Mainstream—the largest firm in the group in terms of active cultivation centers—has its production capacity distributed in all macrozones, but is strongly concentrated in macrozones 2 and 3. Marine Harvest—the third largest in the group—has 15 active cultivation centers mostly concentrated in macrozone 2.

[12] Notice that the elasticity involved in the model reflects a certain amount of discretion. It was chosen with the advice of industry experts.

[13] The exercise is carried out only for the Los Lagos region due to data availability.

Table 5.10 Number and percentages of active cultivation centers in the Los Lagos region by firm and macrozones, July 2011

Firms	MAC1	MAC2	MAC3	MAC4	Total no. of active centers by firm
Aquachile	54.5 %	18.2 %	27.3 %	0.0 %	11
Caleta Bay	100.0 %	0.0 %	0.0 %	0.0 %	5
Camanchaca	57.1 %	14.3 %	0.0 %	28.6 %	7
CM Chiloé	40.0 %	60.0 %	0.0 %	0.0 %	5
GMT	25.0 %	0.0 %	75.0 %	0.0 %	8
Holding – Trading	0.0 %	50.0 %	50.0 %	0.0 %	8
Invertec	0.0 %	75.0 %	25.0 %	0.0 %	8
Mainstream	10.0 %	40.0 %	45.0 %	5.0 %	20
Marine Harvest	13.3 %	73.3 %	0.0 %	13.3 %	15
Mirasol	0.0 %	0.0 %	0.0 %	100.0 %	3
Multiexport	0.0 %	0.0 %	0.0 %	100.0 %	2
Pacific Star	0.0 %	0.0 %	100.0 %	0.0 %	5
Salmones Antártica	12.5 %	37.5 %	0.0 %	50.0 %	8
Salmones Humboldt	33.3 %	0.0 %	0.0 %	66.7 %	3
Trusal	64.7 %	11.8 %	0.0 %	23.5 %	17
Ventisqueros	16.7 %	0.0 %	0.0 %	83.3 %	12
Average part.	26.7 %	23.8 %	20.1 %	29.4 %	8.5
Macrozone total active cultivation centers	40	40	29	30	139

Source: Katz et al. (2011b)
Note: The results reflect cultivation centers active during July 2011
MAC macrozone

Remembering that different macrozones have different risk rates (see Table 5.9), we can now combine geographical location and differences in risk across macrozones in order to calculate a static firm-specific indicator of risk which considers the relative participation of each company in each macrozone. We present this estimate in Table 5.11 to explain the sanitary conditions upon which salmon is being cultivated.

The individual firm coefficients reported in Table 5.11 should be considered 'static' indicators of the risk each company faces as a result of its geographical location and its programmed sowing and harvesting calendar for the period 2011–2014. The parameter does not capture the differences in individual-firm risk resulting from differences in 'control' variables, i.e. those reflecting its sanitary and environmental protection efforts, and the dynamic aspects of collective action.

We notice a certain degree of variance in individual company risk levels. Eleven out of 16 companies in Table 5.11 show a risk coefficient between 19 and 31 i.e. they are relatively close to each other in the level of risk. There are two outliers—Mirasol and Multiexport—which have a low risk indicator of 17, while three firms—Invertec, Marine Harvest and CM Chiloe—exhibit a high-risk parameter above 34.

Table 5.11 Firm-specific risk in the Los Lagos region

Firms	Risk 2011
Aquachile	29.2
Caleta Bay	31.0
Camanchaca	28.1
CM Chiloé	35.8
GMT	22.0
Holding – Trading	29.0
Invertec	34.0
Mainstream	28.1
Marine Harvest	35.0
Mirasol	17.0
Multiexport	17.0
Pacific Star	19.0
Salmones Antártica	27.0
Salmones Humboldt	21.7
Trusal	28.6
Ventisqueros	19.3
Average	26.4
Est. Desv.	6.3

Source: Katz et al. (2011b)

Note: Our estimate of company risk rates was obtained using the risk coefficients of Table 5.9 for each macrozone and the percentage participation of each company in each macrozone, as in Table 5.10. For example: the risk rate for Marine Harvest for 2011 results from: 31*0.45 + 39*55 + 19*0 + 17*0 = 35.4

Individual firm risk can also be seen as a reflection of company-specific control variables—i.e. its sanitary and environmental control routines—and involving dynamic considerations not yet explicitly incorporated in the coefficients of Table 5.11. Although the estimated risk parameters reported in Table 5.11 reflect a certain dynamic—insofar as they include the incidence of company production plans for the period 2011–2014—they do not incorporate dynamic changes in company strategy in a more fundamental sense. This will influence a firm's risk rating in the future. It is also possible for the firm gradually to change their risk factor by changing their geographical location and moving its production activities to less risky environments—even though the firm must realize that this change will probably reduce risk levels in the macrozone the firm leaves but might increase risk levels in the macrozone it moves into. Additionally, the firm could introduce changes in production organization routines leading to more meticulous sanitary and environmental protection practices. More collective action to jointly improve the sanitary and environmental conditions in the *barrios* may also influence the outcome. An increase in a firm's size through M&A may also allow it to exert more control over sanitation measures. By changing its 'control' variables and moving from quantity to quality in its production organization, a firm will reduce company-specific risk and also positively affect its state risk in the *barrio*. These decisions are not taken merely for sanitation purposes, but involve other decisions of a collective nature, such as logistics for transport, infrastructure, and available human resources, making it even more firm-specific and rendering it more difficult to predict the risk.

6 Conclusion

Any country will exploit natural resources for development purposes. As identified in the earlier chapters, the globalization of production and consumption has created an opportunity to exploit the comparative advantages of resources through export so that economic activities can be transformed for greater productivity. However, once the industry is being shaped and has started to increase its production scale, unexpected negative externalities may emerge to threaten the very existence of activity. Environmental/ecological problems are typical of such cases especially because these resources are accessible to all users free of charge, creating the problem of 'free riding'. This is a clear case of market failure in which the policy intervention is justified—in the form of creating rule of law and enforcement mechanisms—to regulate the use of resources and distribution among involved stakeholders. Yet, this is still a difficult task in many countries, particularly developing ones.

This chapter illustrated the process of making 'evidence-based' regulations using the case of the salmon farming industry's challenge to create effective institutions for monitoring sanitary conditions. It did so in two steps: firstly, by understanding the mechanisms behind the sanitary crisis of the Chilean salmon industry in 2007; and secondly, by understanding the process of converting (sanitary) knowledge into indicators to be used in the monitoring process.

The first part identified that various factors such as geographical location, fish density, and the type of fish reared contributed to the worsening sanitary and environmental conditions. The latter part illustrated the attempts made to create a model by simplifying the complex mechanism of risk with 'state' and 'control' variables. The 'state' variable represents the geography/location-specific risks, while the 'control' variable represents firm-specific risk. Despite the lack of data on 'control' variables, this chapter was able to calculate the risk factor of firms based on the locations of their production sites. The development of these measures is still in its incipient stages and requires further fine-tuning with the inclusion of additional data such as information on firm-level biosecurity measures implemented, dynamics of M&A, and density of fish by firm cultivation site, so as to create more detailed 'control' variables. The same is true for the 'state' variable which would need to include geographical, oceanographic, and ecological data (such as depth of water, direction of current, temperature of water, locational ecological conditions, and luminosity) specific for each *barrio*.

As this case shows, creating new institutions to regulate the sustainable use of natural resources requires translating the scientific evidence into implementable institutional mechanisms. As activities based on interaction with the biosphere follow a dynamic evolutionary path, the process of fine-tuning the regulatory indicators for monitoring is expected to continue in a trial-and -error manner.

References

Blomström, Magnus, and P. Meller (eds.). 1991. *Diverging paths: Comparing 100 years of Scandinavian and Latin American development*. Baltimore: Johns Hopkins University Press.

Bustos, H. 2008. *Manejo Sanitario Integral en Centros de Agua Dulce*. Presentation made at Segundo Conferencia Agua Dulce-Skreting, mimeo, Puerto Montt, November 12–14.

De Ferranti, D., P. Perry, D. Lederman, and W. Maloney. 2002. *From natural resources to the knowledge economy: Trade and job quality*. Washington, DC: World Bank.

Dempster, P. 2011. *The Chilean salmon industry: current status, future potential and some views over some short term challenges 2011 to 2013*. Mimeo, Presentation of mimeo at II Taller PMC Puro Salmon, Aysen, 25 Oct 2011.

EWOS Health. 2007. *Comparacion de resultados productivos en salmonatlantico, Noruega y Chile*. Mimeo, Puerto Varas, November.

Fearnside, P.M. 2001. Soybean cultivation as a threat to the environment in Brazil. *Environment Conservation* 28: 23–38.

Feeney, D., F. Berkers, B.J. McCay, and J.M. Acheson. 1990. The tragedy of the commons: Twenty two years later. *Human Ecology* 18(1): 1–19.

Hardin, G. 1968. The tragedy of the commons. *Science* 162: 1243–1248.

Iizuka, M., and J. Katz. 2011. Natural resource industries, tragedy of the commons and the case of Chilean salmon farming. *International Journal of Institutions and Economies* 3(2): 259–286.

Iizuka, M. and J. Katz. 2012. *Globalization and the changing institution for sustainability: The case of the Salmon farming industry in Chile*. UNU-MERIT Working Paper 2012-063.

Iizuka, M. and L. Soete. 2011. *Catching up in the 21st century: Globalization, knowledge & capabilities in Latin America, a case for natural resource based activities*. UNU-MERIT Working Paper 2011-071.

Johnson, A. 2007. *Evaluación económica de la situación sanitaria*. Mimeo, paper presented at Primera Conferenca de Salud de Peces Skretting, Puerto Varas, Chile, November

Katz, J., M. Iizuka, and S. Muñoz. 2011a. *Creciendo en base a recursos naturales, tragedia de los comunes y el futuro de la industria salmonera Chilena*. Serie de Desarrollo Productivo, UNECLAC.

Katz, J., P. Roje, J.P. Zanlungo, and V. Vera. 2011b. *The Chilean salmon farming cluster after the 2008 sanitary and environmental crisis*. Paper presented at Globelics conference, Buenos Aires, November.

Koh, L.P., and D.S. Wilcove. 2007. Cashing in palm oil for conservation. *Nature* 448: 993–994.

Lenzen, M., D. Moran, K. Kanemoto, B. Foran, L. Lobefaro, and A. Geschke. 2012. International trade drives biodiversity threats in developing nations. *Nature* 486: 109–112.

Maloney, W.F. 2002. *Missed opportunities – Innovation and resource-based growth in Latin America*. Policy Research Working Paper Series, 2935. Washington, DC: The World Bank.

Nieto, D. 2009. *Diagnóstico de Situación, Análisis de Riesgos y Propuesta de Plan de Manejo. Mimeo*. Final report for Proyecto Reordenamiento Salmonicultura, Puerto Montt, Intendencia X Región, Chile.

Nieto, D. 2011. Personal interview, Puerto Montt.

Ostrom, E. 1990. *Governing the commons: Evolution of institutions for collective action*. New York: Cambridge University Press.

Ostrom, E., J. Burger, C.B. Field, R.B. Norgaard, and D. Policansky. 1999. Revisiting the commons: Local lessons, Global challenges. *Science* 284: 278–282.

Perez, C., A. Marin, and L. Navas-Alemán. 2009. *The possible dynamic role of natural resource-based networks in Latin American development strategies*. ECLAC-SEGIB project document, Santiago de Chile, UN.

Perfecto, I., A. Mas, T. Dietsch, and J. Vandermeer. 2003. Conservation of biodiversity in coffee agroecosystems: A tri-taxa comparison in southern Mexico. *Biodiversity Conservation* 12: 1239–1252.

Philpott, S.M., W.J. Arendt, I. Armbrecht, P. Bichier, T.V. Diesch, C. Gordon, R. Greenberg, I. Perfecto, R. Reynoso-Santos, L. Soto-Pinto, C. Tejeda-Cruz, G. Williams-Linera, J. Valenzuela, and J.M. Zolotoff. 2008. Biodiversity loss in Latin American coffee landscapes: Review of the evidence on ants, birds and trees. *Conservation Biology* 22: 1093–1105.

Pucchi, H. 2009. *El Salmón Chileno: Experiencia Histórica y Futuro, Material de Presentación*. Presented in April 2009, Casa de Piedra, Santiago, Chile.

SalmonChile. (2009, 2011). *Sección estadística, Revista Aqua*. Santiago: Technopress.

Sernapesca, 2008. *Balance de la Situación Sanitaria de la Anemia Infecciosa del Salmon en Chile de Julio del 2007 a Julio del 2008*. Unidad acuicultura, Government of Chile.

Sernapesca. 2009. *Informe Tecnico 520075309*. Valparaiso, Sernapesca, Government of Chile.

Sernapesca. 2010. *Program specific health surveillance and control of infection salmon anemia (PSEC-ISA) Technical Report*. Valparaiso: Unidad Acuicultura, SERNAPESCA.

Sernapesca. 2012. *Informe Sanitario de Salmonicultura en Centros Marinos*. Semestre Enero-Junio 2012, Valparaiso: Unidad de salud animal, subdirección de acuicultura, Government of Chile.

Sinnoit, E., J. Nash, and A. de la Torre. 2010. *Natural resources in Latin America and Caribbean: Beyond booms and busts?* Washington, DC: World Bank.

Stirling, A. 2008. Science precaution and the politics of technological risk: Converging implications in evolutionary and social scientific perspectives. *Anual New York Academy of Science* 1128: 95–110.

Stirling, A. 2010. Keep it complex. *Nature* 468: 1029–1031.

Vera, V., and J.P. Zanlungo. 2011. *Modelo de evaluación de eventos de riesgos ISAv en base a la programación de descansos, proyecciones de siembra, engorda y cosecha salmonicultura 2011-2014, X Región de los Lagos*. Programa Cluster y Territorio, DII U. de Chile.

Zanlungo, J.P. 2011. *Capitulo crisis sanitaria*. Mimeo, Santiago de Chile.

Zanlungo, J.P., and V. Vera. 2010. *Desarrollo de nuevas herramientas de gestion para la bio-logistica del nuevo cluster del salmon*. Valparaiso: Sernapesca, October.

Chapter 6
Transformation of Institutions: Crisis and Change in Institutions for Chilean Salmon Industry

Michiko Iizuka

1 Introduction

Institutions matter for development but there is no clear consensus on how existing institutions can be transformed to better accommodate economic activities in an inclusive and sustainable manner (Acemoglu and Robinson 2012). Institutions can be defined in various ways. In this chapter, we consider institutions as mechanism that shape agents' behaviors: "a system of social factors that conjointly generate a regularity of behavior" (Greif 2006, 30).[1] Here, a system is considered as the combination of 'rules of the game', norms, beliefs, routines, organizations, and interactions that influence the outcome and the behavior of the various agents involved. It is also "self-sustaining salient patterns of social interactions, as represented by meaningful rules that every agent knows and are incorporated as agents' shared beliefs about how the game is played and to be played" (Aoki 2007, 6). The common point in the above statements is the idea that institutions are the mechanisms that determine the individuals' behaviors as well as the outcomes of complex interaction among stakeholders.

Observing changes in institutions is, hence, not an easy task because it requires untangling a complex web of dynamic interactions among agents, since changes in the 'rules of game' alter how we identify and assign roles to each agent in the game as well as how we define the goal and time span of the game. Furthermore, if the new 'rule of the game' is to have any impact in altering the behaviors of agents, fundamental change at the broad systemic level is required. However, a number of

[1] Hodgeson (1988, 2006), Aoki (2007), Greif (2006), and Nelson (2008) also described the institutions as how (agents') behaviors are formed.

M. Iizuka (✉)
Maastricht Economic and Social Research and Training Center for Innovation and Technology (UNU-MERIT), United Nations University, Maastrciht, The Netherlands
e-mail: iizuka@merit.unu.edu

A. Hosono et al. (eds.), *Chile's Salmon Industry*,
DOI 10.1007/978-4-431-55766-1_6

cases have revealed that changes in the 'rules of the game' do not always accompany behavioral changes of agents unless each agent is *motivated* to change (Greif 2006).

This opens a wider conceptual discussion on how institutional change can be brought about. The existing understandings are at opposite ends of the spectrum: some may argue that change in the rules can alter agents' behaviors (this is a structuralist or top-down perspective); others may argue that change in the rules does not occur without prior changes in each agent (based on the agent, this is a social constructionist or bottom-up view). A more feasible alternative is to consider the combination of the above two views: co-evolutional changes. Aoki (2007) explains institutional change as a sign of profound transformation that involves gradual and wider changes in the way interactions take place among agents. This approach is called evolutionary institutionalism.

In order to understand the evolutionary process of institutional change, this chapter identifies the following distinctions for institutions: regulatory, normative, and cognitive levels of institutions (North 1990, 1991; Scott 1995). The regulatory institutions encompass legislation and government regulations and policies that serve as 'rules of the game'. The normative institutions are embedded in business practices, policies or ethical standards—the way things are done—rather than rules or governing structures that constrain behavior. The cognitive institutions reflect the way people interpret and make sense of the world around them, including cultures, value systems, religions, and norms. In other words, while each level tries to influence the agents' behaviors differently there are also inter-level interactions in a co-evolutive manner. Applying the distinctive level of institutions, it is possible to disaggregate and observe complex interactions accompanying institutional change at three distinctive levels while paying attention to inter-level interactions.

Here in this chapter, we will take a look at the case of salmon farming industry in Chile paying attention to the institutional changes that took place in reaction to the sanitary crisis of the salmon industry in 2007. The institutional change is represented by the passing of the Aquaculture Law (Ley Aquacultura, Ley No. 20.434) that modified the existing General Law of Fishery and Aquaculture (Ley General de Pesca y Acuicultura: LGPA, Ley No. 18.892) in 2010. This change took place at regulatory level with the modification of law and caused changes at normative level, namely granting more authority to the Undersecretariat of Fisheries (SubPesca) and the National Fisheries Service (SERNAPESCA) to ensure sustainable management of aquaculture, particularly in Chilean salmon farming. This was an important turning point that shifted the market-led approach of Chilean aquaculture towards a more regulation-oriented approach. However, whether such change will be able to create new 'routines' in the industry via changing behavior at individual firms to prevent further occurrences of environmental and sanitary crises still remains to be seen.

In this chapter, attempts have been made to disentangle the interactions and institutional changes that took place in the Chilean salmon industry before and after the ISA (infectious salmon anaemia) crisis in 2007. The institutional changes are examined in the following order. First, an overview of the sanitary crisis and corresponding changes in policies and regulations set the scene. After that, the situation leading up to the crisis is illustrated to describe the types of interactions and institutional set-ups that existed in the public as well as the private sector before the crisis. The unfolding events are woven together following the first outbreak of ISA in July 2007 until the end of 2012. In the last section, Attempts were made to put each section together to understand how the motivations of each agent are shaped and aligned to establish a new institutions, which is a "system... that generates a regularity of behaviour" (Greif 2006, 30), applying the regulatory, normative, and cognitive distinctions by Scott (1995).

2 Setting the Scene

2.1 Description of the Sanitary Crisis and Its Impact

In July 2007,[2] the Chilean National Fisheries Service officially confirmed the presence of infectious salmon anaemia (ISA: see Box 6.1) virus in a cultivation center located in the 10th region (Sernapesca 2008). The disease, known to be contagious and to cause high mortality in Atlantic salmon (while not harmful to human health), quickly spread to the nearby cultivation centers. Soon the affected cultivation sites suspended operation (Iizuka and Katz 2011). This incident reduced the volume of Atlantic salmon[3] production by 47.8 %, a drop from 370,000 tons in 2008 to 203,000 tons in 2009 (Baillarie et al. 2010), and sales fell 12.9 % to US $2169 million FOB in 2009 compared to the previous year.[4] The decrease in production caused negative chain reactions: firms started to lay off close to 20,000 employees from the affected cultivation sites and related fish processing plants in the short period of 2007–2009 and numerous salmon firms failed to meet bank loan repayments, leaving a total estimated bank debt of US$1600–2500 million (Larrain 2011) by the end of 2009. As the result, unemployment and chains of bankruptcies increased dramatically in the 'salmon cluster'[5] causing huge damage to the regional economy by 2009.

[2] According to some findings, several generations of the ISA virus developed in Chile, apart from the one believed to have come from Norway (Alvial et al. 2009).

[3] Currently, the ISA virus affects only Atlantic salmon.

[4] The gap is caused by the rise in the price of salmon. The decrease in the value of exports is smaller than that of volume due to the rise in price per kg of salmon caused by the shortage of the supply of salmon, due in turn to the decrease in production in Chile.

[5] See Maggi (2007), Iizuka (2007), and Katz (2006) for details.

Box 6.1: Infectious Salmon Anaemia

Infectious salmon anaemia (ISA) is a highly infectious transboundary disease affecting Atlantic salmon (*S. salar*). This disease was initially diagnosed in Norway in 1984. The disease was later reported in Canada in 1996 and in Scotland in 1998, as well as in the Faroe Islands in 2000 and in the USA. The presence of the virus has also been found in rainbow trout (*O. mykiss*) in reported cases from the Faroe Islands, in coho salmon (*S. kisutch*) in Chile, and in the freshwater stages of brown trout and sea trout (*S. trutta*), although the disease was not clinically present.

The presence of ISA in farmed fish has been detected in both the freshwater and seawater stages. However, the main effects of the disease were presented in the seawater stage, where symptoms are evident from 2 to 4 weeks after infection, and are associated with severe anaemia, leukopenia, and bleeding in various organs. Mortality associated with various outbreaks of ISA can vary significantly among various farming centers and within the same farming center, with reported daily mortalities at the cage level ranging from 0.5 to 1 %, which may increase over time. The cumulative mortality rate may exceed 90 % of the population in the most severe cases.

The ISA transmission mechanism in marine environments is mostly via viral particles present in mucus, feces, or contaminated biological fish material, or via direct contact between susceptible and infected fish. Another source of transmission is via waste from harvesting activities, whether conducted at sea or in processing plants where there is no effluent treatment, or via sharing of equipment and material between farms or between cages with different health statuses and without disinfection procedures that should eliminate the virus. Another transmission route that may explain the spread over large distances is the transport of live fish, during which a critical role is played by wellboats. Experimental research conducted by Melville and Griffiths (1999) suggests the absence of vertical transmission of the virus. However, new evidence suggests the possibility of some type of transgenerational transmission, which would explain the recurrence of outbreaks and the movement of certain viral isolates within Norway. It has been proven that species of sea lice, *Caligus elongatus* and *Lepeophtheirus salmonis*, can act as a vector of the ISA virus, and may exacerbate the spread and dissemination of the disease during outbreaks and endemic situations.

Source: Adapted from Technical Report "Program Specific Health Surveillance and Control of Infectious Salmon Anemia (PSEC-ISA)." Sernapesca Aquaculture Unit, December 2010.

2.2 Establishment of Mesa de Salmon (Salmon Roundtable)

In April 2008, the Mesa de Salmon (officially called the "Groupo de tareas del salmon: salmon working group" or the Salmon Roundtable, and hereafter referred to as the Roundtable) was created as the ministerial advisory commission to solve the sanitary crisis in the salmon industry. The Roundtable consisted of representatives from the relevant public sectors such as the Ministry of Economy, the National Commission of Environment (CONAMA), the Undersecretariat of Fishery (SubPesca), the Undersecretariat of Marine, the National Fisheries Service (SERNAPESCA), the Chilean Economic Development Agency (CORFO), the Maritime Agency (DIRECTEMAR), and the Agriculture and Livestock Service (SAG), and was headed by the former head of the Undersecretariat of Fisheries in 2003–2006, Felipe Sandoval.

Box 6.2: Major Tasks to Be Accomplished by the Salmon Roundtable

1. To analyze the institutional organization necessary for aquaculture activities and propose measures to strengthen the existing institutions in the Ministry of Economy;
2. To propose legal measures, regulations, or operations to improve, coordinate and accelerate the procedures of public organizations related to aquaculture, including, among others, the system of data collection and generation, the system of supervision, and the participation of the government of Chile in creating a system of international certification for the industry;
3. To propose measures in relation to the areas of concessions in regions 11 and 12 in accordance with the existing planning instrument for the use of coastal areas at the regional level;
4. To review the existing regulations with the purpose of proposing measures to update the sanitary and environmental conditions of salmon farming, and to improve the evaluation of operational conditions in the cultivation center;
5. To propose a medium- and long-term program for scientific and technological research into the further development of salmon farming;
6. To propose possible incentive measures to stimulate research into the creation of vaccines and medicine for the industry, and to analyze the situation regarding intellectual property rights.

Source: Comision Grupo de Tareas del Salmon 2009, 3 (translated from Spanish by the author).

Initially, the Roundtable was expected to create a new institutional framework through the following measures: first, modifying the existing norms for sanitation and the environment (RESA (Reglamento Sanitario para la Acuilcultura) and

RAMA (Reglamento Ambiental para la Acuilcultura)); and, second, creating operational protocols to ensure the future growth of this sector (see Box 6.2). The Roundtable was placed directly under the authority of the president of Chile with participation limited to relevant elements of the public sector to ensure maximum authority and a rapid decision-making process (interview, Mr. Sandoval 2011).

Due to a series of events after the crisis, the Roundtable had to deal with the following additional issues: (1) regional unemployment; (2) restrictions on the excessive use of chemicals and antibiotics; (3) financial debt of salmon firms; (4) reform of the concession rights system; and (5) the regional coastal planning. The process by which these issues were incorporated into the tasks of the Roundtable will be discussed in the following sections. What is clear here is that the task of the Roundtable dramatically increased from just fine-tuning the existing regulatory framework to drastically transforming it, which included going through the formal modification of LGPA via the political process. The modification of LGPA was prepared in 2009 and finally passed in the Congress in March 2010, just before the change of government.[6] The Roundtable played a crucial coordinating role among all the agents involved in this process.

2.3 *Main Contents of the Modification of the LGPA and Implications*

The modification of LGPA (Law No. 20.434) in 2010 made the following major changes regarding the sanitary crisis: (1) reforming the concession rights system; (2) strengthening existing sanitary and environmental regulations; (3) introducing collective management via the system called *barrio* (neighborhood) and macrozones; and (4) strengthening the authority of the National Fisheries Service to enforce regulations.

2.3.1 Changes in the Concession Rights System

The concession rights were to be converted into a transferable property or an asset that could be used to guarantee a bank loan. The change was made with the purpose of resolving salmon firms' bank debt problem by replacing their conventional collateral, the biomass (fish), which was destroyed by the ISA crisis. In the course of the discussion about converting the right to conduct economic activities in the

[6] Just after the establishment of this law in March 2010, the government changed from President Bachelet to President Piniera, of the opposition party.

oceanic area to a transferable financial asset, concern was raised over the potential privatization of the ocean. Hence the following two compromises were made: first, limiting the period of concession up to 25 years[7] with the possibility of renewal after complying with environmental and sanitary regulations; and, second, placing a 20 % cap on the area that one firm can own within one region. In addition to the above changes, the payment for concession rights was increased substantially[8] to finance the enforcement of regulations and regulation-oriented research. Finally, granting new concessions for the 12th region (Magallanes) and the 11th region (Aisén) was suspended for 2 years and 1 year, respectively, until the salmon farming concession sites could be integrated into the coastal zoning plan.

2.3.2 Strengthening Sanitary and Environmental Regulations

Strengthening sanitary regulation was the central task for the Roundtable. This was done first through strengthening the existing regulations,[9] which involved setting a basic framework for stricter control over the imports of eggs and movement of fish stocks to restrict the transmission of pathogens. The framework was also aimed to develop specific regulatory indicators such as optimal fish density[10] and fish mortality rates for monitoring sanitary conditions in different geographical zones.

The sanitary and environmental measures for aquaculture were to be integrated into a comprehensive zoning plan for coastal areas. Regulations on the use of chemicals and antibiotics were also strengthened. Most importantly, for the first time, measures, methods, and standards for implementing sanctions were clearly stipulated.

[7] The previous law did not set limits on the duration of ownership.

[8] The law requires a monthly payment of 2 UTM (Unidad de Fomento) per ha of cultivation center, up to the first 50 ha and 4 UTM per ha for the area exceeding 50 ha. 1UTM was US$46.58 as of March 2012. The payment was increased from 2 to 4 UTM per ha per month to 10 UTM per ha per month. The increase of revenue from concessions (*patente* in Spanish) was used to finance enforcement of regulations and research (Sernapesca, interview, Mr. Burgos 2011). In 2012, the fee is expected to rise further to 35 UTM per ha.

[9] These are Appropriate Areas for Aquaculture (AAA), Regulation on the Environment (Reglamento Ambiental para la Acuicultura: RAMA) and Sanitary Regulation (Reglamento Sanitario para la Acuicultura: RESA). AAA share common epidemiologic, oceanographic, operational, or geographic characteristics, and have complied with both environmental and sanitary regulations before granting concessions. The identification of an AAA requires examining various information including alternative uses of the site such as natural reserves, tourist attractions, indigenous population, harbor and natural habitat for other hydrobiological resources.

[10] This is described in Chap. 5.

2.3.3 Creation of a New Institutions to Encourage Collective Action: *Barrios* (Neighborhoods)

The modified Aquaculture Law (Ley No. 20.434) created a new institution called a *barrio* (neighborhood)[11] or “a group of concessions” located within a similar geographical, oceanographic, and epidemiological area. The owners of concessions (firms) are grouped according to these geographically defined *barrios*. All the *barrios* are grouped into *macrozonas* (macrozones), areas determined by geographical characteristics.[12]

The idea of the new institutions is to encourage collective management of environmental and sanitary conditions among firms that own concessions within the same *barrio*.[13] In fact, the law requires all the concessions that belong to the same *barrio* to follow a synchronized production calendar (either 24 or 21 months) and collectively manage sanitary and environmental conditions. This means that these firms must simultaneously implement sowing, harvesting, medication treatment, and 3 months of fallowing. In addition to the above, firms in the same *barrio* are also obliged to jointly implement regulations on fish escapes, and ensure an appropriate distance between cultivation centers and *barrios*, and biosecurity measures for transporting fish, eggs and other necessary inputs by sea. The law also assumes that each *barrio* has different types and levels of risk due to differences in geographical conditions such as topography, oceanography, temperature, current, depth etc.; hence differentiated control indicators are to be defined for each *barrio* and macrozone (explained in Chap. 5, see Fig. 5.8).

The *barrio* is a new instrument that encourages owners of different concessions to collaborate to find the most effective solutions. The decision-making process within the *barrio* follows the democratic rule of one concession, one vote. As represented in Fig. 6.1, currently each *barrio* consists of concessions of different owners (firms) and products (species of salmon: coho, trout, salar (atlantic)), which means the *barrios* bring together various stakeholders with diverse interests. The decision-making process within the *barrio* can therefore be complex, particularly given the lack of trust and social capital within the industry (Vignolo et al. 2007).

A grace period was provided to ensure a smooth introduction of the institutions, *barrios*. During this period, firms were allowed to relocate through transferring, dividing and merging the concessions located in different *barrios* or macrozones to efficiently comply with sanitary and environmental regulations.

---

[11] At the time when law was issued, there were four zones and 23 *barrios* in the 10th region and three zones and 33 *barrios* in the 11th region. In the 12th region, 17 areas are identified but zones and *barrios* are not yet clarified.

[12] In 2010, the 10th and 11th regions were divided into seven macrozones (four in the 10th region and three in the 11th region) and 58 *barrios* (24 in the 10th region and 34 in the 11th region) (RS. No 450; see Fig. 6.1) but this was modified into 61 *barrios* (24 in the 10th region and 37 in the 11th region) in 2011 (Subsecretaria de Pesca 2011 res, extebti 18.96).

[13] The original proposal for dividing fish farming areas into *barrios* in the 10th and 11th regions was made by SalmonChile (interview, Mr. Odebret 2011).

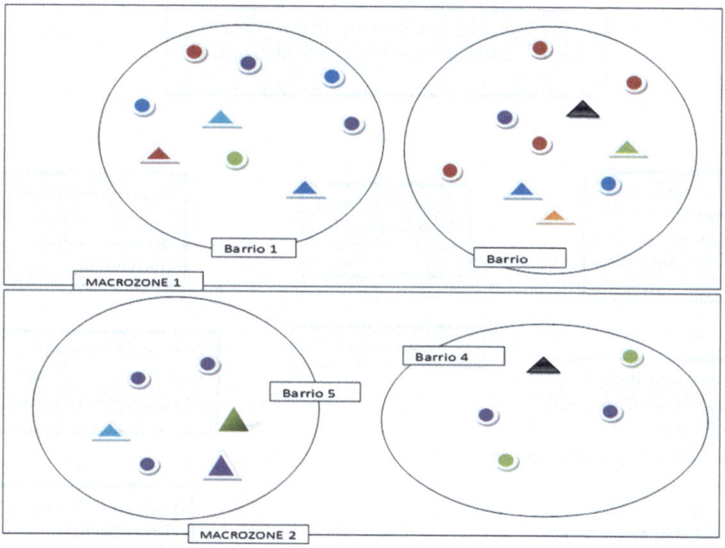

Fig. 6.1 Conceptual map of *barrios* and macrozones (Note: each *circle* represents cultivation of salmon salar, while each *triangle* represents coho producers. *Different colors* represent different companies)

2.3.4 Strengthening the Authority of the Public Sector for Enforcement

The law enhances government authority on aquaculture matters exercised by the Undersecretariat of Fisheries (SubPesca) and the National Fisheries Service (Sernapesca). The Undersecretariat of Fisheries has the authority to establish resolutions based on the issues determined by the modification of the Aquaculture Law (Ley No. 20.434) to specify detailed operational measures (such as the level of fish density in cultivation centers by species or by location) through consultation with experts. The National Fisheries Service enhanced its authority to enforce regulations set by the Undersecretariat and now has authority to inspect and register all the property (farms, stores, warehouses, slaughter facilities (processing plants), fish nurseries, ships, aircraft, trains, vehicles, boxes, packages, and packaging items) related to aquaculture. Furthermore, under the new law, the National Fisheries Service will administer the preparation of the environmental information report (INFA), monitor the sanitary and environmental conditions of cultivation sites, and determine the continuation of business at the site. Before the modification, the neutrality and credibility of this report was compromised as the consultants hired by the firm conducted this task. In addition to above, the National Fishery Service is granted authority to stop any transit of vessels between macrozones as well as between *barrios* in case of sanitary emergency.

After the modification of LGPA by Ley 20.434, the Undersecretariat of Fisheries needed to transform the law into enforceable regulations in the following manner: first, by strengthening the existing measures via adjustments (as can be seen in

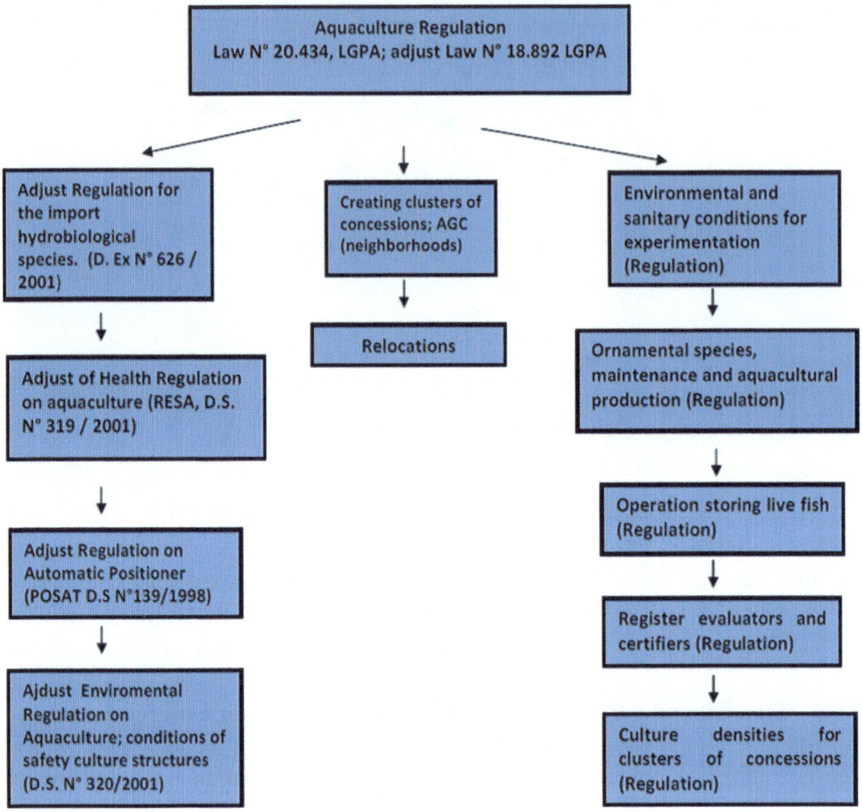

Fig. 6.2 Steps to follow after the modification of LGPA via the Aquaculture Law (*Source*: Undersecretariat of Fisheries (2011))

Fig. 6.3, left side); second, by implementing the new scheme in the *barrios* (Fig. 6.3, center); and third, by creating the necessary complementary regulations to enhance the effectiveness of existing regulations (Fig. 6.2, right side).

At early period of dealing with crisis many efforts were made by public and private sectors to learn from the experiences of Norway and Canada where they had similar problems in the past; however, they soon recognized that many basic conditions—natural conditions, industrial structure, geographical distribution of cultivation sites, production practices—are not the same, so solutions cannot be blindly transferred. Two organizations, the Undersecretariat of Fisheries and the National Fisheries Service are in intense trial and error learning process with regards to new regulations and enforcement of sanitary and environment regulations. In fact, after 2010 numerous *ley exenta*[14] were issued to update details of

[14] *Ley exenta* is a form of law that does not require political approval by Congress. This law can be issued by the Undersecretariat of Fisheries.

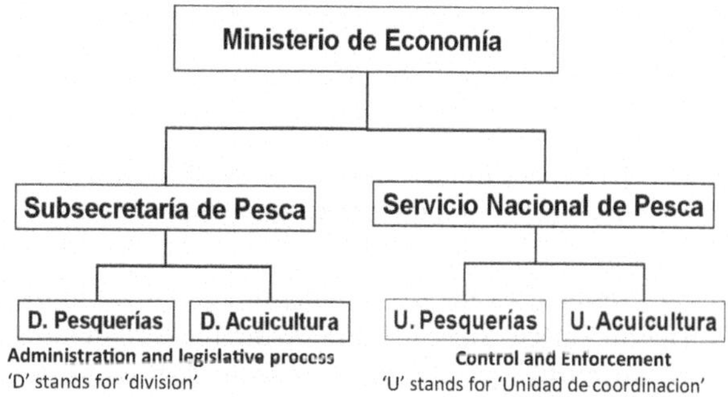

Fig. 6.3 Simplified structure of the fishery administration in Chile (2012) (*Source*: Based on information from respective websites)

specific measures related to sanitary and environmental matters outlined in the law. These specific changes aimed to deal with short-term problems. While the importance of research and development to come up with effective policy measures has been well recognized, not much time or budget was allocated.

2.4 *Organizational Changes in Public Sector*

Organizational change often reveals important aspects of institutional transformation. The new aquaculture law accompanied some changes in organizational structure in the Undersecretariat of Fisheries and the National Fisheries Service, the two main organizations dealing with fishery resources (Fig. 6.3).[15]

For a long time, extractive fishery was the main fishery activity in Chile. The government prioritized extractive fishery by allocating more licenses and budgets. This condition of path dependence continued even after the contribution to exports shifted from extractive fishery to aquaculture in the late 1990s. In Chile, any change in the public sector organization[16] requires legal modification with approval from Congress, and thus cannot be made very easily, making the public organization resilient to the changing reality within the industry. While the above is true, evidence from the interview with a government official (Ms. Saa) in 2011 revealed

[15] The fishery administration was initially placed under the Ministry of Agriculture but was transferred to the Ministry of Economy in 1978. This is due to the export potential of extractive fishery at that time. Tasks related to fishery are divided in the following manner: the Undersecretariat of Fisheries makes regulations and policy while the National Fisheries Service enforces and regulates. There were other fishery associated institutions, such as the Undersecretariat of Marine and The Fisheries Development Institute (IFOP). The former is involved in granting permission for the use of coastal areas as well as control of shipping used in maritime transport. The latter is a private organization with public origins dedicated to conducting applied research on fishery for policy purposes. Until recently, IFOP's research was mainly dedicated to extractive fishery but currently IFOP is increasingly involved in regulation setting research for aquaculture.

[16] Such as changing the organizational structure and the allocation of resources in terms of number of employees, positions, and expertise of employees. It was found that many additional staff are hired as "consultants" due to the limitation in official posts (interview with Ms. Saa 2011).

that gradual de facto organizational adjustments were made a few years before the formal legal changes in 2010.

2.4.1 Organizational Changes in the National Fisheries Service Before the LGPA: Focus on Aquaculture

In the National Fisheries Service, there was no independent section to deal with aquaculture until 2006. In 2006, a small independent unit of eight people, called an Aquaculture Unit,[17] was established to deal with sanitation issues. This unit was created simply by moving a part of the Fishery Administration Unit and the Fish Sanitary Unit to create a unit specializing in the enforcement of aquaculture-related issues such as sanitary and granting concession rights.

This newly founded unit expanded rapidly after the first incident of Calius (2006–2007) and the ISA virus (July 2007). The number of employees increased with additional professionals and a team of inspectors hired on a temporary basis.[18] In 2008, this unit was made to focus specifically on sanitary issues of aquaculture by moving the administrative part (concerning concession rights) back to the original Fishery Administration Unit. The Aquaculture Unit, by this time, increases its number of officers to 15 in order to meet the rising demand for sanitary services. In 2008 with the establishment of the Roundtable, an extra budget of 600 million Chilean pesos was allocated to the National Fisheries Service to deal with problems related to ISA. Part of these funds were used to hire new enforcement officers and experts on sanitary measures. This contributed to an increase of more than 50 officers working on the aquaculture section as of 2010.[19] The modification of the LGPA in 2010, the organizational chart of the National Fisheries Service (Sernapesca 2011) gave the Unidad de Coordinacion de la Acuicultura (Aquaculture Coordination Unit) equal importance to the Unidad de Coordinacion de Pesca Extractiva (Extractive Fishery Coordination Unit), reflecting the growing importance of aquaculture in the national economy. However, many changes had already taken place at the normative level even before the changes in regulatory levels took place.

In addition to the strengthening of organizational *capacity* (i.e. via number of personnel, the size of the budget, and the political legitimacy) for enforcement of

[17] Initially, this was a small unit consisting of eight people: four officers from the 'Fish Sanitary Unit' and four officers from the 'Fish Administration Unit' (interview, Ms. Gallardo 2011).

[18] These increases in the number of employees came about through increases in contract-based employees rather than increases in permanent staff.

[19] The officers are placed as follows: five in the 10th region, ten in the 11th region after ISA compared to one in the 10th region and one in the 11th region before ISA. At the time of the interview (Nov. 2011), the head of the department, Ms Gallardo, reported that there were about 50 officers in her unit administering the sanitary issues in the following regions: Metropolitan region (RM), 7th, 8th, 9th, 14th, 12th, 11th and 10th. In addition to 50 officers enforcing sanitary regulations, there are additional officers to administer environmental regulations, although environmental staffs are not as numerous as sanitary staff (interview, Ms Gallardo 2011).

sanitary matters in aquaculture, there was an attempt to build *capability* by establishing a National Fisheries Service diagnostic laboratory. In the past, the National Fisheries Service did not have its own laboratory and was obliged to rely on results from external laboratories contracted by the firms. This arrangement could jeopardize the neutrality of the National Fisheries Service because the results from external laboratories can be compromised. In 2008, the National Fisheries Service made an agreement with the Catholic University of Valparaiso to create an independent laboratory where they could bring the collected samples from the firms for evaluation. They also accredited this laboratory with the World Organization for Animal Health (OIE), making it the first reference laboratory in the Latin American region (interview, Ms. Gallardo 2011).

2.4.2 Organizational Changes in the Undersecretariat of Fisheries

Since the first decade of the 2000s, similar *de facto* organizational changes were also taking place in the Undersecretariat of Fisheries with regard to aquaculture, reflecting its increasing importance in the Chilean economy. For instance, although the Departamento de Acuicultura (Department of Aquaculture) was placed below the Division de Administracion Pesquera (Division of Fishery Administration) in the organizational chart of the Undersecretariat of Fisheries, it was given equal status as a division, in terms of the position of the chief as well as the size of its budget after 2003 (interview, Ms. Saa 2011). The *de facto* organizational changes are now formalized legally. The current organizational chart of the Undersecretariat of Fisheries (2011) shows the presence of the Division de Acuicultura (Aquaculture Division) parallel to the Division de Administracion Pesquera (Fishery Administrative Division). In addition to this, regional sub-direction in the 11th region was created to serve needs due to the expansion of aquaculture activities in that region.

More changes, such as increases in budget and personnel, and changes in job descriptions and responsibilities, are expected to take place in these organizations with regard to aquaculture. Some ministers have even referred to the possibility of creating an Undersecretariat of Aquaculture due to the future potential growth of this sector in Chile (not limited to salmon, but including shellfish and algae). Furthermore, to effectively control sanitary conditions, the creation of independent institutions, similar to that of National Agriculture and Livestock Service (SAG) for the agriculture sector in aquaculture has been contemplated (interview, Ms. Gallardo 2011). Instituto Fomento de Pesquero (The Fisheries Development Institute) (IFOP) are also going to involve applied research related to aquaculture policy and regulations. Hence, it seems that there were changes in both the cognitive (awareness of the importance via expressed views in media) and normative levels even before the change in regulatory level.

In this section, we have examined two public organizations in the fishery sector—the National Fisheries Services and the Undersecretariat of Fisheries—to understand their organizational changes in relation to the modification of the LGPA in 2010 (Ley 20.434). The evidence obtained from interviews confirms that de facto changes in governance at the normative level preceded the modification of the

LGPA at the regulatory level. Currently open discussions are taking place on how to create new public institutions dealing with aquaculture. This indicates that there are further changes taking place at the cognitive level.

The above illustrates why the modification of the LGPA—the change at regulatory level—was accepted by existing organizations because the changes were well in line with what is taking place at normative level to cope with worsening sanitary conditions. In other words, a change at regulatory level was the result of cumulative changes at the normative level in each respective public organization. This indicates that the process of change is not top–down, but instead very much bottom–up.

Now the key events that took place before the crisis are examined in private and public sector to understand the background of institutional change observed in this section.

3 Before the Crisis

3.1 The Private Sector Before the Crisis: Salmon Farming Firms and SalmonChile

3.1.1 Dynamic Changes in the Composition of Firms Between the Late 1990s and 2011

The salmon industry experienced fierce competition at the global level in the period from the late 1990s to the early 2000s.[20] This was also a time when firms diversified their products (either by type or level of process) and market destination (Japan, the USA, the EU and Latin America).

Another important change before the ISA crisis was the increase of firm entrants, attracted by the high profitability of this industry. Table 6.1 lists 11 of these firms. The table demonstrates that many of these new entrant firms were associated with Chilean extractive fishery businesses, which aimed to diversify their portfolios to compensate for the declining share of extractive fishery. In addition to these firms,

[20] The average price of salmon was declining from US$5.9 per kg in 1992 to US$3.1 per kg in 1999. As a result, mergers and acquisitions took place in order to (1) increase the scale of production to lower unit costs and (2) secure inputs and services through vertical integration within the main production line of salmon farming firms (including fish feed, eggs and smolt production (pisciculture), the fattening phase, and processing). For instance, the leading Chilean firm, AquaChile, merged with Salmon Pacific Star in 1999, acquired Best Salmon in 2003, Salmon Chiloe, Salmon Cailin, Salmon Maulin and Aquas Claras in 2005 and went into the fish feed business with BioMar as Alitec in 2006. The same was true for Marine Harvest, which was acquired by the Dutch animal feed company Nutreco in 1999, acquired Stolt Seafarm (pisciculture) in 2008 but then sold to Norwegian firm Panfish, which also purchased Fjordo Seafood Chile in 2009. Fjordo Seafood itself was the result of a merger between Salmones Linao and Salmones Tecmar in 1999. These mergers and acquisitions transformed the industrial structure into an oligopoly in 2007, which is discussed in Chap. 4.

Table 6.1 Description of the main newly entering firms into the salmon industry in Chile (As of 2011)

Firms	Activities	Year entered aquaculture	Area of operation	Other activities	Origin of capital	Note
Salmones El Golfo/Blumer seafood	Cultivation center	2005/2011	XI	Extractive fishery and other seafood	Chile	Group Yaconi- Santa Cruz of Pesquera El Golf, extractive fishery merged with ITATA in 2011 as Blumer seafood
Salmones Itata/ BlumerSeafood	Cultivation center	2006/2011	XI	Extractive fishery	Chile	Controlled by Sarquis family, Fishmeal and fish oil. Merged with El Golfo, 2011
Salmones Humboldt	Cultivation center	2006/2011	X	Extractive fishery and other seafood	Chile/ Japan	Pesquera Coloso controlled by Chilean family Lecaros Menendez with group of business man; purchased by Mitsubishi (Japan) in 2011
Salmones Cupquelan	Cultivation center	2004/2008	XI	Seafood business	Iceland/ Canada	Icelandic holding controlled Robert Gudfinnsson the changed the owner to Cooke Aquaculture, Inc.
Salmones Aysen	Cultivation center	2006	XI	Extractive fishery, seafood	Chile/ USA	Icicle Seafoods y Pablo Barahona, of ex executive of Salmones Tecmar
Provi. Fish Farms	Cultivation center	2006	XI	Extractive fishery	Chile	Pesquera Landes
RiverFish	Cultivation center	2007	XII	Investor (multiple areas)	Chile	Algeciras S A owned by Eduardo Elberg (investor, real estate, automovile, super-market Santa Isabel)
Tornegaleones	Cultivation center	N.R.	XII	Investor (salmon industry)	Chile	Eblen group, Ex owner of Mainstream. Also owner of Marine Farm GMT, Salmones Andes etc.
Australis Mar S. A.	Cultivation center, processing plant, egg and smolt production	2008	XI, XII, IX	Food but con-trolled by invest-ment firm	Chile	Belong to Australis Food Holding but run by the group of investors

(continued)

Table 6.1 (continued)

Firms	Activities	Year entered aquaculture	Area of operation	Other activities	Origin of capital	Note
FoodCorp S. A./ Pacific seafood	Cultivation center	2008	XI	Seafood business	Norway	Leroy group
Acuimag S. A.	Fresh water phase center egg, smolts	2007	XII	Investor (controlled by investment firms)	Chile	Galmez family former owner of Almacenes Paris acquired 80 % of company

Note: N.R. = no records
Source: compiled by the author based on Revista Aqua issue: March 2007, March 2008 and November, 2011

two global seafood giants, Cooke Aquaculture Inc. and Leroy Groups, are included among the new entrants in Chile. The third group of firms are those owned by investing companies. These new firms located their production sites in the 11th and 12th regions because the more favorable production sites in the 10th region were no longer available.

The new entrants transformed the structure and dynamics within the Chilean salmon industry.[21] These new entrants with different business backgrounds and without a shared history created an environment where collaboration and trust were even more difficult to generate. Furthermore, differences in the geographical location of production sites between older firms mainly in the 10th region and new firms mainly located in the 11th and 12th regions subsequently created differences in the degree of damages incurred by the ISA crisis, as ISA mainly affected the 10th region and then spread toward the south. Finally, unlike those incumbent firms whose mainstay of business was salmon farming, the new firms, having other businesses apart from salmon farming, were able to access bank loans even after the ISA crisis.

3.1.2 Role of Industrial Associations: The Association of the Salmon Industry

During the period of high growth, from the late 1990s to the early 2000s, the Association of the Salmon Industry (SalmonChile)[22] was instrumental in the development of the industry. The Association supported exporting salmon firms first by creating uniform quality standards[23] and, second by marketing to different destinations to protect and increase Chilean salmon's position in the global market. The Association also played a critical role in handling the accusation of dumping made by the USA, Canada, and the EU in 1997. Since then, the Association has actively made alliances both in Chile through opening its membership to suppliers of inputs and services, and abroad through extending its own network via establishing the Association of Salmon Producers in Chile, Canada, and the USA

[21] See Chap. 4 for more details.

[22] It was first established in 1986 and called the Association of Chilean Salmon and Trout Producers (APSTC). APSTC limited its membership to producers of salmon and trout. In 2002 it changed its name to SalmonChile and opened its membership to input and service providers.

[23] In the 2000s, the Association created voluntary standards of traceability and systems and quality assurance for the salmon industry in order to respond to increasing international requirements. Instituto Technologia de Salmon (The Salmon Technology Institute, INTESAL), an institute associated with SalmonChile, created Integrated Management Systems (Systema Integrado de Gestion: SIGES) combining major standards in the global market such as ISO, OSHA, HACCP, and best-practice guidelines. SalmonChile was trying to harmonize SIGES to global standards among the members of Salmon of the Americas in 2004. The harmonizing of standards continued until recently, as SalmonChile signed an agreement in 2010 to launch standards called SALMONGAP, the first internationally recognized standards for the cultivation of salmon in Chile following the GLOBAL GAP (Ibieta et al. 2011).

via creating Salmon of the Americas, the Pan-American association for salmon farming. These alliances were aimed to create leverage for future disputes.

The Association (SalmonChile) was well accepted by firms during the period of high growth and SalmonChile acted on behalf of the salmon industry on various occasions both in Chile and abroad. Member as well as non-member firms gained from externality and spillover from their activities in training and trade and technological missions. In Chile, the Association had an important role in negotiating policy decisions regarding aquaculture with the government.[24] The Association was also active in dealing with accusations from Chilean and international NGOs (EcoOceano, Fundación Terram, OCEANO, WWF, Oxfam) and international media on various issues from labor to the environment.

During the high-growth period between the late 1990s and 2007, leading up to the ISA crisis, the industry was in a state of oligopoly (see Chap. 4) and SalmonChile's member firms controlled almost 90 % of total exports of Chilean salmon. In this context, the Association was considered to be the legitimate representative of the salmon industry. Most of the small and medium firms were not members of SalmonChile; however, as they had common external enemies—be they NGOs, buyers or government—these firms were able to enjoy the positive externality from the work done by SalmonChile[25]; hence it is not an overstatement to say that SalmonChile *represented* the whole industry until the early 2000s. The dynamics, however, gradually changed with the emergence of new entrants from the middle of the first decade of the 2000s and transformed significantly after the outbreak of ISA at the end of 2007.

3.2 The Public Sector Before the Crisis: Undersecretariat of Fisheries and National Fisheries Service

3.2.1 The Evolution of Public Organizations for the Aquaculture Sector

The Undersecretariat of Fisheries and the National Fisheries Service are the two main public organizations dealing with fishery resources. The role of these two institutions during the 1970s, 1980s, and 1990s regarding aquaculture, particularly the salmon industry, was more developmental than regulatory, trying to encourage the incipient salmon farming industry to grow rather than to regulate its activities. This was because "there was nothing to regulate as the scale of production was not so big" (interview, Ms. Saa 2011).

[24] In the early 2000s, the Association took part in formulating the National Aquaculture Policy (PNA) by the National Aquaculture Commission, and was a party to signing the cleaner production agreement with public sector organizations at the regional level.

[25] This view was also shared by the Mr. Odebret, the Manager of SalmonChile (interview, Mr. Odebret 2011).

One of the first significant regulations concerning aquaculture was the General Law of Fishery and Aquaculture (LGPA) in 1991. However, LGPA was mostly about extractive fishery and very little reference was made to aquaculture except for the following two issues: clarifying the responsibilities of public organizations[26] with regard to aquaculture; and establishing the method of identifying the areas appropriate for the conduct of aquaculture (AAA). These were aimed at simplifying the legal procedures to promote aquaculture while avoiding possible conflicts with existing extractive fishery by restricting the areas of operation by AAA.

Several additional regulations concerning aquaculture activities were established in the 1990s. These are: the Supreme Decree No. 475(1994) to define the use of Chile's littoral coastline by the Ministry of National Defence, DS No. 499 (1994); the National Register of Aquaculture and DS No. 464 (1995) to disclose information about fishery and aquaculture activities; and the Basic Environmental Law (LBMA), which took effect in 1994 (Law No. 19.300) and obliged firms to incorporate the Environmental Impact Assessment System (SEIA) before starting any aquaculture activities. In general, the basic legal infrastructure on how to coordinate aquaculture was established in the 1990s. However, several interviews with the policy makers suggest that these regulations were not considered the priority at that time; nor were they based on rigorous scientific evidence.

3.2.2 Sentiment Among the Public Sector Towards the Salmon Farming Industry from 2000 Until the Crisis

In the early 2000s, the government recognized the importance of aquaculture in the national economy. The first action taken by the public sector was promoting its growth further. The Undersecretariat of Fisheries established the National Commission for Aquaculture in 2001 and created the National Aquaculture Policy (PNA) in 2003, aiming to develop the industry with a clear target: to double the value of exports of salmon in 10 years from US$1200 million in 2004 to US$2400 million by 2014 (interview, Mr. Norambuena 2011; interview, Mr. Sandoval 2011). In addition to the above, supportive measures for the industry were taken, especially to speed up the granting of concession rights.[27] As a result, granting of concessions increased significantly from 2003 to 2005 (Iizuka and Katz 2011) (see Fig. 6.4) and changed the proportion of distribution of salmon cultivation sited in the Regions.

---

[26] These were the Office of the Undersecretariat of the Marine, the Office of the Undersecretariat of Fisheries, the National Fisheries Service, the Hydrographic and Oceanographic Service of Marine, the General Water Authority, the National Commission for Environment, and the General Treasury of the Republic. Many organizations were involved in permitting aquaculture; hence the law was created to simplify the procedure.

[27] In order to cultivate salmon in the open ocean, firms were required to obtain concession rights; however, this process took rather a long time (on average between 7 and 8 years (interview, Mr. Sandoval 2011). A shorter process was achieved during the period 2003–2006. This corresponds to the period when Mr. Sandoval was Undersecretary of Fisheries.

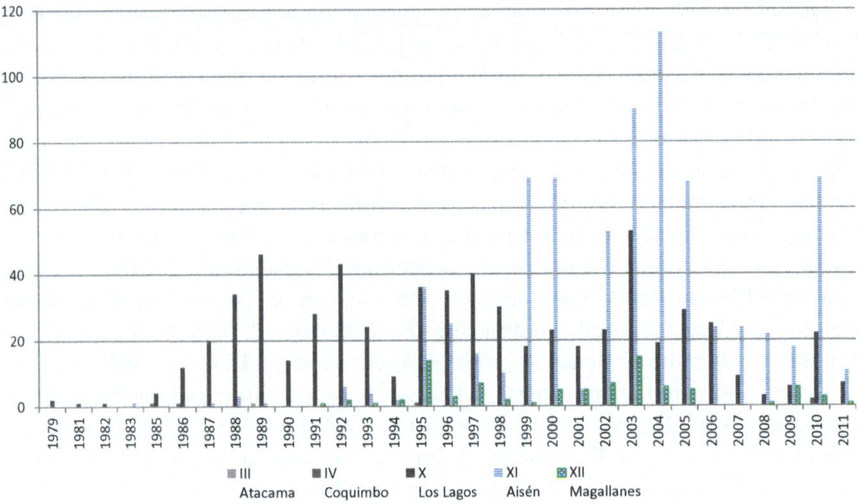

Fig. 6.4 Growth of concession rights granted by the Undersecretariat of Fisheries (*Source*: Undersecretariat of Fisheries. Note: *2011 is preliminary figure)

Parallel to the government's active support of the industry, regulatory measures were also being introduced due to: (1) the growing impact of the industry's increasing scale of production on the environment; and (2) increasing international pressures to have regulatory measures of a global standard for bilateral trade agreements. As a result, the following regulations—DS No. 320 on environmental regulations for aquaculture (RAMA) and DS No. 626 on measures for protection, control and eradication of high-risk diseases for hydrobiological species (RESA)—were both passed in 2001. These regulations required firms to comply with international environmental and sanitary standards; nevertheless, no additional resources were provided for enforcement and monitoring of these regulations (interview, Mr. Norambuena 2011). Hence, even though the regulations existed in as early as 2001, these were not effectively enforced due to a combination of pro-growth sentiment within the country, a lack of resources for enforcement, and a lack of motivation by the firms. In such an environment, private–public agreement schemes for controlling and monitoring the environment and sanitary performance were taken (i.e. Clean Development Agreement (Acuerdos Produccion Limpia: APL)) during this period.

In the early 2000s, the industry grew successfully and the government promoted this growth. While the regulatory institutions were being established, neither budget nor strong political will were present to enforce them. The public sector relied on the private sector's capacity to self-regulate member firms on enforcement of environmental and sanitary regulations. With almost all the large and important players belonging to SalmonChile, which accounted for 92 % of total exports, SalmonChile was the legitimate entity to coordinate the activities of the industry. This self-regulation and governance under SalmonChile had reached its peak in the period just before the ISA crisis because the government "left the industry alone" during 2006–2007 (interview, Mr. Sandoval 2011).[28]

4 Situation During and After the Crisis

4.1 Behavior of Firms After the Crisis

In July 2007, the ISA virus was officially detected in Chile (Sernapesca 2008). Although the seriousness of this disease was well understood by the farming community at the time of its discovery, this incident was considered as strictly a sanitary problem that could easily be contained in the Los Lagos (the 10th region) (Ibeita et al. 2011). Firms had never imagined that this incident would lead to a serious crisis that will transform the Chilean salmon industry within a very short period.

The initial actions taken by the affected firms were threefold: (1) search for the cure and a technological solution to the ISA virus; (2) reduce operation costs by laying off employees at the suspended cultivation centers and associated processing plants; and (3) transfer salmon farming operations to the non-contaminated area in the south, in the Austral regions (Aysen and Magallanes) (the 11th and 12th regions). These were the "reactionary" measures taken by the firms. No one imagined at the beginning that these actions would lead to a chain of incidents that would eventually transform the institutions within the industry.

4.1.1 Finding the Technological Solutions: G6

At the beginning of the crisis, several attempts were made by a group of large firms to control the situation. The so-called G6 (Salmones Mainstream, Salmones Multiexport, AquaChile, Camanchaca, Los Fiordos, and Marine Harvest), the six large exporting salmon firms and the large producers of Atlantic salmon in Chile, got together and tried to find a solution to ISA (Aqua.cl, 21 Nov. and 11 Dec. 2007). They invited international and domestic experts on ISA and representatives of Chile's public sector to organize a seminar in order to find a way to control the situation. The G6 also participated in technical missions sending government officials to salmon producers in the Faroe Islands, Canada, and Norway, trying to find a solution to this problem (Aqua.cl, 3 July 2008). Various technical options were explored such as vaccines and medications; however, it soon became evident

[28] No contact was made between the Undersecretary of Fisheries and SalmonChile between 2006 and 2007. This is due to the difference in the priority put on this sector (more on small-scale fishery) by the new Undersecretary of Fisheries, a successor of Mr. Sandoval, at that time (interview, Mr. Sandoval 2011).

that ISA could not be solved by technological solutions alone; it required environmental management. The collective efforts of the G6 were short-lived and did not take the industry to the next level of collaboration.

At the early stage, efforts were made to identify the source of the virus in order to identify the infection route and the root causes. Marine Harvest, the Norwegian firm operating in Chile, was the first firm to report the presence of ISA and became a target for criticism for transmitting the disease. After studying the virus, however, it became evident that it had been present in Chile for some time but had not been reported officially (Alvial et al. 2009). The currently accepted source of the virus is imports of contaminated eggs from Norway, as it is difficult to detect the virus in the egg during the quarantine period. The virus was transmitted rapidly and spread quickly due to unsustainable production practices including overcrowding of the fish stock in cultivation tanks (Iizuka and Katz 2011). On the whole, the process of finding the cause of ISA exposed various faults in the current production system such as overreliance on imported eggs, excessive use of antibiotics in feed, too much of a concentration of cultivation sites in a small area, no resting period (fallowing) between cycles of production, overlapping production schedules among producers in similar areas, not to mention overcrowding of fish stocks in each cultivation center.

As a result of a series of discussions at the Roundtable, SalmonChile took the initiative in creating a new system of production in 2008 (Aqua.cl, 21 Nov. 2008). This included 44 suggested measures for improvement, monitored and measured by INTESAL (The Salmon Technology Institute), the associated institute of SalmonChile, and including sanitary controls on farming practices. The main points of these 44 measures are as follows:

1. Production coordination: establish a *barrio* (neighborhood of concessions) where all the firms participate in joint management of sanitary and environmental conditions by complying with measures such as resting periods (fallowing) and biosecurity.
2. Control of eggs and smolt: improve control of sanitary conditions for both imported and national eggs to reduce risks of contamination. This includes control of domestic eggs by INTESAL via certification and implementation of government quarantine for imported eggs.
3. Restrictions on rearing smolt in lakes and tanks: install biosecurity measures and series of restrictions.
4. Restrictions on the transport of fish: prohibit the transport of fish contaminated or suspected of being contaminated with the virus.
5. Improved biosecurity of freshwater sites: conduct diagnostic tests to check minimum biosecurity, incorporating a program of routine inspection controlled by INTESAL. (Adapted from Aqua.cl, 21 Nov. 2008)

Forty out of 44 suggestions made by SalmonChile were included in the measures later published by the government in Ley Acuicultura (Ley 20.434). In other words, modification of LGPA at the regulatory level was not solely a top–down process by the government but very much a bottom–up process as well. At the same time, it is noteworthy that the initial suggestions made by the Association insisted on self-regulatory methods of enforcement by its subsidiary organization, INTESAL (Aqua.cl, 17 Mar. 2008).

4.1.2 Layoff of Employees: Leading to Fierce Union Conflicts and Affecting the Regional Economy

In 2008, many cultivation centers were suspended from salmon production due to the ISA virus in the Los Lagos (the 10th region). This not only stopped production at the cultivation centers but also left subsidiary processing plants without work. As a consequence, in the short period from 2007 to 2009, the industry reduced 60 % of its labor force. The salmon industry, over the years, had employed 90,000 people (35,000 direct and 55,000 indirect) in the 10th region where there are very few alternative economic activities. The measures taken by firms had a major impact on the regional economy (Iizuka and Katz 2011).

In fact, fierce labor disputes at the regional level followed, involving unions such as the Labor Union for Salmon Industry (La CONTRASAL: Confederacion Nacional de Trabajadores del Salmon de Chile). Union actions gradually started to involve violence, such as the takeover of a plant by the workers protesting job cuts. The situation had worsened and reached to the level where SalmonChile had to ask the government to intervene.

The unemployment issue, since this incident, was incorporated as a key issue for the Roundtable. The union movement, however, did not die away. Instead, it started to involve NGOs and the international media to generate a wider public awareness campaign, making it very difficult for the industry to ignore. As a result, SalmonChile started to help workers find jobs (the project was called RED SALMON). This is still an incipient attempt but a step towards social corporate responsibility.

The labor dispute left bitter feelings among the firms and labor unions, and some firms were reported to have suppressed union activities. On the other hand, through these incidents, firms discovered that the local community held favorable perceptions of the presence of the salmon industry in the region despite some disagreements about the way the business was run (Aqua.cl, 8 August 2008). The opinion survey (Kapital social, 2011) made it apparent that the large majority of the local community think of this industry as necessary for improving their livelihood via its generation of jobs. These sentiments may provide support for the industry against campaigns on salmon farming by international NGOs and media (interview, Mr. Perez 2011).

4.1.3 Exodus of the Salmon Firms to Austral Regions (11th and 12th Regions): Raising Fear and Resentment in the Regions

Due to the spread of ISA in the Los Lagos (the 10th region), many large firms started to relocate their cultivation sites to the south, first to the Aysen (the 11th region) then to the Magallanes (the 12th region). The increase in the number of applications submitted to the government for concession rights demonstrates how the ISA incident created a massive exodus of firms towards these two regions. There were already limited areas for cultivation in Los Lagos (the 10th region) but the ISA crisis accelerated the move towards the southern Austral regions. The boom in applications started in 2007 in the Aysen with an increase of applications from 962 to 1,249 by 2008. In 2008, the authority gave out 520 concessions to the Aysen, while the Los Lagos got 391 out of 474 applications (Aqua.cl, 12 Nov. 2009). In the Magallanes, there were only 14 concessions before 2007. This has increased to 70 in 2008 and by 2010 the government had received 1600 applications (Aqua.cl, 18 Nov. 2009).

The rapidly increasing presence of the salmon industry in the Aysen and Magallanes alarmed regional stakeholders such as small-scale fishermen, the tourism industry, and civil society, just to mention a few. Their concerns were expressed via relevant representatives (civil society, NGOs such as ECOCEANO, AustroChile: La Asociación Magallánica de Empresas de Turismo, etc.) to the various regional authorities (governors, senators, congressmen). Concerns of the regional stakeholders were justified when the epicenter of the ISA virus gradually moved towards these southern regions. The rapid migration of farming activities without any changes in production methods led to the rapid transmission of the ISA virus to the southern regions. The ISA virus was soon detected in the Magallanes in the latter part of 2008 (Aqua.cl, 3 July 2008) and by the beginning of 2009, Sernapesca officially declared the Aysen the new epicenter of the ISA virus, with a total of 31 cultivation centers under suspicion of ISA out of 51 at the national level (Aqua.cl, 12 Jan. 2009).

As a result, despite the positive economic impacts the industry had, the regional authorities expressed concern over the rapid expansion of salmon farming activities in the regions without proper environmental assessment or coastal planning, and warned of potential conflicts with existing regional economic activities. To appease fears of the rapidly increasing presence of the salmon industry in the regions, SalmonChile had to make an official statement agreeing that development would take place with consideration given to sound regional coastal planning and the identification of appropriate areas for aquaculture (AAA).

The rapid exodus of the salmon industry towards southern regions created a need to integrate this activity into the regional zoning plans. The decision-making process of zoning and regional planning would require the involvement of a wider set of agents, including regional government. The initial actions taken by the firms—searching for a cure, laying off workers, and moving production sites to the south—created a wave of reactions and created challenges for the industry and authorities. In particular, each incident added new agents such as associations, labor unions, regional government, and regional agents into an already complex network of stakeholders.

4.2 Parallel Incidents and Additional Agents: Extending the Influence via Global Value Chains

Apart from the above process taking place within the industry, various reactions were also being observed at different levels owing to global nature of this business.

4.2.1 International Media Influences the Behavior of International Buyers and Consumers

The Chilean salmon industry came under the scrutiny of the international media as a result of globalization. As the ISA crisis started to unfold, the *New York Times* (*NYT*) published a critical article about the practice of salmon farmers in Chile on 27 May 2008. The article accused the industry of environmental malpractice and overuse of antibiotics. These claims were not new, as similar claims had already been made by domestic NGOs (such as Fundación Terram and ECOCEANO) as early as the beginning of 2000. Nevertheless, the accusations made by a widely distributed and well-respected international newspaper such as the *NYT* had different impacts on international buyers and consumers (Barton and Floysand 2010). Soon after the publication of this article, an international buyer in the USA, Safeway, announced a reduction in its salmon procurement from Chile. All the stakeholders related to the industry in Chile—SalmonChile, the Chilean government agencies, Chilean Chambers of Commerce (SOFOFA), and the Chilean Embassy in the USA—rushed to defend the industry against the claims by the *NYT*; nevertheless, similar media coverage of the salmon industry continued: *The Economist* (30 June 2009, "Chile's stricken salmon farms: Dying assets, a bankrupt industry faces reform"), *Nature* (17 June 2010, "Call for cooperation to contain damage by Chile's salmon farms") and *Time* magazine (22 June 2010, "The price of Chilean Salmon") all questioned the environmental sustainability of this industry. These international media put the production methods of the Chilean salmon industry under the scrutiny of international buyers and consumers. In other words, as the industry came to be recognized as an important player at the global level, international media became an additional monitoring and enforcement mechanism to shape the behavior of firms and of the industry.

4.2.2 Local NGOs: Building International and Local Networks

Another important feature is the growing power of Chilean NGOs working on the sustainability of the salmon industry. There has been an increase in the number of environmental NGOs in Chile[29] since the end of the 1990s and particularly in the early 2000s. These local NGOs started to make alliances with international NGOs as well as with local civil movements from the latter half of the first decade of the 2000s.

For instance, in 2006, a joint venture among international and domestic NGOs, such as Oxfam, Terram, Canela de Nos, CENDA and the National Trade Union Confederation (CUT), created an organization called OLACH[30]—the labor and environment observatory of Chile—in July 2006 (Barton and Floysand 2010). Following the establishment of OLACH, several campaigns against unsustainable salmon farming practices took place, such as a joint campaign between Oxfam and Fundación Terram under the slogan "Sin miedo contra la corriente" ('Against the current without fear') in 2008 as well as the "Pure salmon campaign" by a Norway-based NGO in the middle of the first decade of the 2000s. The tactics and financial bases of these Chilean NGOs have also become more sophisticated as they collaborate with the international media to pressure the industry through influencing international buyers and consumers. These NGOs, unlike in earlier times, have started to gain more power in influencing international consumers and buyers through their extended networks and eventually started to influence the issues at the local level.

4.2.3 Financial Debt and Banks: Influencing the Firms' Financial Viability

Large private salmon firms continued to invest in their businesses even after the crisis until mid-2008. These investments were mainly made in order to: (1) transfer their production sites to Austral (southern) regions; and (2) secure a supply of domestic eggs and smolt (freshwater phase) to deal with tighter restriction on imports of eggs. Major exporters such as AquaChile, Marine Harvest, Multiexports, Salmones Friosur, and Pesca Chile all planned to invest in closed system pisciculture equipped with recycled water plants. In addition to the large existing players, new entrants to this business (Salmones el Golfo, Humboldt, Itata etc.) also made substantial investments in infrastructure and acquisition of cultivation centers in 2008.

---

[29] Detail is documented in Iizuka (2003).

[30] As of 2013, OLACH does not seem to be in operation.

When a decrease in salmon production became evident in 2009, banks started to show concern over loans made to salmon firms (Baillarie et al. 2010). The common practice of banks to make loans for the salmon industry was to take the salmon (biomass) as collateral. Hence banks were in trouble when they learned that their collateral was dying of the ISA virus. The financial issues soon developed into a debt crisis and became an important task to be solved by the Salmon Roundtable.

The debt crisis had differentiated impacts on firms and influenced power dynamics within the salmon industry. From the latter half of 2008 to 2009, salmon firms started to divide into "winners" and "losers." The winners were those who were less affected by the ISA virus either because they had cultivation sites in the less affected locations of Aysen and Magallanes,[31] had taken sanitary management methods,[32] or produced less affected species such as coho and trout.[33] The losers, on the other hand, were those whose cultivation centers were in Los Lagos,[34] who followed intensive production methods, and who farmed the most affected type of salmon, salar (Atlantic) salmon.

The debt crisis enlarged the financial gap between these winners and losers. As discussed earlier in Sect. 3.1 (Table 6.1), the new entrants consisted of firms that were relatively smaller, whose cultivation sites were in the Aysen and Magallanes (the 11th and 12th regions), and who had alternative economic activities apart from salmon. In other words, these firms were, in general, less affected by the ISA virus and were able to get the banks' financial support for further investment, while most of incumbent large firms struggled to do so. These differences in access to finances transformed into differences in export capacity. Figure 6.5 shows that the share of exports by the top five firms decreased during this period while the proportion by the rest of the firms increased from 2008 to 2010. The growing gap in capacity to invest created further power relations among the large salmon producers, and was particularly complex within SalmonChile.

---

[31] These are mainly the new entrant firms. For instance, Salmones Cupquelan, whose cultivation center was in a secluded area in Aysen (the 11th region), was considered to be one that may have had good sanitary management until its cultivation site was also affected by the ISA virus in 2011.

[32] Salmones Friosur was considered to be one, as it was not affected by ISA for a long time. It was suspected that it might have had different sanitary management due to more experience in sanitary conditions as it also deals with chicken and pork.

[33] Those firms that produced a higher percentage of salmon coho, for example, Mirasol.

[34] For instance, Marine Harvest was the top exporter in 2007 but in the first half of 2011, it is the 11th exporter of salmon by value.

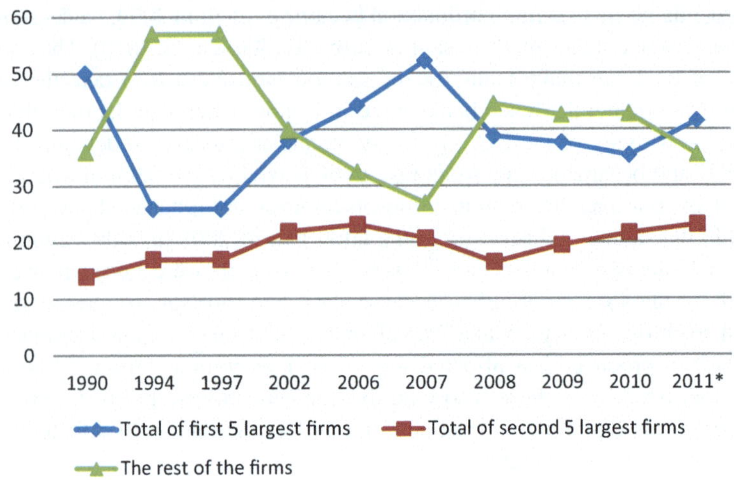

Fig. 6.5 Share (%) of exports by size of firms (*Source*: Based on Bjorndal and Aaland (1999), *Aquanoticias*, May 2002, *Revista Aqua*, 2008, 2010)

4.3 Subsequent Impact on the Salmon Industry in Chile

4.3.1 SalmonChile: Changes in Power Dynamics Among the Member Firms

In 2008, salmon firms were faced with various managerial challenges: (1) increased price of fish feed (feed consists of 30 % of total production cost; see Chap. 4) rising commodity prices (soy, fish oil etc.) ; (2) scarcity of eggs due to tighter restriction of imports via the Resolution of ISA 1803 of 2008; and (3) impact left by the ISA crisis on the performance of firms which are varied due to portfolios of products (percentage of Atlantic salmon), the locations of their production sites (whether they were in Los Lagos, the 10th region or not), and access to finances.

These challenges caused by ISA crisis influenced internal power dynamics within SalmonChile. For instance, a number of salmon firms, particularly those new entrants with extractive fishery origins (such as Salmones Itata, Golfo, Humbolt), accelerated investments in new cultivation sites as well as in freshwater plants (in Biobio, the 9th region) while many incumbent firms had difficulty getting funds for investment. It is easy to imagine that there were growing tensions between new entrants and the incumbent large firms. The tensions among the large firms led to the departure of AquaChile—the founding member and the pioneer of Chilean salmon farming—from SalmonChile in 2009. Other large players in the industry, such as Invertec Pesquera Mar de Chiloe and Salmones Antartica, also left SalmonChile in 2009. Relatively smaller firms such as Trusal and Marine Farm GMT followed suit in 2010.

The reasons for the departure of the above five firms were slightly different. AquaChile wanted to have stricter preventive measures against ISA, namely greater distance between cultivation centers (3.2 km) to ensure the sustainability of operations, while other firms (mainly those of extractive fishery origin such as Camanchaca, Itata, Golfo, Humboldt, etc.) wanted a slightly shorter distance (2 km) (Aqua.cl, 2 Sept. 2010). The shorter distance between cultivation centers would generate a greater number of concessions for those who could still acquire the sites to expand their productive capacity, especially in the Aysen and Magallanes (the 11th and 12th regions). On the other hand, AquaChile and other large producers already held the most concessions and were more interested in ensuring sanitary conditions (Aqua.cl, 2 Sept. 2010; Undersecretariat of Fisheries (Subsecretaria de Pesca) 2010). Invertec Pesquero Mar de Chiloe left the Association due to a disagreement about who would supervise and monitor compliance with the sanitary rules. At that time, the Association was trying to establish self-regulation by creating a committee inside the Association, consisting of selected representatives of firms, to determine the suspension of cultivation centers in cases of non-compliance. In the interview in Aqua.cl, the CEO of Invertec clearly expressed that he was against being monitored and evaluated by competitor firms (Aqua.cl, 8 July 2010). On the other hand, Salmones Antartica and Trusal left the Association in 2009 and in 2010 respectively due to dissatisfaction with the disproportionate representation that SalmonChile had (Aqua.cl, 20 Sept. 2010). All of the above indicate that power dynamics within the SalmonChile changed significantly.

At the beginning of the crisis in 2007 SalmonChile's member firms (25 producers and 50 suppliers) consisted of 92 % of total Chilean salmon exports (Aqua.cl, 18 Jan. 2008). In December of 2011 Salmon Chile represented about 70 % of total exports with 34 firms (of which 17 were pisiculture and 14 suppliers) (interview, Mr. Odebret 2011). Despite some decline in the share of representation in terms of export value, SalmonChile was still a dominant player in the salmon industry. Its role within the industry as the "representative" nevertheless changed significantly after the crisis.

4.3.2 Rise of the Rest: ACOTRUCH and Association of Service Providers

4.3.2.1 Creation of ACOTRUCH by Small and Medium Salmon Producers

In September 2009, a new association of salmon farming industry, the Association for Producers of Coho salmon and Trout of Chile (ACOTRUCH), was established among five small and medium coho and trout salmon producers in Chile (Comercial Mirasol S. A., Cultivos Marinos Lago Yelcho S. A., Salmones Aysen S. A., Salmones Caleta Bay S. A.). These producers produce mainly coho salmon and trout, types of salmon not affected by ISA. The Association was established due to their dissatisfaction that their voices were not being well represented in the current setting of SalmonChile. ACOTRUCH was soon incorporated into the Commission Nacional de Acuicultura and started to participate in discussions at the Roundtable.

ACOTRUCH considered that the government favored Atlantic salmon producers while penalizing non- Atlantic salmon producers in their handling of the crisis. For instance, joint management of the *barrio* included coordination of the production calendar. This was difficult for small and medium-scale coho and trout producers. First, coho, trout and Atlantic salmon are different species and have distinctive production calendars; second, smaller producers that did not have alternative cultivation sites in different *barrios* were forced to go out of business during the 3 months of the fallowing period. Furthermore, complying with numerous biosecurity measures to prevent the re-occurrence of ISA was costly for smaller producers without economies of scale, while these measures largely benefit the larger Atlantic salmon producers.

ACOTRUCH attracted new member firms since its establishment.[35] Some of these firms are former member of SalmonChile. In other words, alternative organizations to SalmonChile are on the rise to change the power balance.

4.3.2.2 Association of Suppliers

Suppliers of services were strongly affected by the crisis, especially from 2009 to 2010[36] due to decline in demand (interview, Ms. Zorzano 2011). The formal supplier firms[37] were represented by the associations, such as Association of Net and Net Service Industries (ATARED), the Association of Regional Ship-owners and Maritime Services (ARASEMAR), and the Association of Diving Companies (ADEB) (all established in 2001), the Association of Veterinary Laboratories (ALAVET) and the Association of Southern Ship-owners (ARMASUR). In 2011, the Association of Transport was created. Almost all the associations were established in the early 2000s.

In 2011, five different associations of service suppliers (ATARED, ARASEMAR, ADEB, ARMASUR and ALAVET) came together to make a joint claim (interview, Ms. Zorzano 2011). They felt that they were left out from the process of creating a new production system for the salmon industry, even though their activities were closely linked with the industry and would be subject to monitoring by the new regulations. In fact, they were not included in discussions neither at the National Commission for Aquaculture nor at the Roundtable. In order for their positions and realities to be reflected in the new system, they jointly demanded the following: (1) the government to focus on its original responsibility—making regulations through the Undersecretariat of Fisheries, and monitoring

---

[35] The following firms joined ACOTRUCH in addition to the original founding members: Salmones Chile, Salmones Ice Val in 2009, Piscola Entre Rios and Sea Salmon Ltda in 2010, and Trusal in 2011. Trusal left SalmonChile to join ACOTRUCH.

[36] The shock from ISA did not affect the suppliers immediately. Even after the suspension of cultivation sites, washing and maintenance work on nets continued.

[37] There is a high percentage of informal activities in the service suppliers of the salmon industry.

and enforcement through National Fisheries Service—rather than diversifying into other activities; (2) Fishery management to be decentralized at the regional level in order to reflect regional realities; (3) IFOP to be strengthened as the independent public research institute with its own budget to formulate research for regulatory purposes; and (4) salmon farming industry to treat suppliers of inputs and services fairly.

Parallel to making claims for their position in the salmon farming industry, suppliers of services also made strategic decisions. They acted collectively to integrate common areas of operation, such as treatment of waste materials and setting standards for services, and jointly diversified their market to include areas beyond Chile, such as Brazil and Peru. The Association, after over a decade of existence, established a trusting relationship among the member firms and obtained the capacity to represent and negotiate with the government and the salmon industry. However, even with the increasing importance of their voice, the ISA crisis made them aware that depending on the Chilean salmon industry alone was a risky strategy. With this new understanding in place, their negotiating power with the industry and its presence may further transform its structure in future.

5 Unexpected Outcome of the Modification of the Law

The Ley de Acuicultura (Aquaculture Law: Ley No. 40.434) has outlined a framework for controlling the sanitation and environmental conditions in the new production system for the salmon industry. Effective implementation depends on the willingness to convert the framework into implementable measures and actually enforce them. The trial-and-error process of implementation gave rise to some unexpected outcomes.

For instance, the National Fisheries Service encountered several challenges in actually implementing contingency measures when it had to act upon the detection of ISA in the 11th region in 2011. Although the law and regulations were in place and firms were willing to comply, due to a lack of infrastructure (such as a processing plant, a port with biosecurity measures, etc.) it was not possible either to dispose of the contaminated salmon (biomass) on site or to secure a biologically safe route to transport it to the nearby port. Furthermore, unlike the Agriculture and Livestock Service (SAG), the National Fisheries Service does not have overruling power. This means that its decision to suspend plant operation or disposal of biomass may require a court order if a firm refuses to accept the decision. This lack of ultimate authority may endanger the sanitary conditions in an emergency, particularly when dealing with diseases about which there is little shared knowledge among the firms.

The lack of authority by the National Fisheries Service and Undersecretariat of Fisheries may stem from the absence of a scientific base in setting up regulatory measures or norms. As the study by Bravo et al. (2007) indicates (see Chap. 4), much of the research conducted in aquaculture had been aimed at mainly enhancing production capabilities and did not address fundamental research issues specific to the Chilean context, such as environmental carrying capacity based on local specific natural conditions stemming from oceanography, biology, and geography. Hence it became apparent that investment was needed in research on this area, particularly to establish regulations that fit local environmental and biological conditions. Currently, increasing the role of the Instituto de Formento Pesquero (Fisheries Development Institute, IFOP) in aquaculture is being discussed. IFOP has been actively involved in forming regulations and norms (such as decisions over fishing quotas and prohibition periods) in extractive fisheries. It is said that part of the income from the increase in fees for concession rights is used to finance research by IFOP for applied research to formulate policy.

Firms' access to finance did not improve very much even after the modification of LGPA, which transformed concession rights into transferable property to be used as collateral when firms applied for bank loans. Unlike banks in Norway, which have accumulated information about the salmon farming industry, the majority of Chilean banks were not able to evaluate the value of concessions correctly because each concession site has different characteristics (location, area, size, and biological and environmental conditions). These banks preferred stocks over concession rights for guaranteeing loans. As a result, many large-scale firms, such as AquaChile (2011), Camanchaca (2010) and Australis (2011), opened on the stock market and those already on the stock market, such as Multiexport Foods (2007) and Invertec (2005), added their capital in 2010. In other words, these firms' strategic decisions are now dependent on shareholders and banks. It is not difficult to imagine that these investors—either domestic or international—are now the new subject of influence by the international media and NGOs. These co-evolutionary outcomes from modification of LGPA are gradually making the institutions more complex and global in structure, involving new and different stakeholders.

In 2010, after the completion of modifications to the LGPA, the public–private Roundtable was re-established by the Minister of Economy in an attempt to maintain a space for dialogue among various agents from both the private and public sectors to define implementation and enforcement measures, including representatives of two associations (SalmonChile, ACOTRUCH), private firms, the adviser to the Ministry of Economy, the Unit of Animal Health (Subdirection of Aquaculture, National Fisheries Service), the Undersecretariat of Fisheries, and other related agents. The Roundtable was divided into five thematic groups: Institutions, Territorial Planning, Productivity Model, Infrastructure, and Research and Science. The public sector, represented by the Undersecretariat of Fisheries, the National Fisheries Service, and the Ministry of Economy, coordinated each thematic group. This space for discussion among distinct agents in the sector was considered useful in identifying effective enforceable solutions in the sector and it was suggested that this organization should become a permanent body as Mesa de Salmon[38] (the Salmon Roundtable) in January 2012 (Sernapesca 2012).

---

[38] This Mesa de Salmon, although the name is the same, is different from the one organized in 2008.

6 Conclusion and Lessons Drawn from This Chapter

This chapter tried to capture the institutional transformation process using the case of the salmon industry before and after the ISA crisis in 2007. The ISA crisis was a key event because it clearly exposed the change that was taking place at distinctive levels: regulatory, normative, and cognitive. The regulatory change, the modification of the General Law of Fishery (Ley General de Pesca No. 18.892) by the Ley Acuicultura (Ley No. 20.434), officially created the following changes: strengthening the role of the Undersecretariat of Fisheries and the National Fisheries Service to regulate firms' activities concerning sanitary management of aquaculture, and creating a mechanism of concession rights and new institutions—*barrios* and macrozones—to manage sanitary conditions in production centres. Looking just at these regulatory changes suggest a top–down institutional shift towards stronger governance by the public sector from a market-oriented model that is more familiar to Chile.

We examined the historical context before and after the crisis and learned that the changes in regulatory institutions—the modification of LGPA by the Ley Acuicultura—was partly the outcome of a gradual and more profound co-evolutional change among stakeholders over the years. When we observe the public sector, the Undersecretariat of Fisheries and the National Fisheries Service had made de facto organizational changes before the crisis in an attempt to adjust the monitoring activities to more closely reflect actual economic activity. When we look at the industry, we see that seeds of change in the existing industrial dynamics had already been planted in the period leading up to the crisis in 2007, as follows: the emergence of new entrants in the middle of the first decade of the 2000s; reports on deteriorating ecological and biological conditions in production sites starting in the 2000s; the establishment of a labor union for the salmon industry (Contrasal) in 2006; the emergence of domestic NGOs working on sustainability of the salmon industry since the late 1990s; the consolidation of suppliers of services to the salmon industry (small and medium sized) in the form of associations since the early 2000s; and growing attention of international media to the industry since the middle of the first decade of the 2000s. These small events cumulatively started to form the new institutions, "a system of social factors that conjointly generate a regularity of behavior" (Greif 2006, 30). Nevertheless, the above changes were not clearly articulated until the crisis.

Under the current institutions-in-the-making, governance of self-regulation by SalmonChile is no longer the "legitimate" option as it was in the past. Firm behavior is currently monitored constantly by various agents and influenced by the following: (1) civil society, particularly by local NGOs on environmental issues; (2) labor unions on labor issues, and (3) global media (such as the *NYT*, *Time*, *The Economist*, *Nature*); (4) investors and banks; (5) different associations of industries with conflicting interests (SalmonChile, ARCOTRUCH and associations of suppliers); (6) other sectoral (small fishery and tourist sector etc.) and regional

(regional planning, coastal use etc.) stakeholders; and (7) other firms in the same barrio, the new institutions to conform firms behaviour.

In face of such numerous monitoring entities, what the industry needed was a clear set of rules based on science to legitimize their actions with fair and transparent enforcement mechanisms. In other words, the strengthening of the regulatory power of government with more scientific rigor was a mutual, yet unconsciously negotiated, decision of all parties involved. If we apply the definitions of institutions by Scott (1995) mentioned earlier in this chapter, we can identify how the legislative level, Ley Acuicultura; the normative level, the actual actions and behaviors shown by agents; and the cognitive level, those shaped by international media, NGOs, labor unions, all interacted with each other, shaping the new institutional set ups.

With the above understandings, we can say that changes in the "rules of the game" to enhance state authority were not caused solely by the top–down attempt to improve sanitary management in the industry. The forces for change towards stronger state governance were also supported by bottom–up forces due to the vacuum in leadership created within the private sector, making this a two-way process.

There are still many unresolved issues for the practical implementation of existing law while various mechanisms, e.g. *barrios* and macrozones, are already in place to create new institutions. With such a mechanism in place, the authorities will eventually be able to fine-tune the regulations in accordance with geographical and natural conditions synchronized in a collaborative manner at the level of the *barrio* with scientific evidence. This will present a great challenge to the firms, which up until recently have been acting in an independent manner with regard to their decisions on when, how much, and how to produce. As has been demonstrated, institutional change cannot be achieved overnight; it requires many years of continuous alignment of interest among agents.

The current change in institutions in Chile is a step in the right direction towards sustainable aquiculture; nevertheless, whether the speed of institutional change can match the speed of biological and ecological degradation still remain as a question. Of course, we must not forget the current rapid changes taking place in Chilean society, represented by the emergence of civil society with an interest in the fair distribution of wealth, justice, sustainability, and governance over pecuniary interest. This overall maturity of society may hold the key to determining the speed and trajectory of institutional change in the future.

Several lessons can be drawn from examining the institutional transformation, taking the case of the salmon industry in Chile. First, the change in "the rule of law" is merely the tip of the iceberg of institutional change. The magnitude of dynamics can only be understood by examining the inner workings and processes of how such change came about because of its co-evolutional nature. This understanding may allow us to speculate about the future prospects and impacts of the change in "the rule of law." Second is the importance of creating a space for interaction between various agents, particularly involving the private and the public sector. Such space will provide opportunities to align the interests of different stakeholders both at the normative and cognitive levels. As we have observed in the creation of the new Mesa de Salmon, creating real changes in firms' behaviors requires cumulative efforts of building trust and understanding between different entities. The third point is a general lesson in creating a non-traditional export industry based on natural resources in developing countries. This process often suffers from lack of traditional institutions and local knowledge due to lack of prior history. If the industry successfully takes off and increases its scale, local environmental sustainability may collapse without a sound management system. The provision of institutions at an earlier stage to monitor sustainable environmental conditions would be critical for the sustainability of such economic activity.

Appendix: Some Further Institutional Changes Taking Place in Chile's Fishery Sector

Institutional change in Chile with regard to aquaculture is an ongoing process. The above chapter contained information until 2011. The following details some of the changes that have taken place while this chapter was being written.

The new fishery law (Ley de Pesca, Ley No. 20.657) was published in the official newspaper on 9 February 2013. This law focuses mainly on the extractive fishery part of the law, modifying the LGPA and its modifications (Ley No. 18.892); however, some of the issues apply to aquaculture (*Revista Aqua*, 9 Feb. 2013). Some of the principles demonstrated by this law (Ley No. 20.657) clearly show the change of perspective within the ministry and the sector as a whole towards managing natural resources for long-term economic activity. For instance, it is noteworthy that this law states that government's principal focus is 'sustainability of hydrobiological resources' rather than just 'administration of access to resources', as in the past. The following lists some of the main points of this law:

- The central issue of the new regulation is **sustainability of fishery resources**. The new law incorporates **maximum sustainable yield standards** so that resources can be used for the **medium and long term**. These criteria have been shared and evaluated by **international NGOs such as Greenpeace, OCEANA, and WWF**, among others.
- **Decisions need to be made according to scientific and biological criteria**, not just according to the high participation of stakeholders in the sector. Various scientific committees are to be created to support such a process.
- **Incorporate more social protection** for workers, such as incorporation of a social platform for industrial workers, including life insurance etc.
- **Strengthen research capacity** through creation of a National Research Programme for Fishery and Aquaculture. The basic research of this program will be done by the Instituto de Fomento Pesquero* (IFOP), whose budget will be directly dependent on the Ministry of Economy. The existing programme, administered by the Fishery Research Fund (Fondo de Investigacion pesquera:

FIP), will be integrated with the above programme. The evaluation system involving external evaluators will be established to evaluate quality of researches conducted by the program.
- **Strengthen the institutional capacity of the National Fisheries and Aquaculture Service**** to monitor and enforce regulation.

* Up to now the IFOP was an independent research organization; the budget from the government for contract research was not on budget basis (interview, IFOP, Mr Guzman 2011).

** The National Fisheries Service changed its name to the National Fisheries and Aquaculture Service by Ley No. 20.597 published in *Diario official*, 3 Aug. 2012.

As can be seen from the above, some changes are already taking place in the right direction, such as incorporation of the sustainability concept, incorporating third-party evaluation (NGOs etc.), emphasizing scientific rigour, transforming institutions to strengthen research (IFOP, FIP), incorporating and strengthening evaluation, checking (technical committees, incorporation of NGOs and others) and enforcement (strengthening the National Fishery and Aquaculture Service) mechanisms.

Source: Undersecretariat of Fisheries (Subsecretaria de Pesca), 23 Nov. 2012. www.sernapesca.cl (accessed 10 Feb. 2013).

References

Acemoglu, D., and J. Robinson. 2012. *Why nations fail: The origins of power, prosperity and poverty*. New York: Crown Publishers.

Alvial, A., J. Mancilla, and F. Avendano. 2009. *Aplicaciones del primer estudio Epidemiológico de ISAv en Chile, powerpoint presentation Mimeo.*

Aoki, M. 2007. Endogenizing institutions and institutional changes. *Journal of Institutional Economics* 3: 1–31.

Aqua.cl (various years; see below) *Revista Aqua*, Technopress, Santiago, Chile.

Baillarie, C., J. Kehdy, and P. Auszenker. 2010. Sector Salmones—Renace de una Industria> *Renta Variable*, Genencia de Estudios, BCI corridor de Bolsa.

Barton, J.R., and A. Floysand. 2010. The political ecology of Chilean salmon aquaculture, 1982–2010: A trajectory from economic development to global sustainability. *Global Environmental Change* 20: 739–752.

Bjondal, T., and K. Aarland. 1999. Salmon aquaculture in Chile. *Aquaculture Economics and Management* 3(3): 238–253.

Bravo, S., M.T. Silva, and C. Lagos. 2007. *Diagonostico de la proyección de la investigación en ciencia y tecnología de la acuicultura Chilena*. FIP, Mimeo.

Burgos, J.M. Current Director of Aquaculture division, Undersecretariat of Fisheries. Interview by author. November 30, 2011.

Claudio Perez, C. Director of Kapital Social. Interview by author. December 1, 2011.

Comision Group de Tarea del Salmon. 2009. *Informe final Comision asesora ministerial, Denominada 'Grupo de Tareas del Salmon'*. Santiago de Chile: Gobierno de Chile.

Gallardo, A. Chief of Aquaculture unit, National Fisheries Service. Interview by author. November 25, 2011.

Greif, A. 2006. *Institutions and the path to the modern economy: Lessons from medieval trade.* New York: Cambridge University Press.
Gusman, L. Chief of Aquaculture division, Instituto Fomento de Pesquera (IFOP). Interview by author. December 1, 2011.
Hodgeson, G. 1988. *Economics and institutions.* Cambridge: Polity Press.
Hodgeson, G. 2006. What are institutions? *Journal of Economic Issues* LX: 1–26.
Ibieta, Pablo, Valentina Tapiza, Claudia Venegas, Mary Hausdorf, and Harald Takle. 2011. Chilean Salmon farming on the horizon of sustainability: Review of the development of a highly intensive production, the ISA crisis and implemented actions to reconstruct a more sustainable aquaculture industry. In *Aquaculture and the environment: A shared destiny,* ed. Barbara Sladonja, 215–246. Croatia: InTech. http://www.intechopen.com/books/aquaculture-and-the-environment-a-shared-destiny.
Iizuka, M. 2007. *Global standards and local producers' knowledge governance and the rise of the Chilean salmon industry.* PhD dissertation, University of Sussex.
Iizuka, Michiko, and Jorge Katz. 2011. Natural resource industries, 'Tragedy of the Commons' and the case of Chilean salmon farming. *International Journal of Institutions and Economies* 3 (2): 259–286.
Kapital Social. 2011. Encuesta de Percepcion Industria del Salmon: Regiones de Los Lago, Aysen y magallanes, presenation slides, Puert Montt.
Katz, J. 2006. Salmon farming in Chile. In *Technology, adaptation and exports,* ed. V. Chandra, 193–224. Washington, DC: World Bank.
Larrain, F. 2011. *Financiamiento de la Nueva Etapa de la Industria, presentación en Encuentro nacional del Salmon.* Paper presented at Primeno Encuentro Nacional de Salmon, Puerto Varas, Chile, November, 30, 2011.
Maggi, C. 2007. The salmon farming and processing cluster in Southern Chile. In *Upgrading and governance in clusters and value chains in Latin America,* ed. C. Pietrobelli and R. Rabellotti, 109–142. Boston: Harvard University Press.
Melville, K.J., and Steven G. Griffiths. 1999. Absence of vertical transmission of infectious salmon anemia virus (ISAv) from individually infected Atlantic Salmon, Salmon Salar. *Diseases of Aquatic Organisms* 38: 231–234.
Nelson, R. 2008. What enables rapid economic progress: What are the needed institutions? *Research Policy* 37: 1–11.
Norambuena, R. Former Director of Aquaculture division, Undersecretariat of Fisheries. Interview by author. December 1, 2011.
North, D. 1990. *Institutions, institutional change and economic performance.* Cambridge: Cambridge University Press.
North, D. 1991. Institutions. *The Journal of Economic Perspectives* 5(1): 97–112.
Odebret, C. Managing Director of SalmonChile. Interview by author. December 1, 2011.
Saa, E. Former secretariat member of Mesa de Salmon. Interview by author. December 2, 2011.
Sandoval, F. Former Undersecretary of Fisheries. Interview by author. November 24, 2011.
Scott, W.R. 1995, 2001. *Institutions and organizations.* Thousand Oaks: Sage.
Sernapesca. 2008. *Balance de la Situación Sanitaria de la Anemia Infecciosa del Salmon en Chile de Julio del 2007 a Julio del 2008.* Valparaiso: Unidad Acuicultura, Sernapesca.
Sernapesca. 2010. *Program specific health surveillance and control of infectious salmon anaemia (PSEC-ISA).* Technical Report. Valparaiso: Unidad Acuicultura, Sernapesca.
Sernapesca. 2011. *Marco regulatorio y el rol de SERNAPESCA: Encuentro Nacional de la Industria del Salmon.* Paper presented at Puerto Montt, Chile, November 30, 2011.
Subsecretaria de Pesca. 2010. *Ley no 20.434 que modifica la LGPA en materia de acuicultura.* Subsecretaria de Pesca, Government of Chile.
Subsecretaria de Pesca. 2011. *Implementation of the aquaculture law.* Subsecretaria de Pesca, Government of Chile.
Subsecretaria de Pesca. 2012. Principales de Cambios en la Nueva Ley General de Pesca y Acuicultura. www.sebpesca.cl. Accessed 10 Feb 2013.

Vignolo, C., G. Held, and J.P. Zanlungo. 2007. *Strategic management of clusters: The case of the Chilean salmon industry*. Documentos de Trabajo Serie de Gestion no. 83, Centro de Gestion (CEGES). Santiago de Chile: Departmento de Ingenieria Industrial, Universidad de Chile.
Zorzano, S. Representative of ATARED, provider of net service. Interview by author. November 29, 2011.

List of Articles Used from Aqua.cl

2007, 21 Nov. Salmonicultores y gobierno realizaron simposio por virus ISA.
2007, 11 Dec. El 'G6' busca solucionar lso desafios de la salmonicultura.
2008, 18 Jan. Sernapesca desmiente informacion sobre posibles responsabilidades en aparicion de virus ISA.
2008, 17 Mar. Salmonicultores adelantan nueva estrategia el ISA.
2008, 3 July. Positivos resultados arrojo mission tecnologica sobre medidas de bioseguridad.
2008, 8 August. Encuesta analizo la percepción de la industria salmonicultora en la región de Los Lagos.
2008, 21 Nov. Industria del salmon acuerda Neuvo sistema de Produccion.
2008, 10 Oct. Industria del salmon anuncia cambios en su modelo productive para el 2009.
2009, 12 Jan. Epicentro de virus ISA se translada a la Region de Aysen, y Sernapesca confirma presencia en truchas.
2010, 2 Sept. Mario Montanari se refiere a las proyecciones de Invermar y a la actual situacion gremial.
2010, 2 Sept. En conflicto en el gremio salmonicultor que termino con la salida de AquaChile.
2010, 8 July. Alberto Montanari afirma que SalmonChile no debiera hacer el papel de fisicalizador sanitario.
2010, 20 Sept. Salmones antartica renuncio a SalmonChile.
2013,9 Feb. Fue Publicada en el Diario Oficial nueva Ley de Pesca No. 20.657.

Chapter 7
Public Goods, Regulation and the Expansion of the Natural Resource Exploitation Frontier: The Future of Salmon Farming in Chile

Jorge Katz

1 Introduction

The process of globalization of the world economy is strongly affecting natural resource rich countries catering for the expansion of world demand for industrial commodities, such as oil and gas, minerals, soybean oil, pulp and paper, timber, flowers, foodstuffs and more. A number of important—and yet badly under-researched—questions emerge in relation to the impact said process will have upon the long term sustainability of natural resources in peripheral economies, the knowledge base upon which the expansion of the resource exploitation frontier is to take place, the governance and regulation of natural resource based activities—which frequently involve the exploitation of a 'common', like oil and gas reserves, mines or forests—and the extent to which local communities are to share in the benefits of a more intensive exploitation of natural resources.

As far as Latin America is concerned many of these industries have been growing fast over the past two decades, catering for the expanding demand from East Asian countries, particularly China and India. The expansion of production has taken place in many countries in the region through a more intensive exploitation of existing natural resources, but very seldom serious consideration was given to the vast array of new conceptual and policy questions that come up concerning environmentally-friendly forms of exploiting natural resources, long term resource sustainability, social inclusiveness and fair treatment for the local communities living in the areas where the expansion of the natural resource exploitation frontier is taking place.

Lack of knowledge concerning the resource 'loading capacity' in different locations, very poor understanding of the ecological and biological equilibrium in which the resource is embedded, scarce government regulation and limited law

J. Katz (✉)
University of Chile, Santiago, Chile
e-mail: jorgekatz@terra.cl

A. Hosono et al. (eds.), *Chile's Salmon Industry*,
DOI 10.1007/978-4-431-55766-1_7

enforcing capacity from the part of public sector agencies, as well as very little 'collective action' from the part of firms engaged in the exploitation of the resource caring for its long term protection, have frequently resulted in a less than satisfactory outcome, i.e. in the overexploitation and degradation of the resource, in more than one case. Salmon farming in Chile—examined in this book—constitutes a clear example in this respect.

With the benefit of insight we now know that the expansion of the natural resource exploitation frontier involves a major episode of social engineering, the creation of markets and new institutions, the expansion into ecologically more frail environments which requires the participation of many different stakeholders with quite different objective functions in mind. It demands public/private coordination if it is to occur in an efficient, environmentally sustainable and socially inclusive way because many different forms of market failure crop up during the process accounting for less than socially optimal results. We now know that proceeding along this path involves more than having access to exploitation permits, process technologies and engineering know how. It also requires a host of new institutions and norms of social interaction ensuring an ecologically and socially sustainable exploitation of the existing natural endowments. Many intangible forms of knowledge, public goods—under the form of roads, energy, trained human capital, schools, health care services, transport facilities and more—and also different forms of collective action regulating access and protecting resource degradation are needed if a negative impact is to be avoided affecting biodiversity, desertification, depletion of resource biological properties and else. Contrary to conventional wisdom these intangible forms of knowledge and 'social capital' demand location-specific R&D efforts of various sorts and different public/private mechanisms of coordination which are not frequently present. Urged by the need for expanding exports and for attracting direct foreign investment, most Latin American countries frequently pay little attention to the above mentioned aspects of ecological equilibrium and public/private coordination and leave the door open to many disastrous consequences which are now beginning to be perceived in terms of increasing desertification, climate change, falling biodiversity and more.

Different intermediate inputs and services are demanded for the production of natural resource-based commodities. Some of them are public goods in nature—in the sense that their use by any one firm does not preclude the use by any other firm—as it is the case with R&D efforts producing knowledge and understanding of the location-specific ecological and environmental properties associated to the resource, the legal framework specifying the rules under which it is to be exploited—property rights, royalties and cannons and else—bilateral or multilateral trade agreements facilitating exports, labor codes regulating legal aspects of labor market functioning, an adequate physical infrastructure in terms of docks, roads, telecommunication services, waste disposal facilities, and more. Said public goods are essential to attain an adequate process of industry expansion and more exports. In addition to the above mentioned public goods others are also needed—education and health services, transport and housing facilities, for example—if the resource is to be exploited in a manner that ensures local communities to receive a fair share of the benefits of the expansion of the natural resource exploitation frontier. The much criticized case of the enclave economy with weak economic and social ties to the territory in which the resource is being exploited has been extensively discussed in the academic literature and in the popular press, to require further consideration.

The nature of the needed public goods can be expected to change over time—from industry inception to maturity—reflecting the likely initial lack of local technological and production organization capabilities, finance and physical infrastructure, and the subsequent development of technological capabilities and supporting institutions pari pasu with industry expansion.[1] Timely intervention of public sector agencies supporting R&D activities and the creation and diffusion of technology and production know how, as well as providing long term finance for the erection of new production facilities appear to be quite important in the early days of industry inception[2] as our study of salmon farming in Chile has shown. The crucial role of public sector support seems to diminish as the industry expands, markets develop and the process of capital and knowledge accumulation is set in motion. Instead, other public goods associated to the social upgrading of the local communities directly involved in the exploitation of the resource—schools, infant care wards, health care services, transport and telecommunications—continue to have primary importance. The image of isolated and overexploited mining communities is all the more notorious to require further discussion. This topic will be extensively discussed later on in this chapter in relation to salmon farming in Chile.

An immediate question comes to mind when we look at the expansion of the natural resource exploitation frontier as from this perspective: Can conventional market forces deliver the required economic, technological and institutional advances demanded for the expansion of the natural resource exploitation frontier, or is government intervention required as a result of the various forms of market failure and uncertainty likely to be present in the process? Can free market processes ensure long term environmental sustainability, the preservation of 'commons' and the emergence of the institutions required for a socially inclusive process of development? What does it take in terms of public/private cooperation to reach a satisfactory process of expansion of the resource exploitation frontier? Studying the expansion of the US agricultural frontier in the nineteenth century Prof. Rosenberg, from Stanford University, pointed out to the complexity of the process, showing that together with farmers, property rights and agricultural machinery the colonization of the US western frontier demanded banks and financial institutions, knowledge and production know how coming from universities and agricultural

[1] A case can be made, justifying government subsidies for a limited period of time for a so called 'infant regions' as the one normally made justifying temporal support for 'infant industries' during the initial learning period.

[2] We have shown this to be the case of Chilean salmon farming in the early years of industry inception.

extension agencies, transport services which came along with the expansion of the railway system and much more (Rosemberg 2000, Chapter 3). Far from being the result of well-functioning markets the expansion of the US agricultural frontier has to be seen as a major episode of social transformation, marked by the transition from a traditional (peasant) to a market economy. Transitions of this sort have been characterized by Sir John Hicks in *A Theory of Economic History* (1969), as involving the co-evolution of economic, institutional and technological forces which interact in a rather unplanned and out-of-equilibrium way. Moreover, said episode has been shown to be far from socially equitable and inclusive if we are to judge by the destruction the colonization process imposed upon the life style and organization of original indigenous communities displaced by the expansion of the US agricultural frontier. Similar circumstances have been shown to prevail in connection with the mining or the petroleum industries.

In other words, the expansion of the natural resource exploitation frontier usually involves an episode of vast social dimensions which requires a great deal of government intervention correcting different forms of market failure and uncertainties, as well as the creation of new institutions and markets, if it is to result in a sustainable and equitable process of development.

Previous chapters of this book have studied how a process of this sort obtained in the case of Chilean salmon farming. Chapters 2 and 3 of the book examine the mechanisms by which the country initially got access to basic production technology and knowhow, in the early days of industry inception. Public goods—made available by international cooperation agencies like JICA from Japan, and various foreign academic institutions from the US and Canada, and also by Fundación Chile, a public/private corporation which took major responsibility for the inception of the salmon farming industry in the country in the 1970s and 1980s—played a major role developing and diffusing basic production know how and technological knowledge, erecting the initial production plants showing that salmon could be produced in captivity in Chile and exported. As from this perspective, the inception of salmon farming in Chile is far from being the result of free market processes and demanded many public goods and a strong, pro-active, presence of the State. Chapter 4 examines the gradual expansion of a domestic salmon farming cluster and the gradual transition to 'contract aquaculture' with many knowledge intensive SMEs developing as subcontractors to the industry in different activities along the salmon farming production chain. The evolving market structure and behavior of the industry and of its intermediate input and service suppliers is studied in this chapter, looking at new entry, M&A, innovative behavior and more. Chapter 5 examines the gradual expansion of public sector regulatory agencies and their changing role monitoring sanitary and environmental behavior of salmon farming companies. The Chilean salmon farming industry started with a notorious lack of public sector regulation and monitoring and with frail law enforcing capacity from the part of public sector agencies responsible for assuring environmental protection. Such initial state of affairs gradually started to change as a result of the 2007 sanitary crisis. Chapter 6 examine the more recent structural and institutional transformation the industry and public sector agencies have gone through as a result of the above mentioned crisis, which started by being a sanitary and environmental phenomena but ended up by being systemic when banks, trade unions and municipalities became involved in it. Although the industry has experienced a dramatic recovery after the 2007 crisis we notice that it still is in transition to a new long term model of production and institutional organization. New institutions and forms of company production organization have emerged in response to the crisis, and public sector regulatory agencies have significantly strengthened their monitoring capacity over the past 5 years. A new public/private dialogue is gradually emerging in the industry but it is still much too early in the process for us to be able to say what the final outcome of the transition is going to be.

This book shows that the industry can simultaneously be regarded as an outstanding success—growing at two digit rates in the 1990s and 2000s, and becoming second to Norway supplying world markets for salmon—and also as a major failure, if we consider its record in terms of environmental sustainability and social inclusiveness. The production of salmon grew exponentially for nearly two decades—a major achievement—but increasing signs of negative sanitary and environmental consequences emerged in more recent times, questioning its long term record of success and opening up an interrogation mark concerning its future sustainability. On the other hand, the industry is far from being a great success in terms of local equitable and inclusive growth. Even in spite of having created employment at the local level the industry is not particularly welcome in the localities where it operates. The popular feeling is that local communities have remained fairly excluded from the benefits of growth. Labor unions bitterly complain about unfair treatment, of hiring contracts lacking adequate social security protection, of lacking of social services and on-the-job training, and more. Local communities speak about low corporate social responsibilities and scarce company involvement in community and municipal affaires. In other words, Chile has managed to 'catch up' with Norway in terms of tons of farmed salmon, but it has not managed to do so in an environmentally sustainable, socially equitable and inclusive model of growth. Many expectations have remained unfulfilled indicating that a new set of institutions and new forms of social and production organization are needed if said promises are to be honored in the future.

Having in previous chapters of the book examined how the industry originally came into being, how it grew over the past two decades, and how it reacted in recent years to the 2007 sanitary crisis, in this chapter we shall briefly recapitulate some of our research findings and explore what now needs to be done if Chile is to move into a better, and more socially committed, model of industry organization in the future. We argue here that it is the lack of public goods, of 'collective action' from the part of firms, and of a workable public/private dialogue concerning R&D activities, environmental sustainability and the creation of institutions for an equitable and inclusive process of growth, that need to be revised if salmon farming is finally to become a major success story in Chile.

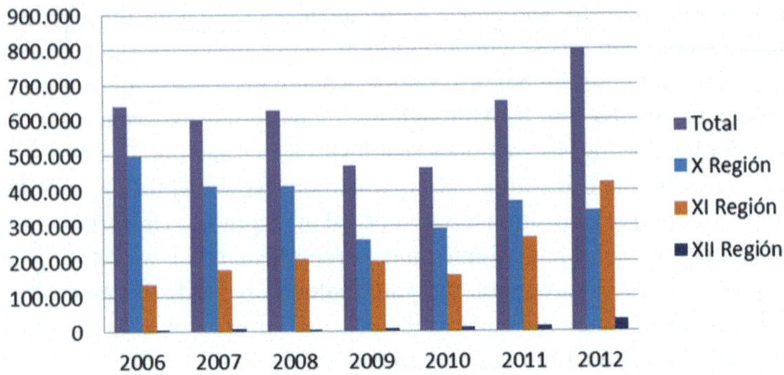

Fig. 7.1 Total salmon production by region and the growing participation of Aysen and Magallanes Regions. 2006–2012 (Note: Production is in volume (tons). *Source*: Zanlungo et al. (2013))

2 Natural Resource-Based Growth and the Expansion of the Resource Exploitation Frontier

In order further to expand production the Chilean salmon farming sector needs to expand its activities southwards from Puerto Montt, the area in which the industry originally started. In fact, this is already occurring, as salmon farming is moving southwards to the territories of Aysen and Magallanes since 2006, as Figs. 7.1 and 7.2 below show. The process gained momentum in 2010–2012.

By mid-2000s it had become clear that there are no more space was available for new cultivation centers to be erected in the proximity of Puerto Montt. On the other hand, as shown in previous chapters of the book, the option of increasing fish density in the existing cultivation tanks proved to be disastrous, as it increased the rate of fish mortality and favored the diffusion of new diseases. Expanding the biomass under cultivation in a given geographical area negatively affects salmon's quality of life and its auto-immune response, negatively affecting growth and the survival rate of the individuals under cultivation. Lack of understanding of this basic biological fact -, and no collective action from the part of firms protecting the 'common' and/or more stringent surveillance efforts from the part of public sector regulatory agencies—triggered off the ISA sanitary crisis in 2007. Local veterinarians and biologists saw the problem coming up many years in advance but their voice was not heard. In the hype of rapid growth and euphoria resulting from the catching up with Norway in volume of production nor the government neither salmon farming companies paid much attention to the falling biological and ecological indicators which were signaling an impending crash.

The Public Sector response to the constraint imposed by the exhaustion of the Puerto Montt 'frontier' was to accelerate the issuing of new cultivation permits in the Aysen and Magallanes regions, inducing the establishment of new cultivation

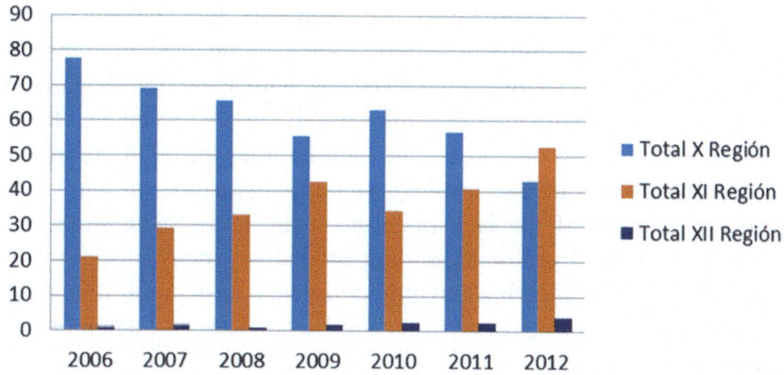

Fig. 7.2 Regional distribution (%) of salmon production. 2006–2012 (Note: Share (%) of production in volume (tons) by regions. *Source*: Zanlungo et al. (2013))

centers south of Puerto Montt. The expectation of expanding salmon farming in a new, virgin, territory induced many firms to reallocate their activities southwards.

With the benefit of insight we now understand that the expansion of the natural resource exploitation frontier constitutes a major episode of economic, institutional and social change which demands not just engineering know how and exploitation rights, but also a vast array of public goods—schools, sanitary posts, housing facilities, trained human capital, docks, waste disposal plants, transport and communication services and else—if the process is to result in an efficient and socially equitable operation. In actual fact, this is not how the expansion of the salmon farming frontier to the territories of Aysen and Magallanes was originally conceived by Chilean authorities. Given the strong free market ideology underlying Chilean public policy making local authorities thought that it was just a matter of handling more cultivation licenses to salmon farming companies, letting decentralized market processes to do the rest, i.e. to cater for the provision of the other goods and services demanded by the expansion of the resource exploitation frontier. Little ex ante consideration was given to the vast array of other goods and services needed, including R&D efforts better to understand location-specific ecological and environmental circumstances, resource 'loading capacity' in different locations and other 'merit' goods—education, infant care and health care facilities, transport services and more—the new arriving families would demand.

It has now become clear that conventional market processes did not adequately cater for the above mentioned goods and services in the quantity, quality and time scale required. Lack of qualified human resources and long term finance, inadequate housing facilities for the arriving new families, a poor local transport and telecommunication infrastructure, lack of schools and health care wards, and much more have resulted in a rather traumatic process of expansion to the salmon farming frontier into the Aysen region. From the point of view of individual salmon farming companies the consequence has been that unit production costs have increased, affecting international competitiveness. For example, that the lack of a waste disposal plant in the proximity of Aysen forced companies to transport their mortalities and waste by track over long distances, with an obvious negative impact upon production costs. Many other examples of this sort can be given. On the other hand, from the point of view of workers and their families the rapid expansion of the industry into the Aysen region resulted in more hardship for family life and organization as a result of the lack of an adequate housing facilities, transport services and else. In the hype of expanding production many of these aspects of urban planning, social engineering and public/private coordination were simply left out of consideration both by private firms and by public sector agencies and have now emerged to the surface.

In all fairness it could be said that market processes are slowly starting to respond to the emerging new demands—a new private dock has been recently erected, some universities and research labs have started R&D activities exploring local biological specificities and resource 'loading capacity', technical schools are offering new academic programs in aquaculture—but this has occurred in homeopathic doses, not yet having much of an impact on the local situation. The need for government intervention and for public/private coordination has become all the more clear in recent times. It is important to notice that Aysen is by no means the only case of this sort in Chile. A similar situation has emerged in recent years in northern Chile in relation to the expansion of the mining industry in Antofagasta. A public/private Regional Development Agency—Creo Antofagasta (Clark et al. 2010)—was created in this case with the specific purpose of designing and implementing a broad Regional Development Plan, addressing the needed for urban planning, the provision of public goods of various sorts—including schools, health care units, transport services and more—catering for a rapidly expanding population of mining workers and technicians coming into residence in the area. If the region is to become socially attractive as a long term residence area for new families quality of life needs to be explicitly taken into consideration and a variety of public goods is to be offered to the community. The example of Creo Antofagasta suggests that Aysen could in the near future follow a similar path erecting a private/public corporation exploring alternative ways of catering for the broad set of public goods and institutions now demanded by the community. We will return to this topic later on in this chapter.

There is another example of Chinquihue Foundation (Box 7.1) which also tries to improve the lives of small fishermen, who are left out from the successful development of the salmon industry but slightly in different manner by offering alternative means to earn living owing to decrease in natural resources. Here again, government used the support from international cooperation came up with longer term solution through capacity building.

Box 7.1 Chinquihue Foundation

The Chinquihue Foundation was established in 1989 in the outskirts of Puerto Montt, the capital city of the Los Lagos Region, where Chiloé Island, one of the areas that had remained impoverished in Chile, was located. The Chinquihue Foundation worked to improve the capacity of artisanal fishing communities within the Los Lagos Region as part of its efforts to increase their income. It also needed to cope with depleting fishery resources resulting from overfishing.

The regional government of Los Lagos, through Chinquihue Foundation, tried to make a shift from capture fisheries to culture fisheries with the introduction of aquaculture as part of efforts to address the depletion of coastal fishery resources and the poverty of artisanal fishers. Chinquihue Foundation provided trainings aimed at transferring technology for farming Pacific oysters and other shellfish as well as organizing artisanal fishers in Los Lagos Region. The foundation also supported them with procedures to obtain a license to operate fisheries management areas ("Áreas de Manejo" in Spanish) off the coast of their communities at their request.

Chinquihue Foundation's program to support artisanal fishers came as a timely helping hand for local fishers who were exploring new directions for themselves having realized dim future prospects for extractive fisheries. This is substantiated by a growing share of income from aquaculture in the total income of artisanal fishers. The fishers' organizations that received assistance are now putting the technologies they have acquired in farming Pacific oysters to good use for natural seed collection and farming of chorito, a kind of mussel to be exported to European countries. They are now standing on their own. Through the cultivation of shellfish, local fishers have learned to work together to improve their livelihoods. In short, the training program for artisanal fishers jointly managed by Chinquihue Foundation and JICA has culminated in the application of the experience in farming shellfish and organizing fishers to cultivate new fields. The fishers had actually 'learned' and enhanced their capacity to self-sustain. This had consequently improved the quality of lives for artisanal fishers.

The learning process took place not only for the fishers but also at organizational level. Chinquihue Foundation has conducted many projects for artisanal fishers under contract to the regional and central governments. In the process, it has been gradually developed its capacity in the field of aquaculture, playing an important role similar to that played by the Agricultural Development Institute (INDAP, Instituto de Desarrollo Agropecuario) in the field of agriculture. In this way, the foundation has become a pioneering organization that supports production activity of artisanal fishers, although its scale and scope are much smaller than those of INDAP, technology transfer and institutional capacity development for artisanal fishers in this region would not have been possible without Chinquihue Foundation.

(continued)

Box 7.1 (continued)

The salmon industry had brought prosperity to the 10th region however, failed to reduce the economic disparities within the region and vulnerable population such as artisanal fishers are left behind. Chinquihue Foundation is one of few examples in Chile that targeted capability building to those who left behind of progress to create more equitative society. This is still a very small efforts and scaling up of this type of activities is very much needed in future.

Source: Hosono (2010)

3 Different Stakeholders and the Need for Coordination and Cooperation

Previous chapters of the book have shown that many different stakeholders—salmon farming companies, intermediate service providers, banks, trade unions, public sector regulatory agencies local municipal authorities, universities, public research labs, NGOs, artisan fishermen—with very different views and perspectives as to what the more convenient expansion of salmon farming in Chile should be, actively interact on a daily basis debating the functioning of the industry. These stakeholders normally operate with incomplete information and understanding of the multiple issues hereby involved and with less than adequate comprehension of the fact that salmon farming involves the cultivation of a biomass in captivity which has its specific biological, genetic and health needs if it is to grow in a sustainable way. As shown in previous chapters of the book pathogens and viruses mutate in a random way and nor firms, neither public sector agencies, possess adequate ex ante knowledge and understanding concerning the path biological and ecological forces are likely to follow. This is why cooperation between companies and public sector regulatory agencies is particularly crucial to secure long term sanitary and environmental sustainability.

With the benefit of insight we now know that the 2007 sanitary crisis induced changes of behavior from each one of the previously mentioned stakeholders adapting to a new circumstances imposed by ecological and biological forces. New institutions have emerged, such as the 'Mesa del Salmon' (an instance of public/private dialogue and coordination), the re-structuring of the industry in 'neighborhoods' (barrios) of closely located cultivation centers, the recent implementation of a risk score mechanism allowing public sector agencies to monitor individual firm sanitary behavior and future production plans, and more. These new institutions have to be seen as emerging from the sanitary crisis and helping to develop new forms of coordination between public sector agencies and firms, new forms of collective action previously unheard of in the industry. Although they are certainly welcome we should notice that it is still much too early in the transition process to a new industry governance regime to be able to judge as to their final long term impact. A new equilibrium between the economy and the ecology is now in the making as both, firms and public sector agencies have started to work together looking for a new status quo.

Many challenges remain to be tackled. A waste disposal plant is not yet available in Aysen, and will have to be erected. Similarly so, energy is expensive and in short supply. Transport services are lacking as well as housing facilities. How to induce new investment in all these needed areas? A Regional Development Agency could become a major catalyzing force in the years to come organizing the cooperation of public sector agencies and salmon farming companies into a new model of production organization and integration into local community life. More on this issue later on in this chapter.

4 'Tragedy of the commons' in Salmon Farming

Producing salmon is very different from producing shoes or garments. When two salmon farming firms cultivate salmon in the same ocean bay or lake they both share on the use of water, and are therefore exposed to the 'horizontal transmission' of pathogens and predators, that cannot be stopped from moving from one cultivation center to the next. Firms cannot therefore be thought as acting arm-length from each other, as producers of shoes or garments are. The management of Common Pool Resources (CPRs) reflects an inner tension between the individual user of the common, and its attempt to maximize profits, and the performance of other users. As each individual firm attempts to maximize its private use of the 'common' it eventually inflicts welfare losses to the rest by depriving others from access. At variance with the canonical market model of production theory where arm-length relations among producers can be assumed, interdependency among firms is to be regarded as the norm and not the exception when we deal with 'commons'. 'Free riding' and opportunism, solidarity and reciprocity, constitute important features of individual firm behavior that strongly affect market functioning and outcome in commons.

In 1968 Hardin addressed the potential overexploitation of the resource in the case of CPRs and called it 'the tragedy of the commons'. He concluded that CPRs could only be managed through government regulation (role of state) or private ownership (role of markets).

Nobel Prize winner E. Ostrom (1990) reacted to Hardin's argument considering his case much too simple. She claimed that some social groups can successfully respond to the threat of resource overexploitation and degradation through self-governing institutions involving solidarity and reciprocity, i.e. forms of collective action. Studies of CPR management also emphasize the uniqueness of each case and the fact that the successful management of commons requires *local institutions,* capable of responding both to local as well as to global forces. 'Bottom up' solutions seem to work better and be more sustainable in the long run than 'top down' arrangements. Although a great deal of advance has been attained in recent years understanding the important role institutions play in the governance of commons still very little research has been carried out concerning the link between ecological and economic forces, the set of 'location-specific' institutions that develop connecting the economy and the ecology. This is an area in which evolutionary economics has yet to make progress in the years to come.

Continuing with the exploration of these issues in the case of Chilean salmon farming we now consider the change of institutions that obtained in response to the 2007 sanitary crisis.

5 Salmon Farming 'Neighborhoods' (Barrios) as a New Institution

The 2007 sanitary crisis dramatically brought to the surface a major weakness of the Chilean salmon farming model: lack of collective action from the part of firms protecting the common and lack of adequate public sector monitoring and law enforcing capacity to discipline company compliance with the prevailing environmental and sanitary norms.

As previously explained in the book, the ISA crisis—which involved the closing up of nearly 60 % of the industry's cultivation centers and laying off of some 25,000 workers—resulted in the creation of the 'Mesa del Salmon' (a new institution), which introduced a new style of public/private dialogue in the industry. This was the first time ever the industry demanded "more regulation" i.e. more discipline to be imposed by public sector agencies upon company behavior. It is in this context that another new institution—neighborhoods or 'barrios'—came into being imposing a common calendar of planting, harvesting and fallowing to closely located firms. This is done in order to facilitate the restoration of water biological properties after any production campaign.

Although in theory this new institution—barrios or salmon farming neighborhoods—constitutes a rational way of caring for long term environmental sustainability and for the renewal of water biological properties, it should be noted that it brought other, unintended, consequences. Cultivation permits are unevenly distributed among firms and many SMEs considered that imposing a compulsory resting period imposed a serious discrimination against their market functioning. Lacking a portfolio of alternative cultivation permits allowing them to move to other locations these companies considered that the new institution in fact affected their competitive capabilities vis a vis larger firms holding more cultivation permits. As a result of the above a number of SMEs left SalmonChile—the association of salmon producers—and created a new business association of small producers. Moreover, many of these firms changed their output mix expanding the production of trout and reducing their commitment to Atlantic salmon.

This new institution is still under experimentation and should be considered susceptible to change in the future, but has to be understood as part of a new regulatory environment and public/private dialogue now being established in the industry. Public sector agencies are trying to improve in bargaining power and law enforcing capacity vis a vis the private sector recognizing that they have lost much of it during the previous two decades in which public sector agencies took a back seat in industry affairs and accepted to playing a subsidiary role in this field. On the other hand, salmon farming companies which traditionally defended self-organization and free market principles and pushed State regulatory agencies into a subsidiary role now seem to admit that they cannot enforce the needed cooperation and collective discipline to stop a new critical sanitary episode as the one they went through in 2007. So they are gradually accepting a new, more stringent, regulatory environment.

6 Risk Scores as a New Institution

Taking a species—salmon—that freely grows in nature and trying to grow it in captivity attempting to reproduce in the cultivation tanks the biological dynamics that obtains in rivers, lakes or at the open sea, constitutes an act of extreme audacity which ignores the very poor understanding we have of the oceanographic, environmental and sanitary conditions which affect the welfare and growth of said species, the variance of said conditions across regions (and even across localities in a given region), and the difficulty of codifying and predicting their mutation through time.

In previous chapters of the book we have dealt at length with the impact State and Control variables have on the functioning of the industry. State variables are those the firm cannot change at will—temperature of the water, marine currents, nutrients in the water, and more. Control variables are those the firm can freely act upon making its own strategic choices, as for example, fish density to be planted in the cultivation tanks, vaccination practices, food supplements, quality of the eggs and smolt sown for cultivation, and so forth. A combination of state and control variables determines the biological and economic conversion rates of inputs into output and therefore the biological and economic results of any production campaign i.e. kilograms of harvested salmon per planted egg or smolt, length of the cultivation period, fish weight at harvesting time and more.

State and control variables determine the risk rate of different cultivation sites, groups of companies in a given 'neighborhood' (barrio) and geographical areas. Risk scores reflect, on the one hand, the relative incidence of the ecological conditions of each zone and, on the other, firm-specific sanitary and environmental protection practices. In principle the risk score constitutes a valuable indicator that permits public sector agencies to monitor activities and maximum fish cultivation density to be allowed in specific areas. It reflects the aerobic condition of each location (a state variable), the expected mortality rate in each cultivation centre and zone (difference between planted and harvested individuals), and a certain 'low risk' average density reflecting past performance and estimated 'loading capacity' of the zone.

The risk score constitutes a new institution facilitating market governance. Firms now have to inform Sernapesca at the start of any new production campaign how many individuals of a given species—Atlantic salmon, coho salmon and trout—they expect to plant for cultivation next year and Sernapesca then has to respond—after estimating the risk score—accepting the proposed planting program or revising it downwards or upwards. Calculating the risk score demands information disclosure from the part of firms, stronger law enforcing capacity from the part of public sector agencies, and the transition to a new style of dialogue between salmon farming firm and government.

In preparation for the enforcement of this new model of market governance Sernapesca started by collecting information and building its own data base in 2012. Early 2013 it started to use the risk index in an experimental way, expecting to have it in full operation by mid-2014. Firms are now required to disclose information concerning the rate of fish mortality, the use of antibiotics and many other factors they previously kept secret. This new modus operandi constitutes a significant advance with the past which assures a great deal more of transparency and public sector scrutiny of individual firm operation.

As indicated before the risk score is a new institution intended to regulate industry sanitary practices and environmental and ecological parameters and it is not yet in full operation. It began to be used in an experimental way late in 2013 and it reflects a significant change in the public/private dialogue likely to prevail in the industry in the future. It should be noted that this new institution involves information sharing among firms and with public sector agencies and a global assessment of the risk status of each salmon farming center, zone and neighborhood.

We have so far examined how new institutions have developed as a result of the 2007 sanitary crisis and how these new institutions are beginning to affect firm and industry behavior and public/private coordination in the industry. It was argued before that it is not just production organization aspects that demand being reconsidered in the years ahead if Chilean salmon farming is to be better accepted in the local communities in which it presently operates, and by the public in general. For this to happen it has to become more socially committed, inclusive and equitable. Many aspects concerning labor market functioning and participation in community life demand improvement jointly with environmental and sanitary practices. We now turn to these aspects.

7 Institutions for a More Equitable and Inclusive Model of Industry Development

7.1 Labor Legislation and Labor Market Functioning

Aquaculture has increasingly turned into an industry in which independent subcontractors provide services to salmon farming companies. Large companies have proceeded to outsource many activities previously performed ‘in house’. Veterinarians, divers, net cleaning services, and more now belong in the field of subcontracted activities. This has had a tremendous impact upon the functioning of labor markets. The role of subcontractors and the extent to which labor legislation provides a reasonable protection umbrella to salmon farming workers has become under strong scrutiny in recent times. Large salmon farming companies, and their subcontractors, have in their payroll a large fraction of workers not adequately covered by the Chilean social security legislation.

On the other hand, Chilean labor codes do not explicitly address the singularity of aquaculture activities providing them specific treatment and consideration. Diving activities, the handling of hazardous materials (such as ammonia in the refrigeration areas of salmon processing plants) and more, provide examples of areas in which labor unions recurrently complain of lack of adequate legislation and insufficient training programs from the part of companies providing workers with the adequate knowledge in high risk activities.

Another area in which labor market functioning has been strongly affected in recent years is the now prevailing model of production organization which has forced workers to accept living in precarious housing facilities at the cultivation centers, only returning to their families a few weeks per month. Besides seriously affecting family life the new production organization routines demand more transportation time which workers claim not to be adequately taken care of in the working contracts.

Many of the above mentioned aspects have been present in the industry for many years, but have now become more open and understood with the expansion of the salmon farming frontier to the Aysen region. Inadequate labor legislation and company hiring and subcontracting practices have resulted in a tense labor market atmosphere in the region, scarcely leading towards collaborative solutions and for better forms of production organization leading to productivity growth. Labor market institutions demand significant reconsideration in the salmon farming field in the years to come.

7.2 Education, Health and Other ‘Merit’ Goods

Expanding the salmon farming frontier into Aysen and Magallanes without simultaneously having considered the need for a Regional Development Plan involving urban planning, an enlarged public education and health infrastructure, more housing and recreation facilities, more public transportation and else reflects a serious misconception concerning what economic development is all about. Following a strong market oriented ideology Chilean policy makers acted under the expectation that free markets would cater for the above mentioned needs. Their expectations have not been fulfilled and Puerto Aysen has turned into a rapidly expanding city with lack of energy—energy prices are 20 % higher than in Santiago—very few new offerings of residential housing, lack of transport and recreation facilities and an unfriendly atmosphere for newly arriving families. Lack of schools—at the secondary level in particular—of infant care wards and of health care facilities have further compounded the image of a somewhat turbulent process of expansion which in many ways recalls the previously mentioned image of the nineteenth century expansion of the US agricultural frontier, with its rush to capture Ricardian natural rents, its destruction of traditional community life, its fever for short term enrichment, at the expense of environmental sustainability and a more equitable process of growth.

The transition from a traditional agricultural society to a market based economy—very much what is behind the arrival of the salmon farming industry to Aysen—involved for many families leaving behind the model of production for auto-consumption and the entry to a less protected market environment in which family life and relations are more affected by uncertainty, anomia and by the lack of shared community values.

Assuming that the transition from a traditional to a market economy could be adequately guided by conventional market forces, with the public sector playing a subsidiary role in the process, involves a serious misreading of how transitions of this sort have taken place in other parts of the world in the past. Transitions of this sort have been shown to demand new roles from the public sector, new institutions and new forms of community organization if they are to result in socially equitable and inclusive pattern of development.

8 New Roles for the Public Sector

Previous chapters of the book have shown how the role of Chilean public sector agencies varied in the course of time in the field of salmon farming. From being a pro-active agent during the inception period of the industry, catering for the production and diffusion of know how in salmon farming and for access to long term finance, the Chilean public sector took a subsidiary role during the period of rapid industry expansion, accepting a back seat in industry affairs for more than two decades. The 2007 sanitary crisis encountered Chilean public agencies marginalized and rather weak, initially incapable of adequately responding to the crisis and to the new set of circumstances that require attention as a result of ISA.

Chile did not have at that time a legal framework distinguishing aquaculture from industrial fisheries, two quite different industries with different constraints and opportunities. It had to start by passing a new law through Parliament to this effect. In addition to the above Sernapesca and Subpesca found they lacked trained human capital to deal with the emerging new issues and had significantly to expand their in house personnel incorporating professionals and technicians in various disciplines. They had to open regional offices capable of operating much closer to cultivation sites. They had to start building up their own data base rather than acting on the basis of secondary information provided by the firms. Coordination efforts among public sector agencies were poor and had to be improved, and so forth. A country-wide strategy concerning the future of Chilean aquaculture was absent and had to be gradually developed answering the question as to how much Chile could expand production without affecting world prices and local sanitary and environmental sustainability.

Five years have now passed since that moment and a great deal of progress has been attained. New resources have been allocated in the national budget for Subpesca and Sernapesca. Skilled manpower has been brought on board, regional offices have been established and surveillance missions monitoring industry compliance with sanitary and environmental protection rules have increased by an order of magnitude. In parallel to the above a new set of institutions has emerged—'barrios', risk scores, and more—that reflect the changing balance of power in the industry. Public sector regulatory agencies have gained bargaining power and law enforcing capacity vis a vis the private sector recently.

In spite of the above, however, not much progress has so far been attained in terms of a more equitable and socially inclusiveness model of salmon farming. This has become dramatically clear in recent years with the expansion of the industry into Aysen and Magallanes. Both these regions are lacking in public goods and institutions to ensure that together with a better long term sanitary and environmental protection behavior the industry also develops better patterns of integration in the communities in which it operates. It is argued here that public/private cooperation on this front is required in order attain progress in equity and inclusiveness. A change in the public sector mind setting admitting that the expansion of the natural resource exploitation frontier necessarily demands public goods and new institutions, and a similarly important change in corporate social responsibility (Pedersen 2010, pp. 155–166) better caring for labor market functioning and community welfare, appear now as sine qua non for a more socially equitable and inclusive model of industry expansion.

9 Back into the Future

This book has shown that Chilean salmon farming managed to grow at a very rapid pace over the past three decades, catching up with Norway as far as volume of production is concerned. Both countries cater now for about one third each of total world output of farmed salmon. We have shown in this monograph that the Chilean public sector played a very important role in the early years of industry inception, supplying knowledge, long term finance and other forms of support to the emerging new industry. Different forms of market failure and uncertainty could be avoided by timely intervention of public sector agencies that focuses on long term capacity building such as the one from JICA, a public sector Japanese agency.

The initial dramatic success the industry attained was called into question two decades after inception by the fact that it did not manage simultaneously to develop strong institutions, local technological competencies and forms of collective action capable of securing both a sanitary and environmentally sustainable industry nor a socially inclusive and equitable model of growth. The ISA crisis crudely brought that to the fore in 2007. The ISA crisis triggered off the search for new institutions. 'Mesa del Salmon', salmon farming 'barrios' and 'risk scores' are all new institutions which are gradually being brought to bear, rebalancing the relative bargaining power of public sector regulatory agencies vis a vis salmon farming companies. Over the past 5 years a new public/private dialogue has emerged in the industry with private companies for the first time accepting they demand being regulated by the State given their lack the capacity to act collectively in defense of the common.

The expansion of the natural resource exploitation frontier to the Aysen and Magallanes regions has shown the extent to which Chilean policy making has not so far brought an board idea that the transition to a more equitable and inclusive model of industry expansion demands not just technology and cultivation permits, but also a host of public goods and institutions which would permit local communities better to share in the distribution of the benefits of expanding the natural resource exploitation frontier. Lack of schools, of health care facilities, of transport and telecommunication services, inadequate labor market institutions and very poor urban planning have resulted in a rather unsuccessful episode of expansion into Aysen and Magallanes. So in the new forms of public sector intervention also a major change is required in the sphere of corporate social responsibilities if the expansion of the industry is to result in a socially equitable and inclusive process. This is particularly notorious in aspects of labor market institution and community welfare where the low degree of company involvement has been notorious. We conclude that the provision of public goods from the part of State agencies and a pro-active new pattern of involvement of salmon farming companies in local community affairs appear today as two sides of a cooperative public/private program which demands being implemented in the future. Social inclusiveness is unlikely to improve if these two sides fail to attain progress into a new model of industry organization.

References

Clark, G., J. Huxley, and D. Mountford. 2010. *Organizing local economic development*. Paris: OECD.

Hicks, Sir John. 1969. *A theory of economic history*. New York: Oxford University Press.

Hosono, Akio. (2010) *Nambei Chile wo Sake Yushutu Taikoku ni Kaeta Nihonjintachi* [The Japanese who changed Chile into a Great Salmon-exporting country]. Tokyo: Diamond, Inc.
Ostrom, E. 1990. *Governing the commons: Evolution of institutions for collective action.* New York: Cambridge University Press.
Pedersen, E. 2010. Modeling corporate social responsibilities: How managers understand the responsibility of business towards society. *Journal of Business Ethics* 2010: 91.
Rosemberg, N. 2000. *The Graz Schumpeter lectures.* London: Routledge.
Zanlungo, J.P., J. Katz, C. Araya, and J.P. Mingo. 2013. Diagnostico de las brechas y /o problemas que afectan la red I+D+i en los territorios de bordemar de Aysen (informe final).

Chapter 8
Conclusions and Policy Implications

Michiko Iizuka, Akio Hosono, and Jorge Katz

This book examines the development of the Chilean salmon farming industry, paying special attention to public goods, namely: 'knowledge development', 'environmental sustainability', 'institutions' and 'inclusiveness/social welfare'. Normally, policy interventions in managing public goods are justified by the market failure argument. There are; however, several scholars who question assumptions made by neoclassical approach and extend their argument for the policy intervention in correcting systemic failure as well as coordination failure (for example, Cimoli et al. 2009; Stiglitz 1999).

These different aspects of issues on public goods were applied to our specific case study on the Chilean salmon farming industry in each chapter. The following research questions were addressed with regard to each of the aspects of public goods and comprehensively analyzed: (1) how did the newly emerging non-traditional activity begin and grow, overcoming barriers of initial knowledge creation and diffusion to build capacity, thereby allowing the country to catch up in an already competitive global market (Chaps. 2, 3, and 4)?; (2) how did the expansion of the new non-traditional export activity lead to environmental degradation, endangering the sustainability of the industry (Chap. 5)?; (3) how did new institutions emerge to manage the sustainability of non-traditional export activities (Chaps. 5 and 6)?; and (4) how can the growth of new non-traditional export activities be made more sustainable and socially inclusive (Chap. 7)?

M. Iizuka (✉)
Maastricht Economic and Social Research and Training Center for Innovation and Technology (UNU-MERIT), United Nations University, Maastrciht, The Netherlands
e-mail: iizuka@merit.unu.edu

A. Hosono
Japan International Cooperation Agency Research Institute (JICA-RI), Tokyo, Japan

J. Katz
University of Chile, Santiago, Chile

A. Hosono et al. (eds.), *Chile's Salmon Industry*,
DOI 10.1007/978-4-431-55766-1_8

In this final chapter, we try to go beyond the lessons learnt from our case study of salmon farming in Chile and look at each question mentioned above from more general perspective, recognizing that issues addressed in this particular case can be found in other natural resource-based industries in developing country settings. In fact, as natural resource-based export activities are rapidly expanding in developing countries, we believe these countries are likely to face similar challenges to the ones we have examined in the earlier chapters.

1 Escaping from the "Knowledge Deadlock"

Investing in knowledge is highly risky and uncertain, and many individual firms might refrain from allocating significant sums of money for this purpose due to the non-excludible and non-rivalry properties of knowledge as a public good, making any investment in knowledge suboptimal from the point of view of society (David 1993). The risk of investing in knowledge is particularly pronounced in activities based on natural resources (e.g. agriculture, fishery, forestry, mining and renewable energy) as a result of the lack of scalability (Padrey et al. 2010). This is due to the high degree of variability and location-specificity caused by the biological and ecological circumstances that productivity hinges upon. In other words, different combinations of knowledge are needed in different locations depending upon the endowed resource, climate conditions, soil types, topography, locational characteristics such as distance from markets, and other factors, making it difficult to benefit from economies of scale resulting from simply investing in knowledge on its own.

The success of non-traditional exports (salmon, timber, fresh fruits and wine, biofuel and more) is usually associated with liberal trade policies. Chapter 2 examined the development of salmon farming before Chile introduced market-led open trade policies in the mid- and late 1970s. We unfolded the 'untold story' of this industry from the late 1960s to early 1970s when Chile had just begun to explore the possibilities of salmon farming in local fiords and lakes. Chapters 2 and 3 described early efforts made by Chilean governmental agencies such as SAG and SERNAP in scoping the international scientific and technological knowledge frontiers and accumulating a knowledge base from scratch. They did this by utilizing the technological transfer scheme of international cooperation from countries including Japan (via Japan International Cooperation Agency, or JICA) as well as the US and Canada. The technological cooperation from Japan, in particular, continued for an extensive period (from 1969 to 1989) in broad areas of the production process (Chap. 3). Based on the cases we have seen, we can say that for establishing a new industry, government plays a critical role at the early stages in stimulating knowledge development, actively utilizing exhaustive means to access available advanced knowledge elsewhere and encouraging its transfer to the local context. To this end, the government needs to bring together locally available human capital and external scientific and technological know-how with the goal of creating new domestic production capacity, and using this to provide a basis from which to expand exports in foreign markets.

Even though governments do not have clear industrial policy or strategy, some guidance in encouraging the learning process is necessary in order to create a knowledge base for industrial development at the start. The case demonstrated that there were several actors—Japan-Chile Salmon Project, Fundación Chile etc.—that were able to fill this gap by creating such a knowledge base. The process of establishing an effective alignment of each of the stakeholders is also largely a trial and error process, with high uncertainty and few guarantees of success. In fact, salmon farming was one among many options that Chile was exploring at that time for creating new export industries. Not all explorations are likely to be successful; some will fail, as in the cases of Fundación Chile with regard to timber and furniture, for example. Even though investment may not bear the fruit of profits, exploration and investment in knowledge is essential to be at the entry point of competitive global markets. The process of creating a new export industry, therefore, cannot be entirely left to market forces but requires policy interventions that go beyond just fixing market imperfections. This does not mean that government should be in charge of everything in developing an industry. Nevertheless, the government can play a pivotal role in creating the systemic conditions conducive for entrepreneurs to emerge in the subsequent period. The gestation period, at times, can continue over an extended period of time, because local capability needs to be cumulatively established and has to come in alignment with windows of opportunity in the market.

Starting new activities requires creating a critical mass of firms. This requires knowledge diffusion and a broad array of firms and individuals adapting the frontier technology. Knowledge diffusion and adaptation efforts take place when the new idea is considered to be 'better', more 'applicable' or 'manageable', and 'easily available' by firms and individuals (Rogers 1995). This means that potential adopters need to have the technological capability (Lall 1992; Kim 1998; Bell and Pavitt 1995) to identify new knowledge as better, more manageable and applicable, using their absorptive capacity, created by the existing knowledge base and learning efforts (Cohen and Levinthal 1990). The diffusion process is facilitated by the presence of intermediaries that can decode the foreign knowledge into more accessible specifications for local users. The role of such intermediaries can be played by the private sector (e.g. MNCs, engineering associations) as well as public sector agencies (such as extension services from public research laboratories, universities etc.) in different combinations.

Chapter 3 focused on the details surrounding the start of the salmon farming on a commercial basis in Chile. In the early phase, there were pioneering entrepreneurs (Nichiro and Piscicultura Lago Llanquihue) who were willing to take risks to enter this business. They were highly inspired individuals who were willing to share their knowledge and experiences between each other and in small circles. They were followed by other pioneering firms. These early pioneers were supported by various agents such as Fundación Chile, Japan-Chile Salmon Project and foreign firms (primarily buyers) in transferring and diffusing knowledge concerning salmon production and commercialization. This evolutionary sequencing of knowledge transfer ensured successful development of an 'infant industry' over the subsequent years of scaling up by attracting followers to enter into the business until a critical mass had been created. Here, we can observe the evolutionary process of knowledge diffusion and creation that worked well in the context of the salmon farming industry. Numerous agents were involved in creating a knowledge base from the production process to bridging the product to export markets. In other words, amalgamation of interacting actors created a condition that promoted knowledge creation and diffusion in reflexive manner. This created positive dynamics and synergy with the growth sequence of the industry.

The globalization of the world economy and the diffusion of communications technology improved access to frontier scientific and technological knowledge for many developing countries. However, it should not be forgotten that domestic technological capability (Lall 1992; Bell and Pavitt 1995; Kim 1998), local absorptive capacity[1] (Cohen and Levinthal 1990; Kim 1998) and indigenous knowledge (Fu et al. 2011) are crucially needed to internalize and adapt external knowledge to local conditions. Such knowledge should not be considered as exclusively referring to process technologies and engineering know-how but can also be extended to local institutions (Pietrobelli and Rabellotti 2011), facilitating international marketing and environmental protection, and other co-evolving fields (Bell and Pavitt 1995; among others). This is particularly so in the case of natural resource-based economic activities that involve interactions with highly local specific biospheres (Pardey et al. 2010). Received literature considers that access to external knowledge does not automatically translate into domestic capabilities. Local technological efforts and domestic R&D activities (Katz 1984; Lall 1992; Bell and Pavitt 1995) are needed in order to stimulate the learning process and the adaptation of foreign know-how to the local social, economic and environmental conditions.

Chapter 4 described the period when the Chilean salmon farming industry became integrated into the global market. The volume of production, as well as exports, grew at a very rapid pace in response to the expansion of demand in the global market. The increasing scale of production was accompanied by increased diversity and complexity in the organization of a newly emerging industrial cluster. Various innovations were achieved in relation to specialized equipment, production services, and in-house production organizations contributed to improving productivity in an incremental manner. Despite innovation efforts in the form of R&D expenditure (with public sector support for R&D activities), little attention was paid to the accumulation of local knowledge to manage natural resources sustainably over the long term.

The important question for many developing countries is how to start building up such capabilities from scratch, when sufficient prior knowledge, human capital and financial resources are lacking. The important challenge is to overcome the knowledge deadlock at each phase of development through timely and appropriate

[1] The concept of absorptive capacity is defined as "the ability of a firm to recognize the value of new, external information, assimilate it and apply it to commercial ends" (Cohen and Levinthal 1990, 128).

interventions. The lesson hereby learnt from the case of salmon farming in Chile is that interventions are needed for knowledge generation at each phase—initial, growth and globalization—but its nature changes at each phase. In the incipient phase, exhaustive efforts should be made to make frontier knowledge accessible to local stakeholders in order to create a knowledge base to start commercial activities.

When the knowledge base is sufficiently established at the local level, the core area of intervention should shift towards making the environment more conducive for entrepreneurs and foreign investors so that the infant industry can emerge and scale up. Various types of incremental innovations can facilitate the scaling up process to increase productivity. Such rapid surges in productivity may not always be accompanied by increases in the local capability, the increased understanding of highly diverse and variable natural environmental conditions where the production activity are dependent on. This indicates that even after industry has been sufficiently scaled up, the need for interventions in terms of local capacity building do not disappear. The intervention is still needed in establishing good mechanisms for knowledge development is critical as public goods (such as environmental and sanitary conditions, creating standards, regulatory measures) for the sustainability of industrial activities, in cases where such knowledge does not exist elsewhere due to being specific to the country or region.

2 Dealing with the Negative Consequences of Industrial Development

After a natural resource-based industry is installed and has successfully expanded its activity to a substantial level, the kinds of negative externalities that are most likely to crop up in the form of environmental problems, as natural resources are prone to being overexploited. The use of environmental services constitutes a major aspect of production organization in natural resource-based activities, which is not adequately accounted for in current production functions (Costanza et al. 1997; Hawken et al. 1999; UNEP 2013). Although attempts are currently being made to introduce environmental considerations into production processes under the concept of a green economy (UNEP 2013), the environmental resources (biosphere, water, air, land, forest just to name a few) are still prone to mismanagement and overexploitation when 'proper' institutions are absent or unable to monitor long-term sustainable exploitation. For many emerging 'nontraditional' industries, the most difficult challenges are to identify the optimum level of loading capacity in different geographical locations, and to come up with appropriate regulatory mechanisms and methods to effectively enforce them. This requires location-specific knowledge on the biosphere and productive process, as well as the ability to codify the knowledge into institutional language and socio-political dynamics, in order to change the behavior of firms and stakeholders involved in production process.

Chapter 5 of the book described the sanitary crisis of Chilean salmon industry in 2007. The first half of chapter illustrated how such a crisis occurred. The crisis emerged as a result of resource overexploitation without proper institutions in place, and occurred in a similar manner as the 'Tragedy of the Commons' (Hardin 1968), by which each firm added more salmon to limited areas of cultivation in response to growing global demand. The crisis did not happen due to the spread of a virus or pathogen alone. The crisis happened as the result of combination of factors cumulatively causing the next event in order: a rapid growth in scale of activities causing overcrowding of the fish cages in the sea, which had gradually decreased the regenerative capacity of environment and weakened the immune system of fish, making the fish more susceptible to the diseases. Furthermore, the weakness or absence of institutions to control such individual firm behavior provides the underlying conditions for such a 'tragedy' to take place. The case has shown how natural resources in developing countries are becoming increasingly predisposed to overexploitation when exposed to global demand. The finding is well in line with other existing studies. For instance, Lenzen et al. (2012) indicated that an increase in world trade and consumption of imported commodities—such as coffee, tea, sugar, textiles and manufacturing products—by developed countries contributed to 30 % of biodiversity loss in commodity producing (mostly developing) countries. Under such circumstances, strong public sector agencies, an adequate legal framework and strong law enforcement capacity seem to be urgently needed at the local level to counterbalance the growing influence of market demands for commodities. These institutional issues were explored in the latter half of Chaps. 5 and 6 in this book.

3 Establishing Institutions to Meet Emerging Challenges

Many developing countries are now trying to turn their rich natural resources, or common pool resources (CPR), into exportable products catering for the current boom in commodities. However, this comes with a risk of overexploitation if effective institutions are not in place to manage the resources, as was discussed in the previous section. A study by Hardin (1968) suggested that CPR should be managed either through strict regulation (role of the government) or exclusive private property ownership (role of the market) (Ostrom 1990; Ostrom et al. 1999), however, considered Harding's view as grossly "simplistic" and claimed that local self-governing institutions are important in dealing with the threat of resource degradation. She claims that stakeholders can learn from interaction and therefore develop institutions capable of preventing overall environmental degradation will emerge.

Chapter 5 in the book, with a clear example, demonstrated that without appropriate institutions to maintain and manage the adequate use of natural resources, the strong pressure of global demand can easily induce local entrepreneurs to overexploit the local commons because they tend to maximize short-term profit (benefit) at the cost of long-term social losses.

Establishing and implementing effective regulation to manage sustainable use of natural resources requires identifying critical indicators of optimal loading capacity and that said, indicators demand knowledge and understanding of the local biological and ecological environment so as to figure out probable causes (possibilities) and predictors (probabilities) of environmental mismanagement. This learning process for 'construction' of institutions, as Ostrom sees it, demands a rather lengthy period of time, which might simply not be available for many developing nations. In the case presented here, we observed the emergence of institutions such as neighborhoods (barrios) and risk scores to ensure the sustainability of industry via policy intervention. These changes are an important step in the right direction, however it generally takes a rather long time for new institutions to become operational and incorporate a better understanding of outcomes on the interactions between the economic activities and biospheric conditions. This issue is particularly pronounced for non-traditional products whose antecedent knowledge of managing the natural resources is limited, while at the same time, the industry grows at a rapid pace owing to growing demand in global market.

Hence, Ostrom's findings may not be relevant, or applicable, within the present-day situation, especially given the rapidly changing global context. First, even though she claims that the institutions will 'self-emerge', this may not happen on a time scale sufficient to prevent disaster due to the magnitude of demand involved. Second, the game-theoretical dynamic interaction by Ostrom does not consider other factors, such as technological change, scientific progress or increasing global interaction and increasing involvement of new actors. Her model, therefore, captures the dynamic notion of interaction among stakeholders but may not sufficiently reflect the evolutionary context in which the stakeholders are situated.

Chapter 6 illustrated the complex process of institutional change that lay in the context of introduction of barrios and risk scores following the ISA crisis. The chapter demonstrated that transformation of institutions should be considered an outcome of a top-down and bottom-up, bi-directional process. In other words, contrary to what seems to be the top-down change in the institutions marked by changes in the legal framework, many small adjustments had already taken place at the practical 'routine' level to enable the change. These incremental changes were proposed by the stakeholders who are normally being governed by the regulatory mechanism. Such 'bottom up' flow of interactions is considered critical in providing motivation to make changes in behavior and eventually in contributing in creating effective institutions (Greif 2006). The successful changes in institutions should follow what Aoki (2007) refers to as 'evolutionary institutionalism' which understand that institutions evolve to fit to the local context as the result of interactions among local settings, internal and external selection criteria.

4 Attaining Social Inclusiveness

The Chilean salmon farming industry succeeded in becoming a major export sector, strongly contributing to Chilean external trade accounts. It is not clear; however, how much the industry has contributed to improving social welfare in the regions where production of salmon takes place. Some interviews and opinion survey (Perez 2011; Kapital Social 2011) suggested that inadequate functioning of labor market institutions may have permitted highly questionable hiring and firing practices on the part of salmon farming companies, and this may have negatively affected the quality of labor relations in the industry.

Chapter 7 of the book paid attention to these questions, together with issues of sustainability in an attempt to draw out the future direction of this industry. There have been some isolated successful attempts, such as Fundación Chinquihue, on improving the social welfare of the population that were left out from the growth generated by the salmon industry. Fundación Chinquihue provided trainings to the small-scale fishers to engage in aquaculture (shell). These attempts have had some impact in improving welfare. Nevertheless, these are far from being sufficient to address the existing magnitude of problem.

The importance of inclusiveness of institutions is gaining increasing prominence in the new policy agenda. Acemoglu et al. (2005) and Acemoglu and Robinson (2012) made an important distinction between inclusive and extractive institutions in both political and economic spheres. This distinction was considered useful for analyzing how types of institutions can determine long-term prosperity of a locality, region or nation. They claim that inclusive institutions can cause a virtuous circle of economic activities over a long period of time through nurturing social cohesiveness. This approach has attracted attention from international development organizations and several of them have started to mainstream this concept into their discourse.[2] Despite the increasing interests, there are still large gaps to be filled between the concept and practicality of bringing it into reality.

[2] For instance, in 2006, UNDP created an initiative called 'Growing Inclusive Markets', which tries to make business inclusive and beneficial for the poor in ensuring that development is something that "marginalized groups take part in and benefit from, regardless of their gender, ethnicity, age, sexual orientation, disability or poverty." It also seeks "to address the deepening inequality across the world that has arisen despite unprecedented economic growth" (UNDP 2008). In 2008, 'inclusive and sustainable globalization' became the vision of the World Bank group. Similarly, Asian Development Bank (ADB), in 2007 published "Propoor to inclusive Growth: Asian Prescriptions" (Ali 2007) and "Inclusive Growth toward a Prosperous Asia: policy implications" (Ali and Zhang 2007) and has positioned 'inclusive growth' as one of the three agendas in its long-term strategic framework of Strategy 2020 in 2008 (Rauniyar and Kanbur 2009). In 2011, ADB created Framework of Inclusive Growth Indicator (FIGI) and this has been updated annually (ADB 2011). In 2012, OECD published a report on innovation for inclusiveness trying to understand how innovation can support making economic structures that are relevant for the marginalized populations. UNEP's Towards a Green Economy (2013) also considers inclusiveness as one of the most important pillars for a 'green economy'.

For instance, we need to look at the welfare consequences of the salmon farming industry moving towards Southern regions to seek sustainable production. In order to expand the natural resource exploitation frontier, producers will gradually move the production activities to distant and isolated regions. These regions rarely have an adequate physical and social infrastructure, public goods in some sense, such as education and health services, transport and telecommunication facilities, roads, docks and waste disposal plants and other areas. Under such circumstances, there are two key actors that can play a major role to change the prevailing situation of deprivation. First, public sector agencies should intervene in providing education and health services and urban planning to handle the many social problems in rapidly expanding new territories. At the same time, as most of the beneficiaries for such investments are the employees of the firms in these areas of expansion, these firms should also share the burden of responsibility. In other words, there are potential areas to explore for public/private cooperative programs to deal with the lack of goods and services in the expanding localities to enhance welfare of population (Nissanke and Thorbecke 2010).

While inclusive development is recognized as important in the current policy agenda, it necessitates overcoming long-term limitations in terms of lack of skills, physical infrastructure and sources of finance. In order to improve access to the above goods and services, local communities need better links with the national setting. A continuous learning process cannot be achieved without interacting more strongly with national, regional and global agents. This network of learning is essential for accessing new knowledge and markets. Corporate social responsibility can play a critical role in this field by expanding the frontiers of social interaction to the national level and beyond. The image of the enclave economy exploiting local natural endowments and not developing social roots in the localities where it operates has been heavily criticized in the academic literature and in the conventional press so as to require further examination. OECD (2011) established guidelines of good conduct for multinational enterprises (MNEs) in following areas: corruption, human rights, employment, industrial relations, environment, consumer interest, science and technology, competition and taxation. We can also suggest extending the coverage of guidelines to incorporate the goal of enhancing local inclusiveness and community welfare. Of course the fruits of such provisions can only be enjoyed if the local counterparts—namely, civil society, the local community and public sectors—are willing to put in concerted efforts towards the same ends.

5 Conclusion

We have reviewed the chapters of this book under the four inter-locking thematic headings of public goods—knowledge development, sustainability, institutions and inclusiveness (welfare)—with the intention of extending what we learned from the case to draw more generic policy lessons. After examining these four areas that require particular attention by policy intervention, we recognize that these areas are integral components for success in creating sustainable natural resource-based activities in developing countries. Each issue evolves in its own way and requires a distinctive type of intervention at each phase in an evolutionary manner. At the same time, each issue also requires input from one another to create dynamic outcomes.

Furthermore, we now know that, against the backdrop of such industrial development, there are complex layers of interactions between different levels, such as the local biosphere to production process, and production process with global market demand. These correspond to the increasing dynamics of interaction at each level—competition for local natural resources among stakeholders involved in different activities (i.e. tourism vs. fishery for water resources etc.), competitions between stakeholders of the cluster (suppliers, completion among domestic firms, foreign direct investments etc.) and pressures from global interest groups (buyers, media, civil society, consumers). Under such dynamic and highly complex context, it is not possible to draw a single stylized prescription for industrial development; neither market nor government is possible to solve all the problems that can emerge.

The public policy in managing public goods requires coordination of stakeholders and available resources to overcome the barriers of knowledge flow via building institutions to effectively allocate means to improve sustainability and inclusiveness. And to do that, policy makers need to be aware of holistic and dynamic aspect of industry and react to changes reflexibly.

References

Acemoglu, D., and J. Robinson. 2012. *Why nations fail*. London: Profile Books.

Acemoglu, D., S. Johnson, and J. Robinson. 2005. Institutions as a fundamental cause of long-run growth. In *Handbook of economic growth*, vol. 1A, ed. P. Aghion and S. Durlauf. Amsterdam: Elsevier.

Ali, Ifzal. 2007. *Propoor to inclusive growth: Asian prescriptions*, ERD Asian Development Review Policy Brief, vol. 48. Manila: ADB.

Ali, Ifzal, and J. Zhuang. 2007. *Inclusive growth toward a prosperous Asia: Policy implications*, ERD Working paper, vol. 97. Manila: ADB.

Aoki, M. 2007. Endogenizing institutions and institutional changes. *Journal of Institutional Economics* 3(1): 1–31.

Asian Development Bank (ADB). 2011. *Framework of inclusive growth indicators; key indicators for Asia and pacific 2011, special supplement*. Manila: ADB.

Bell, M., and K. Pavitt. 1995. The development of technological capabilities. In *Trade, technology and international competitiveness*, ed. I.U. Haque, 69–102. Washington, DC: World Bank.

Cimoli, M., G. Dosi, and J. Stiglitz. 2009. *Industrial policy and development: Political economy of capabilities accumulation*. Oxford: Oxford University Press.

Cohen, W.M., and D.A. Levinthal. 1990. Absorptive capacity: A new perspective on learning and innovation. *Administrative Science Quarterly* 35(1): 128–152.

Costanza, R., R. d'Arge, R. de Groot, S. Farber, M. Grasso, B. Hannon, K. Limburg, S. Naeem, R. O'Neill, J. Paruelo, R. Raskin, P. Sutton, and M. van den Belt. 1997. The value of the world's ecosystem services and natural capital. *Nature* 387: 253–260.

David, P. 1993. Intellectual property institutions and the panda's thumb: Patents, copy rights and trade secrets in economic theory and history. In *Global dimensions of intellectual property rights in science and technology*, ed. M.B. Wallerstein, M.E. Mogee, and R.A. Schoen, 19–64. Washington, DC: National Academy Press.

Fu, X., C. Pietrobelli, and L. Soete. 2011. The role of foreign technology and indigenous innovation in the emerging economies: Technological change and catch up. *World Development* 39(7): 1204–1212.

Greif, A. 2006. *Institutions and the path to the modern economy: Lessons from medieval trade*. New York: Cambridge University Press.

Hardin, G. 1968. The tragedy of the commons. *Science* 162(1968): 1243–1248.

Hawken, P., A. Lovins, and H. Lovins. 1999. *Natural capitalism: Creating the next industrial revolution*. Boston: Little Brown Publications.

Kapital Social. 2011. *Encuesta de Percepción Industria del Salmón: Regiones de Los Lagos, Aysény Magallanes*, presentation slides. Puert Montt.

Katz, J. 1984. Domestic technological innovations and dynamic comparative advantage: Further reflections on a comparative case study program. *Journal of Development Economics* 16(1–2): 13–38.

Kim, L. 1998. Crisis construction and organizational learning: Capability building in catching up at Hyundai Motor. *Organization Science* 9(4): 506–521.

Lall, S. 1992. Technological capabilities and industrialization. *World Development* 20(2): 165–186.

Lenzen, M., D. Moran, K. Kanemoto, B. Foran, L. Lobefaro, and A. Geschke. 2012. International trade drives biodiversity threats in developing nations. *Nature* 486: 109–112.

Nissanke, M., and E. Thorbecke. 2010. Globalization, poverty and inequality in Latin America: Finding from case studies. *World Development* 38(6): 797–802.

OECD. 2011. *OECD guidelines for multinational enterprises*. Paris: OECD.

Ostrom, E. 1990. *Governing the commons: Evolution of institutions for collective action*. New York: Cambridge University Press.

Ostrom, E., J. Burger, C.B. Field, R.B. Norgaard, and D. Policansky. 1999. Revisiting the commons: Local lessons, global challenges. *Science* 284(1999): 278–282.

Pardey, P.G., J.M. Alston, and V.W. Ruttan. 2010. The economics of innovation and technical change in agriculture. In *Handbook of economics of technical change*, ed. B.H. Hall and N. Rosenberg. Amsterdam: Elsevier.

Perez, C. 2011. Director of Social Kapital. Interview by author. December 1, 2011

Pietrobelli, C., and R. Rabellotti. 2011. Global value chains meet innovation systems: Are there learning opportunities for developing countries? *World Development* 39(7): 1261–1269.

Rauniyar, G., and R. Kanbur. 2009. *Inclusive growth and inclusive development, ADB*, Occasional paper, vol. 8. Manila: Asian Development Bank.

Rogers, E. 1995. *Diffusion of innovations*, 4th ed. New York: Free Press.

Stiglitz, J.E. 1999. Knowledge as a global public good. In *Global public goods: International cooperation in the 21st century*, ed. I. Kaul, I. Grunberg, and M. Stern, 308–325. New York: Office of Development Studies (ODS), Bureau for Development Policy (BDP), United Nations Development Programme (UNDP).

UNDP. 2008. *GIM global reports*. UNDP.

UNEP. 2013. *Towards a green economy: Pathways to sustainable development and poverty eradication – A synthesis for policy makers*. http://www.unep.org/greeneconomy. Accessed 23 May 2012.

Index

A. Hosono et al. (eds.), *Chile's Salmon Industry*,
DOI 10.1007/978-4-431-55766-1

The manufacturer's authorised representative in the EU is Springer Nature Customer Service Centre GmbH, Europaplatz 3, 69115 Heidelberg, Germany. If you have any concerns regarding our products, please contact ProductSafety@springernature.com

Printed and bound by CPI Group (UK) Ltd, Croydon, CR0 4YY
25/09/2026
02222894-0007